The Great Giveaway

The Great Giveaway

*Reclaiming the Mission of the Church
from Big Business, Parachurch Organizations,
Psychotherapy, Consumer Capitalism,
and Other Modern Maladies*

David E. Fitch

BakerBooks

a division of Baker Publishing Group
Grand Rapids, Michigan

© 2005 by David E. Fitch

Published by Baker Books
a division of Baker Publishing Group
P.O. Box 6287, Grand Rapids, MI 49516-6287
www.bakerbooks.com

Printed in the United States of America

Library of Congress Cataloging-in-Publication Data

Fitch, David E., 1956–
    The great giveaway : reclaiming the mission of the church from big business, parachurch organizations, psychotherapy, consumer capitalism, and other modern maladies / David E. Fitch.
        p.   cm.
    Includes bibliographical references.
    ISBN 10: 0-8010-6483-X (pbk.)
    ISBN 978-0-8010-6483-8 (pbk.)
    1. Evangelicalism—United States. 2. Mission of the church—United States. I. Title.
BR1642.U5F55 2005
250'.973—dc22
                                         2005023138

Permission was granted for use of materials first published by and from the following sources:

Chapter 2: David E. Fitch, "Saving Souls Beyond Modernity: How Evangelism Can Save the Church and Make It Relevant Again," *Journal of the Academy for Evangelism in Theological Education*, 17 (2001–2002): 17–33.

Chapter 7: David E. Fitch, "The Need for More Preaching in the Psychologist's Office, or Why Therapy Never Should Have Left the Church in the First Place," *Pastoral Psychology* 48, no. 3 (January 2000): 197–209.

Chapter 8: David E. Fitch, "Populist Virtues and the Challenge for Christian Involvement," *Journal of Christian Education* (Australia) 44, no. 2 (September 2001): 31–40.

Chapter 8: David E. Fitch, "Character and the Public Schools: The Challenge and the Opportunity for Christians," *Discernment* 9, no. 1 (Spring 2004): 6–7. Used by permission of the Center for Applied Christian Ethics of Wheaton College, Wheaton, Illinois.

I dedicate this book to my father,
Elmer B. Fitch Jr. (1918–1982),
who by his life taught me daily
what it means to love Christ's church.

Contents

Preface

I know it is common practice for the author to use the preface of the book to acknowledge all the people who have contributed to its writing. Unfortunately, I fear this may not be possible for *The Great Giveaway* because I suspect that I am just not aware of all the many influences that have contributed to my writing this book. I also know it is common in the preface for the author to name such people and then ask the reader not to blame these people for anything written in the book. Such modesty would necessarily mean that I the author take final responsibility for anything written. I also fear this is not possible. Partly, this is because there is a sense in which quite frankly I can take little responsibility for *The Great Giveaway*. It also is because the writing of this book has truly been the result of me being in Christian community with many people, all of whom have had a profound impact upon my life and thinking through the Holy Spirit. It is hard to imagine this book ever being written without these people being in my life.

And so with these caveats, I would like to thank all the people who are part of the Life on the Vine Christian Community in Long Grove, Illinois, who have partnered with me in ministry, challenged me, and allowed me to minister among them. I forthrightly must blame you for this book. There is also a second community where I first began the journeys evidenced in this book, the Metanoia Christian Community in Chicago, Illinois. To each of you, I also blame you for this book. To both of these communities, all I can say is "what a joy" it has been to journey life in Christ together with you. Thanks for making it possible for me to write this book.

I also thank many people for their encouragement and collaboration. To Steve Fowl, Stanley Hauerwas, Robert Webber, Franklin Pyles, Fred

Polding, Jim Van Yperen, Brian McLaren, Geoff Holsclaw, Jim Poole, David Whited, Brian Sutherland, Gordon Hackman, Dave Carlson, Skye Jethani, Roland Kuhl, Linsey Ebert, Melissa Ann Bixler, Ron Friedman, and Andy Meisenheimer, all of whom read parts of this manuscript and made suggestions, comments, or offered words of encouragement. To some extent I must also blame you for this book.

Also thanks to Tim White who suggested the title *The Great Giveaway* to me. Thanks to Mat Barber Kennedy whose artwork graces the cover of this book.

And special thanks to participants in my classes on church in the postmodern context at Northern Seminary, to folks meeting at Up\Rooted (up-rooted.com, a group of pastors, leaders, and students supporting one another through postmodernity), who heard some of these chapters and interacted with them, and to my fellow co-founders of Up\Rooted, who heard me go on about these issues and gave encouragement. To all of you as well, I gladly blame you for this book.

Thanks and recognition to the below publications and their editorial staff, including the Center for Applied Christian Ethics of Wheaton College, Wheaton, Illinois (publisher of *Discernment*), all of whom gave permission to republish parts of the following essays:

David E. Fitch, "Saving Souls Beyond Modernity: How Evangelism Can Save the Church and Make It Relevant Again," *Journal of the Academy for Evangelism in Theological Education* 17 (2001–2002): 17–33.

David E. Fitch, "The Need for More Preaching in the Psychologist's Office, or Why Therapy Never Should Have Left the Church in the First Place," *Pastoral Psychology* 48, no. 3 (January 2000): 197–209.

David E. Fitch, "Populist Virtues and the Challenge for Christian Involvement," *Journal of Christian Education* (Australia) 44, no. 2 (September 2001): 31–40.

David E. Fitch, "Character and the Public Schools: The Challenge and the Opportunity for Christians," *Discernment* 9, no. 1 (Spring 2004): 6–7.

Thanks as well to Robert Hosack, acquisitions editor at Baker Books, who did an expert job of shepherding this book to completion, to Rodney Clapp, without whose encouragement and guidance at the proposal stage, this book surely wouldn't have happened, and to Paul Brinkerhoff, the book's editor, who did an awesome job refining the text and making it a better and more readable book.

I thank my mother, whose encouragement and prayer for many years kept me going in ministry. And most of all, thanks to my wife, Rae Ann, who supported me and journeyed with me not only in starting a church congregation together (her singing saved the day) but in daily supporting my writing and my journey as a pastor/teacher. Lastly, I dedicate this book to my father, Elmer B. Fitch Jr. (1918–1982), who by his life taught me daily what it means to love Christ's church. No words can express the impact of this one example upon my life and work.

To all of these folks listed above I blame this book on them. I offer it in service to our Lord and Savior Jesus Christ in the furtherance of his church.

Introduction

The Great Giveaway:
Toward a Postmodern Evangelical Ecclesiology

The thesis of this book is that evangelicalism has "given away" being the church in North America. Simply put, evangelical churches have forfeited the practices that constitute being the church either (a) by portioning them off to various concerns exterior to the church or (b) by compromising them so badly that they are no longer recognizable as being functions of the church. Admittedly, this is a bold contention, and so I hope to explain in this book the various ways I see that this giveaway has occurred. I contend, for instance, that we give away certain functions of the church when we adopt models for doing these functions from American business. I also suggest that we give away certain functions of the church by farming them out to parachurch organizations. I find that in essence we outsource spiritual formation to psychotherapy when we send our parishioners to therapists' offices in their times of greatest emotional need. I even suggest that we evangelicals have allowed democracy and capitalism to determine the way we do some functions in the church, which in essence constitutes another form of giveaway. In the process, I cringe at considering whether we evangelicals might have quit being the body of Christ in North America.

In this book I will contend that the main culprit in this "giveaway" is evangelicalism's complicity with modernity. For it is our own modernism that has allowed us to individualize, commodify, and package Christianity so much that the evangelical church is often barely distinguishable from other goods and services providers, self-help groups, and social organizations that make up the landscape of modern American life. In light of these developments, I believe the massive critique of modernity sweeping American cultural institutions affords us the occasion to seriously examine our assumptions as evangelicals in the ways that we are doing church. If my thesis concerning evangelicalism is correct, the academic conversations about the end of modernity, late modernity, and postmodernity could not have come at a better time. Likewise, the appearance of the "emergent church" people and other discontented "younger evangelicals" provides a similar opportunity to seek out a recovery of being the church that is not enslaved to the maladies of modernity.[1] For these folk, hopefully this book provides resources for thinking through what an ecclesiology would look like that both maintains an evangelical identity and yet engages the aging of modernity in order to pursue a new faithfulness to being Christ's body in this postmodern time.

> It is our own modernism that has allowed us to individualize, commodify, and package Christianity.

No doubt, the terms *modernity, evangelicalism, church*, and especially *postmodernity* all require significant definition. There are whole books written on each of these terms. So allow me to fill out some of what I mean when I use these terms via some personal biography.

On Being Conflicted with Modernity and Evangelicalism

I have been a conflicted evangelical for years. This perhaps is nothing unusual. In my case, however, my conflictedness was due to evangelicalism's modernism. If we define modernity as the veneration of modern science, the obsession with controlled factual truth, and the unabashed confidence in objective reason as located in the mind of each individual, I have been uncomfortable with modernity since at least college. And since, in my experience, most evangelical theology and churches were built on these things, I became discontent with evangelicalism as well.

The story of my discontent goes like this. My parents did a good job of raising me in evangelical piety during the 1960s and '70s. I went to the most renowned evangelical Christian college in the United States (Billy Graham's alma mater). I spent three and a half years in five seminaries (evangelical, Protestant mainline, and Roman Catholic). Yet, despite it all, I remained discontent with my inherited evangelical ways of articulating the faith. I left the church and ministry entirely for a time and got myself into some trouble. I then had a good old-fashioned second crisis conversion experience (as my holiness backgrounds understood it) at the age of thirty. I entered a Ph.D. program, continued in the business world, ministered in a seeker service church, joined a men's movement for a time, and led a Christian community in Chicago, Illinois. I gave classic Protestant liberalism a serious try during my Ph.D. work. I even explored the various psychological movements that disenchanted evangelicals were diving into (men's movements were big in the '90s among evangelicals). Through all of these things, I remained discontent. Some things remained important to me about evangelicalism, and yet some things remained seriously problematic about its commitments to modernity. Then one year I found some resolution. Under God's providence, I found myself (during my doctoral studies) in the middle of the academic discussions of modernity, postmodernity, postliberalism, and the United Methodist intelligentsia's discontent with professor Stanley Hauerwas. And during this spell of time, as a card-carrying discontented evangelical, I discovered I could actually be a better Christian by dumping modernity.

But could one still be an evangelical and dump modernity? In other words, could I still minister within evangelical churches yet unload the scientific manipulations to defend the Bible, the overstated attempts to make Christianity intellectually attractive to the society at large, the obsession with decisions for Christ and megachurches, the vigorous rationalizations conducted in the name of individualist objectivity, that evangelicals seem so attached to? To me, evangelicals were spending a lot of effort making Christian faith intellectually defensible on modernist terms that were fading in their usefulness. Even worse, these efforts smelled of an evangelical agenda, which of course in modernity is a bad thing. Because, as any good modernist knows, we were supposed to be objective in the pursuit of truth. Evangelicalism then came off as disingenuous. Furthermore, evangelical salvation seemed cheap when it was made into a formula for modernist evangelism. And evangelical individualist morality seemed legalistic and impotent against the sensuality of the day. There was little connection to the cosmic work of Christ's victory over evil, sin, and death as manifested in his chosen people. Could I leave the modernist things behind yet remain an evangelical? Through the works of Stanley Hauerwas, John Howard Yoder, Alasdair MacIntyre, John Milbank, and other theologians critical of modernity, I was released from the shackles of modernity. (Is there an "amen" in the congregation?) Gone were the insecurities of modernist epistemology, and I was now free to pursue the integrity of the Christian faith and the Christian life on its own terms. But could I throw off the albatross of modernity and still minister as an evangelical?

Four years ago now, I attempted to do just that. Under the direction of my denomination (and the brave district leadership I found myself under), my wife and I set out to plant a church named "Life on the

Vine" that was decidedly postmodern and yet maintained its evangelical identity. Piece by piece a number of us thought through what it means to be the body of Christ at "the Vine" amidst the disintegrating vestiges of modernity while staying in integrity to our evangelical traditions. Many of the stories I recount in this book come from the experience of being with Life on the Vine church as well as Metanoia Community, a small, intentional community I helped lead in Chicago prior to Life on the Vine. (In the book, I have deliberately changed the names of persons and disguised the circumstances in order to protect confidentialities.) Life on the Vine has been a wonderful place to experience God's grace. It has also been a struggle. And although we have not reached many of the ideals set forth in this book, we have made significant progress. And for that I thank God and give him the glory. As a result, I believe it is possible to be an evangelical and to also leave behind the problems and baggage of modernity. And I write this book to call more evangelicals to a similar "conversion" out of modernity.

Hopefully, this brief autobiography makes it clear to the reader that I have written this book while remaining an evangelical. Yet I also wish to reject much of modernity's strictures. Many of my cohorts might rightfully ask, if evangelicalism is so tied to modernity, why continue to be an evangelical at all? Indeed, many of my theological allies in academia and the clergy have left evangelicalism in some way or another upon having epiphanies similar to my own. I don't hold it against them, but I believe we are all born into historical contingencies, and I believe God calls us to work from within these contingencies until informed otherwise. God's calling starts with us where we are born. My contingency is the church I was born into (the Christian and Missionary Alliance, a decidedly evangelical denomination).[2] And frankly, I believe evangelicalism still has some strengths to offer to the rest of Christ's church. I consider, for instance, the evangelical impulse to diligently seek to make the gospel accessible to strangers ("the lost" as we call them), the evangelical's commitment to world missions, holy living, and the seeking of the Holy Spirit for the life of following Christ, all to be strengths to offer to the rest of Christ's church, including the more High Church traditions of the established European churches here in North America. Much of evangelicalism is built on these elements albeit in a modernist sense. So, despite its many problems, I resist leaving evangelicalism and instead I have written this book in service to it and the church of North American evangelicalism. I want the reader to know that I remain committed to that part of Christ's church in America that is labeled (often confusingly, I admit) "evangelical." And, it goes without saying, I hope this book will serve all the rest of Christ's church who face the same challenges of ministering amidst a crumbling modernity.

The Dis-ease of Late Modernity and the Cure: "Let the Church Be the Church"

Of course, the reason for writing this book is that I believe the evangelical church in North America is facing a crisis. Perhaps this is saying nothing new either. But my take on the crisis stems from the simple observation made above that evangelicals are aligned with modernity at a time when the cultural consensus on modernity seems to be ending. North American evangelicals learned how to do church in relation to modernity. During the American Revivalism of the eighteenth and nineteenth centuries, we learned a salvation in Christ that was individual and personal. Amidst the fundamentalist-modernist controversies of the 1920s, we learned to defend truth using modern science and methods of historiography. As a result, most evangelicals today are modernists to the core. Yet modernity's bald confidence in science and progress over nature, its uncritical acceptance of Enlightenment individualism as the basis for politics and all of life is imploding. It therefore seems imperative that we evangelicals reassess our relationship to modernity lest we too "go down with the ship."

Many no doubt will counter, saying, "Evangelicalism is alive and well in North America. Compared to our Protestant mainline and even Roman Catholic brethren, our churches are bursting at the seams." But in response I ask, "Are megachurches the sign of vitality in the church?" I am not one who categorically dismisses the contemporizing of the church as a bad idea. Indeed, recontextualizing the church in continuity and integrity with Christian orthodoxy is definitely a good in and of itself. But is what we are witnessing in the evangelical megachurches today what it means to be the church? And if we have shuffled the same amount of people from smaller local parishes into megachurch buildings and become more efficient by doing so, is this necessarily the sign of church vitality we should be looking for? These questions have all been asked before, I am sure. But here in this book I aim to specifically ask the question in terms of what modernity has done to our churches and whether indeed our modernism is not itself the problem. And so I aim to ask these questions anew through the analysis offered to us through the theological developments that have arisen in critique of modernity over the last twenty-five years. I speak specifically here of the work of Yoder, Hauerwas, and MacIntyre, the work of the postliberal Yale theologians, and those who go by the name "Radical Orthodoxy."

Restated then, the main thesis of this book is that evangelicalism by virtue of its marriage to modernity has not only failed to engage the current cultural shifts of postmodernity, it has indeed structured our churches out of meaningful existence. Because evangelicals articulate salvation in such individualist terms and because modern science and individual reason carry such authority for evangelicals, we do not need the body of Christ for daily victorious Christian existence. In some ways, frankly, we can do without it. We don't need the church to live salvation because we have personal salvation augmented by reason, science, and immediate (charismatic) experience. The church is left with nothing else to do but distribute information, goods, and services to individual Christians.[3] And so, for evangelicals, the church in essence is left to be a sideshow to what God is doing for, in, and through individuals. Because of our modernism, we no longer have a need for the church to be the social manifestation of his lordship where he reigns over the powers of sin, evil, and death, the prolepsis, the very inbreaking of the kingdom of God.

As a result, evangelicals are prone to farm out the functions of the church whenever it is more efficient. Our modernist confidences allow us to freely use models of ministry from the secular sciences whenever they seem "to work better." We are after all only seeking to minister to individuals more effectively. Likewise, evangelicals are prone to borrow concepts and definitions of what we are to do and be from society at large as opposed to engaging these things critically out of who we are as the "called out people" of Jesus Christ. Science and technology, marketing and advertising are therefore all modern wonders given to us to do things more efficiently. Sadly, in the process, many of our churches have quit being the church as it has historically been defined. Likewise, our local churches rarely function as organic local bodies of Christ. And even worse, our people look more and more like secular Americans as opposed to Christians. All of this is what I have labeled "the great giveaway" of the church by evangelicalism to modernity. In essence, evangelicalism has portioned off the tasks of being the church to modernity and in the process quit being the body of Christ in North America. And to reverse this "great giveaway," we must pursue the tasks of being the church again, or perhaps better said, we must "let the church be the church."[4] We must receive back from Christ the practices of being the people of God he has called us to be.

The task of this book then is twofold: (1) to examine the ways we have "given away" being the church to modernity by allowing its influence to individualize, universalize, syncretize, and commodify the tasks, truths, and even the very salvation we have been given as a people from God through Jesus Christ, and (2) to offer practices to evangelicals by which we may receive back being the church, the people of God ruled by Jesus as Lord in resistance to such modern influences. In some ways, doing this is like saying the dog's problem is that it barks and has fur. In other words, perhaps evangelicals are so defined by modernity that any attempt to change that would make evangelicalism unrecognizable. Yet I believe if evangelicalism does not deconstruct its own modernity, and seek diligently to practice being the church in North America, we may suffer the same fate that we accuse our Protestant mainline brethren of: we may become a church that is shrinking, culturally liberal, and largely irrelevant. We must therefore deconstruct our modernist commitments and then address our strategy for living as the church of Jesus Christ in North America amidst the crash and burn of late modernity. This is the task of this book.

Diagnosing Evangelicalism's Lack of Ecclesiology

This book goes about this task with eight chapters, each devoted to a function of the church (preaching of the Word, worship, witness, discipleship, etc.). In terms of basic structure, each chapter deals with a particular function that is integral to the church's life and then examines the ways evangelicals are married to modernity in the way we carry out these various functions. Specifically, each chapter

1. addresses how evangelicals undermine the church's ability to perform one of these functions by being aligned so closely with modernity while the foundations of modernity itself are disintegrating;
2. describes ways we have in effect "given away" the core of each function to the experts, techniques, or redefinitions of the function, all of which come from outside the church; and then
3. proposes a renewal of one or more church practices related to the function being discussed—practices rooted in the history of the church.

Hopefully, such practices point us toward the way to recover being the church, as each practice is a gift from God through the Holy Spirit to his church.

I use the word *function* here hesitantly because I want to avoid the temptation to see the church in the sociological terms we have become so accustomed to using when talking in similar ways about modern corporations and other institutions. I also want to avoid seeing the church as a place where we do certain things. The church is a people called out to live under Christ's lordship in anticipation of the final consummation of his reign over all the earth. In this sense the church is a missional people. So we surely should resist defining the church by a set of functions, or values, or even worse (to use a favorite evangelical word), programs. There is a danger in defining the church according to these functions. There is a danger in referring to these functions in autonomy from who we are as the people of God. Let us therefore see these functions as callings given to us from God and his work in Christ to be carried out by virtue of who we are in Christ. We surely need some markers to help us distinguish the church from false simulacra or even worse from those sincere evangelicals doing activities in the name of being the church yet who have lost their way. Making such distinctions is especially important to the aims of this book. For the underlying goal of this book is to diagnose whether the evangelical church is being faithful to its call to be the church in North America at the end of modernity. These functions therefore will provide the basis for my contention that evangelicals have largely given away all the functions that define us as the church; we've given them away to the experts, techniques, and businesslike efficiencies all in the name of modernity. This state of affairs beckons us to ask, Have we given up being the church in North America?

The post-Reformation called these functions "marks" (*notae*). For the Reformers in the sixteenth century (especially for the so-called Anabaptists), it was especially important to have the means to identify who was the real church. For them, in the midst of the breakup of the medieval unity of the church, these marks or notes were the signs of being a Christian people. These were holy possessions given to his people by Christ himself. So Luther and Melanchthon stated very simply the two basic marks in the Augsburg Confession (1530): "The church is wherever the Word of God is properly preached and the sacraments properly administered." The Anabaptists, however, later criticized the lack of any definitiveness to this criterion, claiming that one could merely post a doctrinal statement at the front of the church and have a priest show up to consecrate the Lord's Supper and that would constitute a faithful church. There need not even be any people in the pews. Instead, the church needs criteria that have to do with the congregation rather than solely the official; criteria that have to do with the church's relationship to the world, not just purely define the institution as an existence unto its own.[5] Later Menno Simons added four additional marks to the original two marks: holy living, brotherly love, unreserved testimony, and suffering.[6] In 1539 Luther also expanded upon the original two marks in his *On the Councils and Churches*. His list grew to include seven: the preaching of the true Word, the proper administration of baptism, the correct form of the Lord's Supper, the power of the keys of church discipline, the lawful vocation and ordination of ministers, prayer and the singing of psalms in the vernacular, and persecutions and sufferings.[7]

Perhaps evangelicals have reached a crisis similar to the one in the post-medieval period, which produced these "marks" of the church. Perhaps amidst all of the evangelical versions of doing church we are too confused to distinguish who is really doing church among us from those who are mere imitators for dubious reasons. Perhaps we need to take a new look at what we are doing and ask if this really qualifies as being the church.

In the spirit of these "marks" then, this book offers an analysis of eight such functions of the church that I believe evangelicals have given away to modernity's experts, techniques, and sociocultural forces. This book is not, however, meant to be a systematic treatment of the marks for evangelicals. Rather, what I offer here are theological engagements and cultural critiques of the ways we have gone about doing the functions of the church as evangelicals. I do not follow the marks according to either the Lutheran or Anabaptist tradition. Nonetheless, there is some overlap even though it may not be immediately obvious.

In chapter 1, for example, my analysis of church growth and the evangelical "giveaway" of our understandings of how we are to gauge success in the church coincides with the "mark" Simons addressed in his mark "brotherly love" and what we now call fellowship or community. In chapter 2, my description of how we have excluded the church from being the center for evangelism and witness is a treatment of the mark Simons termed unreserved testimony and what other Mennonites have labeled "witness." In chapter 3, my analysis of evangelical leadership and its capitulation to American business and sociology addresses something similar to Luther's mark of vocation and ordination of ministers. In chapter 4, my analysis of evangelical worship and our "giveaway" of the production of faithful experience in modernity coincides with the marks of the Lord's Supper and Luther's praying and singing songs in the vernacular. In chapter 5, my intentionally provocative engagement of the evangelical love affair with expository preaching addresses the preaching of the Word, the mark of the church that, along with the Eucharist, forms the classic first two marks of the church for the Magisterial Reformation. In chapter 6, my analysis of how we have "given away" our understandings of justice and its ministry to democratic liberalism and capitalism coincides with the marks Simons addressed in holy living, brotherly love, and unreserved testimony. In chapter 7, my discussion of how evangelicals have "given away" spiritual formation and discipleship to modern therapy addresses the mark both Luther and Simons talked about in terms of suffering and "the keys" of church discipline. In chapter 8, my discussion of moral education and how we have too easily "given away" the moral education of our children to American social-political forces outside the church addresses some of the things Luther dealt with in his

> **Perhaps amidst all of the evangelical versions of doing church we are too confused to distinguish who is really doing church among us.**

sixth mark of praying and singing in the vernacular. For in this mark, Luther tells how catechesis is essential for the church to be the church. Each chapter then addresses a function that has some overlap with a mark of the church as defined by the Reformers/Anabaptists. Each of these chapters can be read independently from the others according to the interests of the reader. At the very end, in the short conclusion to the book, I timidly consider what our churches might look like if indeed we did survive the current malaise of modernity and return to the practices of being Christ's church. Hopefully, this ending is the start of many more discussions, potlucks, and discernments as to how we all can practice more intently being Christ's church.

I do not pretend to offer here an exhaustive ecclesiology for evangelicalism in postmodernity. Neither do I pretend to develop here a set of new marks for the evangelical church in postmodernity. There are just too many unanswered questions in this book to suggest that it can provide an evangelical ecclesiology for our times. Instead, these chapters attempt something more modest in scope. Each chapter examines how we evangelicals have defaulted on various functions of the church via our cultural captivity to modernity. Upon accomplishing this task, each chapter then makes some modest suggestions for practices we might pursue if we are to receive back being the church in North America. In the process, I am sure that this book has cleared only beginning ground in the theological work needed to determine what the true church really looks like when modernity has crashed and burned and whether indeed evangelical churches are being faithful to that call.

Thankfully, there have already been a few notable attempts to engage in this discussion of evangelicalism's troublesome lack of a robust evangelical ecclesiology. The 2004 Wheaton College Theology Conference (Wheaton, IL) and the Regent Theology Conference of 2002 (Vancouver, BC) both brought this subject to the forefront of evangelical scholarship.[8] It is my hope that this book participates further in these discussions both in a theological sense as well as in a practical sense.

Defining Some Well-worn Terms

If all of the above does not clarify what I mean by modernity, evangelicalism, and postmodernity, let me offer the following clarifications.

First, when I use the term *evangelical*, I refer specifically to the denominations and association of churches in North America who claim to uphold a high propositional view (often using the word *inerrant*) of Scripture, who subscribe to a "personal" and individual relationship with God through Christ as the defining issue for one's Christian identity, and who maintain a primary allegiance to a Lutheranized view of "justification by faith," plus the substitutionary view of the atonement as the primary definition of salvation in Christ. By and large, when I use *evangelical*, I am not referring to High Church folk who refer to themselves as evangelicals and who are members, for example, of the Anglican Communion. They may in fact be evangelicals, but a lot of the ecclesiological issues I address here do not apply to my brothers and sisters in the High Church traditions.

Second, the word *postmodern* continues to be one of the most misused words in the English language, especially within evangelicalism. For instance, within popular evangelicalism one can barely distinguish between what "postmodernity" refers to and the prototypical characteristics of Protestant liberalism. I believe nonetheless that the word has significant remaining value when it refers to the context of continental European philosophical writings from whence it got its origin. And I believe these writings have influenced a whole culture and academic context. Within the confines of this book, therefore, I shall use the term to refer to the conversations that emanate primarily from continental philosophy including Jacques Derrida, Jean-François Lyotard, Jean Baudrillard, and Michel Foucault, among others, as well as all the developments emanating therefrom in theology, sociology, and culture.

The word *postmodern* continues to be one of the most misused words in the English language, especially within evangelicalism.

Third, I shall use the words *modernity* and *modernism* to refer to all of the traits of society that emanate from the Enlightenment and the philosophical writings of René Descartes, Thomas Hobbes, John Locke, Francis Bacon, and modern science. Fourth, the words *capitalism* and *liberalism* require better definition for evangelicals who normally use these terms in other ways. In this book I use *liberalism* and *democratic liberalism* to refer to the philosophical ideas and culture that undergird modern democracy, the autonomy of the individual, and the identity of the liberated self. The word *capitalism* is used to refer to the philosophical assumptions that undergird the ways we think about exchange and organize our lives for the marketplace. Particularly important for this book are the developments within capitalism such as *late capitalism* (Fredric Jameson) and *consumer capitalism*.

There is no doubt a great confusion these days over the use of the "post- terms" such as *postmodern, postmodernity, postsecular, postevangelical, post-Christian, post-Christendom,* and even *postliberal*. This book may engender some of that confusion as well. Separate literatures are associated with each of these terms. In this book I occasionally use the terms *post-Christian* and *postmodern* in the same chapter and even the same paragraph, which might add to the confusion. To simplify matters for the reader, I intend to use the term *post-Christian* to refer to the present culture that no longer can assume any form of Christian social, political, or moral consensus. In particular I refer to that form of North American Christian cultural consensus that coalesced around modernist versions of Christian society where science, democracy, capitalism, and churches formed into an inherent alliance to support one another. This form of Christendom is one many would say evangelicalism is most attached to. Yet there are parts of this Christendom that depended upon modernity, and those parts have eroded under the social forces of the postmodern critique.

It is impossible then to not talk about postmodernity in relation to the demise of this form of Christendom. Equally, there are parts of this Christendom that have eroded due to the creep of late democracy and capitalism, and the concomitant demise of the Protestant American Christendom of pre–World War II. In this way it is possible to talk about Christian elements of culture which supersede both modern and post-modern concerns yet have vanished under the weight of the demise of a Christian consensus itself.

For the purposes of this book then, I aim to use the word *postmodern* to talk about the erosion of modernity as an intellectual phenomenon as well as a social one. And I use the word *post-Christian* when I am talking more specifically about the erosion of the Christian cultural consensus that was forged out of democracy, modernity, capitalism, and science in pre–World War II North America.

Lastly, as might already be apparent, I intentionally use the adjective *North American* to define the boundaries of the evangelicalism I wish to address with this book. When I use the term *North American* I am intentionally referring to both Canada and the United States. On the other hand, when I use the term *American* by itself, I am emphasizing characteristics more unique to the United States (e.g., American business, American public education). Although some chapters (e.g., chapters 3 and 8) may speak more overtly to United States Americans, generally it is the evangelicalism of both countries I wish to address. Canada is certainly distinct and different in culture from the United States in many ways. I was raised in Canada and am aware of this. The origins, however, of Canadian and United States evangelicalism have much in common. And culturally, it would appear the two evangelicalisms are much closer than any of their relatives in other parts of the world. Today, the main difference between the two evangelicalisms may be that in Canada, evangelicalism has withered further in its hold upon its own culture than in United States.

As a result, Canadian evangelicals have little pretense concerning their rights to speak for a Christian nation, while many U.S. evangelicals still retain such a posture. Canada may be a snapshot of the post-Christian conditions that lie immediately ahead of the United States, especially in the Northeast, Northwest, and certain parts of Metro Chicago and California. Because this book speaks to doing church under such post-Christian and postmodern conditions, it may speak more immediately to Canadian evangelicals and more eventually to evangelicals living in the United States. Whatever these variations, in my judgment evangelicals in both Canada and the United States have enough in common both in who they are and in the challenges they face to allow me to speak to both populations whenever I use the term *North American*.

To the Emergent Church, Younger Evangelicals, and Others

Finally, I offer a note to some people who I hope will read this book. In the past ten years, I have noticed a generation of sons and daughters of evangelicals who are disgruntled with evangelicalism. A lot of these folk have either left the church or joined Anglo or Roman Catholic parishes. On the other hand, a lot of these folk have resonated with the writing of Brian McLaren and the Emergent Village fellowships. Robert Webber has referred to them as "the Younger Evangelicals." I applaud what is going on there and to some extent I have participated in this group through the founding of Up\Rooted, a local group of pastors, artists, and church leaders in the Chicago area brought together to discuss the issues of the church in postmodernity.

As I have interacted with various members of these groups, however, I have noticed on the one hand a propensity to react against evangelicalism's modernity with versions of Christianity that look similar to classic Protestant liberalism. On the other hand, some emergent and/or self-described postmodern churches look like more extreme versions of self-expressivist evangelicalism. They repeat the drive of earlier evangelicalism itself to be new, innovative, free from history, and experiential. I fear if we're not careful, all of this could lead to the same self-indulgent accommodative Christianity we lament today. And so amidst these developments, I discern a need to define what it means to be the church. Several folk in this group make admirable attempts to bring back liturgy and mystery into our church practices. Many seek to revive community. For me, these are significant moves in the right direction. Nonetheless, I believe the movement will fail if we do not reinvigorate an ecclesiology for our times. I hope this book can help lead us toward that direction.

> Some emergent churches look like more extreme versions of self-expressivist evangelicalism . . . new, innovative, free from history, and experiential.

Likewise, I hope this book will be helpful to those who are emerging as the next generation of leadership in evangelical megachurches. It is true that this book critically engages the megachurch phenomenon. Yet I do so not intending to impugn the character of megachurch leaders either as individuals or as a group. I am convinced that the heart of most megachurch pastors (as well as televangelists) is to serve Christ and further his kingdom. Hopefully, I have conducted this project in such a way that the discussion in this book furthers the mission of the evangelical church, not simply tears it down. Where I have used specific examples naming a church pastor or leader to clarify a theological point, I have attempted to send that chapter to the person, pastor, or church in hopes of dialogue and exchange for the furtherance of Christ's kingdom.

On the other hand, when I engage a theologian's or anyone else's published writings I have considered that material "fair game" for dialogue and critical engagement. I assume as members of Christ's church, we all write to further dialogue in the service of clarifying and furthering the mission of Christ's church. I hope this book furthers this dialogue and contributes to the clarifying of our mission in Christ. I hope the emerging leaders of the evangelical megachurches will see my motives behind writing this book in this way and join in the discussion.

In the end I know that some of the academic work done here in this book may put off some who are less inclined toward the study of philosophy, theology, and the history of the church. Nonetheless, I have attempted to combine both the engagement of the theology and philosophy with the practical insights of actually doing and being church. I write this book as much for practitioners as for the academic conversation. I am a church planter as well as an academically trained theologian. My academic training preceded my church planting. And I have learned that often church planters become academics, but rarely the other way around. Church planting requires many skills, including the habits of prayer, loving people, and faith. Sometimes you can get away without these in the academy but rarely in the task of church planting. Oddly enough, my academic work pushed me toward church planting because I learned from people like Stanley Hauerwas how essential the church is to doing the work of theology. I hope this book reveals that this is more than an academic exercise. I sincerely hope these chapters will be helpful to the emergent church and people like them who seek to figure out what it means to be the church going forward at the end of modernity.

1

Our Definition of Success

When Going from Ten to a Thousand Members
in Five Years Is the Sign of a Sick Church

Each builder must choose with care how to build on it. . . . and the fire
will test what sort of work each has done.

1 Corinthians 3:10, 15 NRSV

Over my years in ministry, whenever I get together with other evangelical pastors and denominational leaders, we inevitably talk about numbers. We can't resist it. The first number we often discuss is church attendance. The second number would be number of conversions or baptisms we have experienced in our congregations. From there, other numbers become relevant. No matter how we would try, we simply could not avoid talking numbers. It was an easy way to measure how we were doing. It was a way to measure success.

There are good reasons for church leaders to discuss numbers. We need to know how we are doing, whether we are doing the right thing, and whether at times we can even financially survive. At the same time, however, I believe there are some assumptions that underlie the way we use numbers that are problematic. By and large, evangelicals use numbers of "decisions for Christ" or church attendance to determine church success. These numbers, however, can mislead. There can be a discrepancy between the size of a congregation (or the number of decisions) and the corresponding lifestyle behavior that would indicate these people are indeed following Christ. Hypothetically at least, we could be achieving great success in the number of decisions for Christ and church attendance yet be failing in the ultimate purpose, that of making "disciples of all nations, baptizing them . . . teaching them to observe all that I have commanded you" (Matt. 28:19–20). These numbers will not tell that story. In fact, they may mask thin notions of salvation or business marketing principles that lie behind them.[1] Again, by using numbers in this way, we may subtly displace the pursuit of being Christ's church with the counterfeit goal of achieving success in the terms laid out by the American economy and capitalism. And so evangelicals may be building something akin to a Hollywood Western movie set—its exterior looks real, big, and impressive, but what is actually there is a lot less than meets the eye.

Perhaps most disturbing is the way we evangelicals are attracted to big numbers. It goes with the evangelical territory that the biggest churches get the attention, the acclamation of success. Inevitably we ask, How did they do this? What is their secret? How can we model and duplicate this success? These kind of numbers steer the direction of our churches and the goals we seek to attain. We are attracted to big numbers because we think they measure effectiveness. But herein lies the danger. Because, as the criticizers of modernity teach us, effectiveness can itself become a value that may be at odds with the purposes of the church. Effectiveness and efficiency draw their agendas from American cultural forces that define success in terms of numbers, size, and capital. This kind of effectiveness may be alien to Christ's church. We therefore need to reexamine what is effectiveness in terms of faithfulness to God's call to be the church and why we are so attracted to big numbers. And then, yes, we will still need to measure where we are going and whether we are getting there. We will need practices of accountability that keep us from wandering aimlessly from our God-given mission to build his church.

In this chapter, I examine how evangelicals "gave away" our understanding of church success to these cultural forces outside of our history in Christ and how we can regain a view of success that is faithful to our calling to be God's church. I then suggest some practices to measure that faithfulness which can shape us toward being the body of Christ in North America.

The Problem of Defining Success in Christ's Church: A Hypothetical Example

It is nothing new to say that numbers can mislead in the measurement of a church's success. Yet we need to be explicit as to why this is true. Numbers miss measuring how well a church is functioning as the body of Christ. Numbers often miss measuring the progress of discipleship in a church. Numbers do not reveal how a church group is functioning internally, whether people are building up each other, ministering to each other, and ministering in the outside community as the body of Christ. In short, numbers, on their own, say nothing qualitative about what is going on in the church when viewed as the body of Christ. Indeed, when numbers reach a certain level, a further increase in numbers may deter achieving the goals of being the body of Christ. Consequently, a church that appears to be a success numerically may be a failure in terms of its mission to be a faithful local body of Christ.

Numbers, on their own, say nothing qualitative about what is going on in the church when viewed as the body of Christ.

To illustrate, let us think hypothetically about a church that started with ten people who then gathered to study the Bible and pray. The meeting grew to approximately fifty people over a year, upon which they decided to plant a congregation.[2] Let us say that the church used a "seeker service" format where the Sunday morning service allows for complete anonymity for visitors. The service was characterized by excellent music, captivating drama, and a message that appealed to one's "felt needs" and to Jesus Christ as the answer to those needs. It often used psychology-driven sermons. Five years later the church averages a thousand attendees, of which there is a 60 percent turnover every year. Out of the one thousand attendees, the basic core group of practicing Christians is one hundred. Out of the thousand there are "fifty-nine giving units" (as they call them) accounting for 95 percent of church giving. Let us say hypothetically we know that a majority of the thousand attendees minus the hundred core still work eighty hours a week to support an indulgent lifestyle while neglecting the poor in their midst, still have sex outside of marriage, and have abusive relationships. Is this church a hundred people large or a thousand?

Let us say that this church of a thousand people has a large staff and a senior pastor acting as chief executive officer as opposed to performing pastoral functions such as visiting the sick, overseeing the budgetary direction of the church, counseling with the distraught, conducting funerals and weddings, discipling families, and mentoring adults for lay leadership. The elders basically act as conduits for the pastor because they were picked and affirmed by the pastor and the existing elder board, using a token congregational process.[3] The church is just too large for the people to actually know, nominate, and affirm elders on a regular basis. Let us also say that when any serious moral problems arise in people's lives within the congregation, the church has a counselor trained in therapy and refers those the pastor couldn't handle to outside psychologists. Consequently, it is emphasized that if there are any seriously troubled persons in a small group, then the staff is to direct them to a psychologist. Troubled persons rarely work through their everyday moral problems with someone in the church, such as a pastor or someone they know personally. The church is simply too big and dealing with such problems is uncomfortable.

The church, however, records fifty to seventy new decisions for Christ a year and conducts about thirty new baptisms a year. Let us say, however, that 70 percent of those who made new decisions for Christ and 80 percent of those who are baptized are gone from the church within one year. Only about 20 percent of the congregation know one another in more than casual ways. There are rare evidences of church disciplines or moral accountability between one another. Usually it occurs with someone in a visible ministry position after he or she has fallen. With these facts in mind, how big a part of this church is actually functioning as a body of Christ as outlined in 1 Corinthians 12, Ephesians 4, or Romans 12? How much actual visible life of Christ is being witnessed by outsiders to the gospel? In other words, what size is the actual functioning body? Is the answer closer to a hundred or a thousand? Numbers alone can't answer this question.

Let us say this church instructs engaged couples to see the marriage counselor, where they can get tested for Myers-Briggs personality compatibility and can receive counseling sessions on communication and finances. The church charges a flat fee for marriage services, which includes the pastor, church facilities, plus counseling. The pastor, or pastor surrogate, marries people even when they were not committed to following Christ and were carrying out behavior antithetical to the goals of Christian marriage, such as cohabiting before marriage. Pastors and the like have little time to counsel situations like this and besides, one of the persons they are marrying is contributing to the children's ministry. Let us say that as a result there are as many if not more divorces out of this church's marriages as are outside the church. In these matters, is this church functioning as a body of Christ or as a justice of the peace with some marriage counseling? Again, numbers alone will not answer this question.

If we define the church as a place for those who gather on Sunday morning for worship, as a place that provides some basic spiritually oriented services (counseling, marriages, funerals, etc.), as the gathering of those who have made a decision for Christ and who have a geographical location to gather to receive religious goods and services, this church is one of the larger churches in the country. If we describe the church, however, as the body of Christ whose members are committed followers of Christ, who give of their finances to the kingdom of God and the upbuilding of the body, who choose to follow Christ and God's purposes for their moral lives, who submit to one another and to church discipline, who teach and nurture one another into the ways of Christ, who edify each other and grow into the stature of Christ, who reach out and invite strangers to the gospel into their homes for ministry and witness, who engage the poor with love and material justice, and who participate in the worldwide mission of Christ, this church is more like a hundred members. Indeed, this church is a hundred members who allow much spiritual sickness to flourish among them under the banner of Christ. In other words, this church may not be a thousand strong but instead a church of more moderate size that is quite "sick" despite the flurry of activity surrounding it.

Nevertheless, most evangelical denominational leaders would see this church as a success. They most likely would not ask these kinds of qualitative questions about such a large church. Despite the disclaimers—"we know that numbers are not what is most important but . . ."—we evangelicals remain obsessed with them whether they be decisions for Christ, church attendance, church finances, or otherwise. This is regrettable considering the recent proliferation of statistical data purporting that evangelical churches, despite growing in numbers, show a constituency with higher rates of divorce, materialism, more ministers having extramarital affairs, and a general lack of any effect on their immediate surrounding culture.[4] We are irresistibly drawn to big churches, as attendance at megachurch seminars of all shapes and sizes indicates.[5] Yet there is little or no discussion of how we measure the faithfulness of these churches to the overall mission of the church to be Christ's body in the world. Our understanding of church success is therefore lacking. And this unchecked view of success spurs on new pastors and church planters to measure their own efforts in terms of these models. Meanwhile success according to numbers and church marketing produces bigger and bigger churches, but we have no real understanding of whether these churches are functioning bodies of Christ.[6]

The Roots of Evangelical Success: Individualism and Corporate Efficiency

Why then are we so attracted to large numbers in churches? Where do these notions of church success come from? I suggest that their roots lie in two sources quite at home in American culture: our individualism and our "business-oriented" forms of organization.

In regard to the first, evangelicals are individualists, which in turn enables us to count decisions as the signpost of salvation. We have always seen God as working first in individuals and only then in social groupings of people. It is the individual's "decision to accept Christ's provision by faith" that matters. It makes sense then to count the numbers of "decisions for Christ" as a measure of God working. We learned the roots of this amidst the revivalism of the eighteenth and nineteenth centuries.[7] Here evangelicals learned that people get saved as individuals irrespective of one's relationship to a local church or the church universal. The central moment of salvation is the individual's decision to accept "my status as a sinner and Christ's sacrifice as the atonement for my sin." This makes sense to us evangelicals even though most of Christian history would frown upon the location of one's salvation in a moment-in-time, self-centered decision. In addition, we cherish holiness as an individual experience. Again, for most of Christian history, salvation was a world to be born into, initiated into through baptism, and authenticated through a life of dedication. But for us one's salvation is authenticated by a personal, private, "real" experience.[8] Even our times around the Lord's Supper are individualist. Though symbolic, the Lord's Supper for most evangelicals is largely an individual interior act of intellectual remembrance. All of this works to center salvation in the individual and private experience. As a result, church becomes a place where saved private individuals come to be "fed" intellectually, to serve out of their personal duty to Christ, to get in touch with an individual experience of worship, and to pool their resources as individuals to further the mission of getting the gospel out to more individuals. Though evangelicals will always urge every new convert to get "plugged into" the local church, it is the "decision," one's private personal experience, that is primary. It makes sense therefore to count decisions and church attendance as the primary sign of progress in bringing more people to salvation and a further experience of personal holiness. We do not see the inner dynamic of the social space of the body of Christ as essential to either. The salvific value we place on the "decision" not only makes counting important, it makes it easy.

It is only one step further then for evangelicals to organize churches around the production of decisions. Why not seek to organize for the greatest efficiency in meeting this goal? Once the internal working of the body of Christ is not a legitimate goal in itself, the central focus becomes, How can we best organize to produce the largest amount of decisions and the best quality of services for Christian growth most economically and efficiently to the largest number in this geographical location?[9] This focus assumes that larger size enables you to produce greater excellence in services, better economics, better facilities, and thereby better overall production of decisions for Christ and their further nurturance. It is the "economies of scale" for churches. As a result, success is measured by how large one can build such an organization that produces such decisions. There is no need to organize for any other goal when the salvation of each person is not dependent upon any inner organic dynamic going on in the church itself.

The best models for this kind of organization are found in American capitalism and the world of American corporations. In this world, effectiveness and efficiency rule the day and one never questions the goal to get bigger. Evangelicals embrace these values and "church growth" becomes a strategy. Competition between churches cannot be avoided as churches vie for the latest ever, newest ways of doing church and attracting parishioners. It now makes sense to organize for bigger growing organizations, larger corporate plants and equipment and the pursuit of excellence, and high quality product. It now makes sense for the senior pastor to be a CEO, and churches become franchises that best produce decisions for Christ and best distribute religious goods and services necessary to live the Christian life. All of this is in the name of success, the larger the better because the results represent something of unquestioned eternal value.

Our focus on numbers, bigness, and large institutions is therefore rooted in two of America's sacred cows: the autonomy of the individual and the necessity to organize for economic efficiency. They are two sacred cows closely aligned to modernity. Modernity's agenda, since Descartes, has been to elevate the individual's freedom over against traditions so that individuals can arrive at truth out of their own reason and modern science. Likewise, modernity seeks a social organization devoid of an all-encompassing theocratic God because only this can guarantee freedom. But devoid of God, modernity is left to pursue only a society of efficiency.[10] These two sacred cows of modernity ironically underwrite the culture of numbers that lies within evangelicalism. However, the question is, Are these sacred cows compatible with the goals of being the body of Christ in North America? Have evangelicals given away our definition of success in terms of being the body of Christ to

> **Our focus on numbers, bigness, and large institutions is therefore rooted in two of America's sacred cows: the autonomy of the individual and the necessity to organize for economic efficiency.**

America's culture of success and its agenda of modernity, an agenda that appears to be quickly passing?

Do Decisions Count Where There Is No Sanctification?

Let us look at the first sacred cow, namely, the individual who validates everything in America by making an autonomous, critical, authentic decision. American elections, the setting of prices in the marketplace, and even sexual encounters are all validated by individuals making decisions. Should "decisions" be a measure of success for evangelical churches? The question is not "Do decisions for Christ matter?" Rather the question is "Are decisions for Christ significant and of ultimate importance if they do not represent an individual's actual decision to follow Christ into a life of discipleship and become part of the kingdom of God via the body of Christ?"

In postmodernity, the nature of a decision and what it means has changed. In "late capitalism," American culture has become so commodified that individual decisions are disabled. Capitalism manufactures desires and products to meet those desires so profusely that it leaves the individual with little orientation to make a decision that critically engages the dominant forces. There is little stable subjectivity to make a decision.[11] The isolated discrete decision of the critical individual is a thing of the past of only fleeting significance. Our churches confirm this insight when we see an increasing disconnect between the number of decisions and corresponding life-change. Perhaps it is time then to reexamine the way evangelicals separate one's decision to follow Christ from the outworking of that decision in the transformed life of the believer. In reaction to certain Roman Catholic practices of his day, Luther separated believers' justification from their sanctification. But evidence today suggests that justification by faith measured in terms of individual decisions often does not lead to sanctification. The decisions that we count today may be only vapors in the air. At the end of modernity, evangelicals can no longer oversimplify and just pursue personal decisions of faith from people. We must seek ways to successfully immerse lives into the life of Christ and his kingdom.

Postmodern thinkers reveal the fallacy that individuals can think and reason to an objective decision all by themselves. Instead, the self is formed and shaped by a culture to act and think culturally in certain ways. Decisions therefore are not autonomous, isolated, and discrete. This is the myth of modernity. Decisions are birthed within a given mind-set and shaped within a culture.[12] Decisions therefore need to be tested and placed within a context in order to be intelligible. Philosopher Alasdair

MacIntyre helps us understand this in *After Virtue* where he states that "in successfully identifying and understanding what someone else is doing we always move toward placing a particular episode in the context of a set of narrative histories, histories both of the individuals concerned and of the settings in which they act and suffer." MacIntyre clarifies that we render the actions of others intelligible in this way because action itself has a basically historical character.[13] In other words, an action, or for that matter a decision, is simply unintelligible separated from the rest of one's life story/narrative and one's cultural context because it is not capable of being made sense of.[14] Apart from a context, a decision will appear to be an arbitrary act made on the spur of the moment for short-term immediate gain with little long-term consequences. Decisions all alone, therefore, isolated from an individual's narrative context, do not only carry dubious value. They are unintelligible. They are as plentiful, changeable, and just as arbitrary as today's modern consumer who makes them.

This perhaps is nothing new to us evangelicals. We have experience with decisions that are induced for all the wrong reasons. We are all too familiar with the abuse of the altar call that carries on with ten more verses of "Just As I Am." We see that the majority of the decisions for Christ that take place in our churches do not result in baptisms.[15] Often a new convert makes a decision for Christ solely for the "benefit" of "one's escape from hell." The decision was not presented as a call to repentance and a life of service and redemption under the lordship of Christ. As a result, many decisions are shallow and last only as long as one is concerned about death or never go any further than one's initial ticket out of hell. Many of the decisions we count then are decisions made for self-oriented reasons in the purest of consumer senses, a transaction to get out of hell with no understanding that eternal life is "the end of one's sanctification" (Rom. 6:22, my translation). The critique of modernity then may be true of many decisions that we evangelicals so love to count. These decisions, as the critique goes, can often be arbitrary, they can often be induced emotionally for short-lived results, and they can often be made for immediate benefits that when the benefits disappear the decision does likewise. As a result, "decisions" are often a poor measure of kingdom activity and indeed the focus upon them leads to the abuse of the gospel message into a purely self-serving selfish gospel that rejects the essence of "denying one's self, picking up one's cross and following me."

Theologically, this calls for evangelicals to reexamine the theology that allows us to separate one's justification from one's sanctification, a theological basis for placing so much importance upon one's "decision." For most evangelicals, decisions for Christ have represented the change in the individual's legal status before God. For us, when a person decides to "accept Christ as personal Savior," he or she goes from being the unjustified person outside of the grace of God to the one justified before God and thereby rendered righteous, absolved of all punishment and divine retribution. That decision holds irrespective of one's ensuing life, which renders that decision intelligible. There is a distinct separation of that decision to accept Christ's atonement for sin in faith, one's justification in Christ, from one's ensuing sanctification. Inherited from the Lutheran Reformation, this distinct separation is what keeps us from associating salvation too closely with its outworking in one's life, in other words with a salvation of "works." As inheritors of the agenda of the Reformation, it keeps us from the "Roman error," to make salvation somehow connected to or even dependent upon the outgrowth of works in a new convert's life.[16] The cultural and historical situation that demanded this theological differentiation, however, has changed and begs for reexamination.

Theologically the value of an isolated decision for Christ must now be evaluated in light of a post-Christian/postmodern society that defines a decision differently. I suggest a decision for Christ does not mean today what it meant in other times in Christian history. Whereas a decision in the past may have been a form of immediate immersion into an already Christian society (i.e., the postmedieval world of the Reformation, or the primarily Christianized, well-churched world of post–World War II United States, or reinforced a prior Christian upbringing), it now is often, in post-Christian consumerist America, no more than an immediate induced consumerist decision to respond to an immediate urge. Amidst a fragmented culture, however, with many competing ways to live, a decision must be followed by the serious engagement of that decision maker into a way that makes that decision intelligible. We must preach salvation not just as an escape from hell, but as an overall repentance and turning away from a world gone awry into its own self-indulgences. We must preach salvation not merely as a personal ticket out of hell but as the entrance into the reality of the lordship of Jesus Christ where God is working to bring about his kingdom unto the day that he returns. This may require bringing together justification and sanctification into a more unified *ordo salutis* where one simply cannot make sense without the other.

> **We must preach salvation not merely as a personal ticket out of hell but as the entrance into the reality of the lordship of Jesus Christ where God is working to bring about his kingdom.**

Certainly this makes sense scripturally. Rarely do the New Testament writers use the word *salvation* to focus solely upon justification. Instead, salvation entails justification, the decision to repent, the invitation into new life, sanctification, and healing. Indeed, salvation is the invitation to repent and become a subject of the kingdom of God (Matt. 3:1–3). When one is converted, he is converted to a different way, to following Christ. The decision to repent and turn leads each one to enter the kingdom of God, the rule of Christ. Conversion is the departure from an old world where we still await the messianic rule and the entrance to the new aeon where he has defeated sin and reigns from the right hand of the Father.[17] Such a theological move unifies the *ordo salutis* and it also makes sense in light of the current changes of culture. In a post-Christian culture where so many have no foundation in the Christian life and even worse have been totally immersed into the ways of a self-indulgent consumerist paganism, preaching salvation may require substantive ways of initiation wherein one's decision is led immediately into a path toward baptism, discipleship, and a life of service to Christ in the world.

In summary, the current post-Christian culture can only understand decisions for Christ as something significant if those decisions are tied to a narrative and being transformed by the gospel. Isolated decisions appear lame. This is not to discredit the great evangelicals of our past. Certainly the evangelical focus upon "decisions for Christ," adapting as it was to the new democratic culture, was a necessary piece of cross-cultural work done in order to save Americans in the early to mid-twentieth century. But as we enter a post-Christian age where there is no Christian context, as we enter a postmodern time when decisions must have a narrative in order to make sense, evangelicals need to evaluate whether such isolated decisions mean the same thing. We must take the focus off decisions and onto deeper ways of initiation that take that first decision from its immature beginnings into its full fruition into baptism (confirmation) and a life of service to Christ and his kingdom. In this way that first decision actually means something. When baptism (or confirmation) carries such weight, when it is more than a personal public testimony of one's own private decision, when it is the full renouncement of a former way of life and a turning to a life of following Christ, it will then make sense to count baptisms (or consecrations of baptism or confirmations) as a sign that what we are doing as a church is being faithful to our call in Christ to make disciples and be his body in America. Let us count baptisms (or confirmations) instead of decisions, and let us have a social space where those baptisms can be lived out and brought to full fruition in the body of Christ.

Why Churches Are Doomed from Being the Church if Their Goal Is to Get Big

The second sacred cow of evangelical success is the larger, more efficient organization. Should larger, more efficient organizations be a sign of success for the body of Christ? Here again, the question is not whether harvesting more souls out of darkness into Christ's kingdom is not more desirable than fewer souls. And the question is not whether we should organize churches intentionally. The question is, What kind of organization facilitates the inner workings of a local body of Christ that are necessary to properly mature new believers into followers of Christ and participants in his salvation through the body of Christ? Is the larger organization better? Can the inner workings of the body function as a large and efficient organization? Once we see it is the quality of these inner workings of the body of Christ (not the quantity) that are necessary for the nurturance of each new convert, we can no longer manage the body of Christ as if its size is irrelevant. In fact, in critique of modernity, we should note that largeness and organizational efficiency risk crushing the goals and substance of what it was we were organizing for in the first place. If we make bigness and efficiency a goal in itself, we may leave the church void of its original calling to be the living workings of the body of Christ before a watching world. Therefore it will not do any longer to naïvely measure success via the size and efficiency of an organization to manufacture decisions for Christ. Instead, we must have measures of success that locate whether an organization is indeed functioning as a living breathing body of Christ. This does not require that bigness in itself is antithetical to being the body of Christ. But what it may uncover is that bigness is a hurdle to overcome and not a goal to be sought in being the successful body of Christ.

> If we make bigness and efficiency a goal in itself, we may leave the church void of its original calling to be the living workings of the body of Christ before a watching world.

Modernity extols efficiency and productivity as ends in themselves. Capitalism extols making more things cheaper, faster, and with higher quality. Over against this, those who criticize modernity argue that managerial efficiency and organizing for growth are not morally neutral. Again Alasdair MacIntyre, for instance, argues that managerial effectiveness is "a defining and definitive element of a way of life that competes for our allegiance with other contemporary ways of life."[18] In other words, choosing to manage for efficiency is a choice with moral implications. It presents values and purposes all on its own that may conflict with what it is we are trying to organize for. Such organizational efficiency relies on its own social scientific narratives for its legitimacy, and can in fact be used to masquerade as social control.[19] In the process effectiveness and efficiency become a moral authority unto themselves. Managerial efficiency can become a tyranny. It can take over an organization and separate its management from the mission and goals for which the organization was started. As a result, the underlying purposes of the organization cannot help but change when managed for efficiency, largeness, and effectiveness.

When it comes to matters like these, evangelicals tend to be modernists. We believe in modern science and that includes the social sciences. We are comfortable in capitalism and the freedom of the marketplace. In our churches, we can succumb to the temptation of technique and bureaucracy because of our propensity to focus upon individual decisions and the distribution of services and materials for the nurturance of those decisions into maturity. In other words, the goal of manufacturing decisions fits well with the notion of organizing for efficiency. But if we see that salvation is more than one's personal transaction with God, if we see that salvation is the invitation into God's cosmological work of redemption over sin through Jesus Christ, our idea of church changes and we must organize accordingly. If we no longer separate one's decision as justification from one's sanctification into the salvation of God in Christ and recognize that one's sanctification is dependent upon membership in the body, our idea of the church shifts and we will organize the church differently.

Mennonite theologian John Howard Yoder describes this shift as follows:

> The church is then not simply the bearer of the message of reconciliation, in the way a newspaper or a telephone company can bear any message with which it is entrusted. Nor is the church simply the result of a message, as an alumni association is the product of a school or the crowd in the movie theatre is the product of the reputation of the film. That men and women are called together into a new social wholeness is itself the work of God, which gives meaning to history, from which both personal conversion (whereby individuals are called into this meaning) and missionary instrumentalities are derived.[20]

In other words, it does not make sense for the church to seek decisions for Christ as an end in itself apart from being his visible body on earth, which makes it possible for people to make such decisions. The church is much more than the machinery that produces decisions for Christ. It is the social space, under his lordship where the Holy Spirit works to build up believers and equip the saints (Ephesians 4). It is the social foretaste of his reign where God is taking the rest of the world. It is spatial because we are a people "called out" from the world to be the *ecclesia*. Each church is a body of Christ, his physicality in the world, so to speak, where he is the head. And things happen here under his lordship that can happen nowhere else. The powers of his salvation are set loose in his body through the mutual participation of its members through the gifts before a watching world. It is this new society's life that calls the world to an awareness of their lostness and their separation from God. Out of this new life, the call to a decision for Christ, to repentance from sin and new life in Christ can actually make sense to those who are lost without Christ. When we see the church like this, we cannot organize blindly for the manufacture of decisions. We must organize toward the goal of being the body of Christ, the manifestation of the work of his Spirit among his people, into which the lost are invited to be saved. We must organize for the facilitation of the inner workings of the body, not for the end result of decisions regardless of whatever it takes. We must measure for the quality of these inner workings that mark faithfulness to the call to be his body, not just measure numbers of decisions, which can be meaningless without a context that allows them to make sense.

These inner workings, however, become more difficult the larger a body becomes. As the body of Christ, we speak the truth one to another in love (Eph. 4:15), we bring things out into the light (Eph. 5:8–13), we gather together to resolve conflict and forgive one another (Matt. 18:15–20), we discern and make decisions (Matt. 18:15–20), we share the gifts of the Holy Spirit with one another for mutual upbuilding (1 Corinthians 12, 14; Rom. 12:3–8; Eph. 4:11–13; 1 Peter 4:10–11), we confess our sins one to another and pray for and anoint the sick (James 5:14–16), we gather to take part in the Lord's Supper in his special presence and worship (1 Corinthians 11). Activities such as these define the church as Christ's body. They can happen here in a way like nowhere else. These inner workings, however, rely on interpersonal community that resists larger more efficient forms of organization. The danger (already mentioned) is that organizing such activities according to a management technique in fact changes them. We mega-organize ourselves out of being the body of Christ. These "inner workings" illustrate why largeness and efficiency cannot be autonomous measures of success among the body of Christ.

Take for example the exercise of the spiritual gifts in community. The spiritual gifts define the very essence of the church for the Pauline corpus and beyond in the New Testament (1 Corinthians 12; Ephesians 4; Romans 12; and 1 Peter 4).[21] In order to exercise these gifts, church members need to recognize, affirm, test each other's exercising of the gifts in the arena of Christ's body (1 Thess. 5:19–21). This requires that we know one another. Therefore, the exercise of one's gifts will become more difficult the larger and more impersonal the church gets. It is not impossible, just more difficult. To facilitate largeness, however, we often try to administer systems to funnel people into their giftedness. We mass administer Myers-Briggs personality type and skill profile tests. Yet this misunderstands and changes the very functions of the gifts in community. Gifts are more than just one's inherent talent slots or personality traits best suited to a particular task. They are supernaturally endowed capacities to be discovered and owned within a living body of Christ. They are not merely inherent skill sets or propensities that can be tested for.[22] Therefore, the mass administering of trait analyses is one more capitulation to modernity by evangelicalism.[23] This methodology subdues the Holy Spirit into a technique to mass administer what was intended for the community of Christ to manage, as inefficient as that might be. It is only one more step to organize the church economically so as to pay more staff positions because we cannot seem to get enough volunteers. When finally the senior pastor becomes a CEO of a massive staff instead of a person exercising his pastoral/preaching gifts alongside all other gifts, the church has taken the ultimate step of losing the gift structure of the body to modernity. This completes the transformation by which the church body morphs into a massive organization made possible only when salvation has been commodified and capable of distribution through an efficient organization. In organizing the inner workings of the gifts for largeness and efficiency in this way, we change them and in turn lose the foundation of what it means to be the body of Christ.

There are numerous other inner workings of the body that we risk changing when we manage them for bigness and efficiency. The activity of "speaking the truth in love" and "mutual confession" requires a level of trust and safety that cannot be achieved in large settings. These "inner workings" require intentional discipleship, elder leadership, plus the organization of small "class meeting" type groups, all of which resist mass production. Conflict resolution, "binding and loosing," the creation of boundaries for church discipline, and the "expelling of the immoral brother" for the sake of his salvation (1 Corinthians 5) are activities that require significant familiarity. They are "inner workings" that make possible the community's functioning and identity as the body of Christ. Church discipline, however, will mean something different in a church of ten thousand than it would in a church of three hundred where everyone knows the person and in some way is in relation to the brother or sister being disciplined.

Preaching also changes as the congregation gets larger. Preaching is an inner working because the preacher applies the Word to the issues and concerns of the local community and Word preached is tested by that same congregation. Once we transmit preaching to larger settings, even video simulcasts, radio or TV, the preaching of the Word changes and we lose the local hermeneutic. We lose any significant testing of the preached Word. The preacher ends up being the lecturer and we end up making the application of the Word a privatized and individual distribution of information. This is again one more capitulation to modernity and the commodifying tendency of managerial efficiency. Likewise, the larger a congregation becomes, the more impersonal and privatized our worship can become. Liturgical participation and the communal partaking of the Lord's Supper change as a congregation becomes mega-sized. We start distributing the Eucharist in pre-wrapped containers.

In the same way, true community diminishes with increased size. There simply is no way to efficiently mass-organize thousands of people for the goals of community. Community is inefficient. It is nigh impossible to organize multiple groups who can genuinely come together to pray for one another, edify one another, support and affirm one another, correct and forgive one another. Because in mass, groups will always tend to come together based upon affinity instead of the Lord's Table. Groups will not come together as black and white, Jew and Gentile, woman and man, poor and wealthy. Such groups, when mass organized, easily degenerate into self-fulfillment enclaves that last only as long as we each have need of specific services and supports.[24] Without a pastoral leader to guide this "inner working" of true community, it will be lost. And so, with thirty, forty, or more small groups, there aren't enough pastors to go around. And the mass organization of groups cannot compensate for the lack of community in the church of thousands.

The body of Christ is a way of life lived and practiced, not a set of programs and activities volunteered for.

The "inner workings" of spiritual gifts, speaking truth in love and confession, preaching, and community cannot be produced more efficiently through economies of scale. The body of Christ is an alive organism of the Spirit, which cannot be manufactured. It truly is a culture as opposed to a company.[25] Through our worship and conversations, our reading of the Word and ensuing hospitality, we learn a new way to speak and a new narrative to live.[26] The body of Christ is a way of life lived and practiced, not a set of programs and activities volunteered for. This cannot be easily organized for efficiency and economies of scale.

Evangelicals therefore should pursue a version of success that is formed out of faithfulness to God's call to be his body as opposed to success via numbers. We should organize ourselves consciously away from the goal of getting big toward the goal of being the body. We should reject the de-churching of our bodies through the modern techno-efficiency creeping into our mind-sets that pushes for larger and ever more efficient bodies of Christ. Bigness will be a problem to be overcome along the way, not a goal in itself to pursue. We should therefore reject the ever grander triumph of expertise that seeks to franchise the techniques of any church that gets bigger than a thousand. The body is local, spatial, and difficult to franchise without doing damage to the very substance of what it means to be the body. We need practices of faithfulness, not techniques for success in terms that only make sense in modernity.

Success as Faithfulness

The current day critique of modernity reveals the sources of evangelical churches' stunning addiction to size. Such critique also points us to another version of success, one built on faithfulness to being the body of Christ in the world. This vision for success aims toward the building of his body and the sanctification of believers via that body. The goal is not merely numbers of decisions. The goal is to immerse the stranger into the salvation of Jesus Christ. This success is purged of modernity's individualism and tendencies toward crass commodification of salvation. It reflects a salvation that is from God, embodied in a people's character and a way of life. This vision for success aims toward faithfulness in being the body of Christ before the watching world. The goal is not bigness. The goal is to inflame the inner workings of his body. This success rejects naïve goals of modernist management for largeness and efficiency that overlook the substance of what goes on that makes the church his body. It advocates evangelism, witness, and growth in a way that does not succumb to modernity. Of course, "success" will be an unfortunate word no matter how we use it. It has its roots deep within the capitalist ways of life. Nonetheless, we need an understanding of the goals of our existence as being the body of Christ and a means to test whether we indeed are heading in that direction.

Out of this version of success we can offer different practices for measuring faithfulness, even if in nonquantitative social scientific ways. Such practices would train and form young leaders' character toward faithfulness and perseverance in being the body of Christ, not just success in terms of numbers or organizational size. We still measure success so that we know if we are truly getting somewhere. But we measure it in ways that are inextricably tied to what it means to be faithful to being Christ's body. Such measures based in faithfulness would be the means to understand whether that church that "goes from ten to a thousand members in five years" is actually accomplishing what being the church means and to what extent.

Renewing Practices That Measure Faithfulness

What would it look like to have practices that measure faithfulness? How do we measure success in ways that see success in terms of faithfulness in being the body of Christ before the watching world? No doubt we will still count things, we will still ask questions on surveys, we may still have focus groups. The questions we will ask will shift, however. We will measure or count different things than under the assumptions of modernity.

Count Baptisms instead of Decisions

For example, depending upon the polity of our church I suggest we stop counting decisions for Christ and instead count baptisms or confirmations (in High Church settings). Let us have ways of initiating converts into the salvation of Jesus Christ and the work of God in the world that mean more than an isolated decision. Let us take a person who has made a new decision to follow Christ from that initial decision into a step-by-step process that leads to baptism (or reconsecration or confirmation).[27] In a late capitalist world where isolated decisions are as significant as the decisions we make at the local grocery store, we must look for ways that this decision will become the decision to be a faithful follower of Jesus Christ. This kind of decision can only make sense within the immersion into the body of Christ as carried through in baptism. These baptisms are powerful points of entry into the world where Jesus is Lord, and the new initiate is born into service for Christ and his kingdom. Baptisms (or confirmations) then mean something, and we should count them as a primary indicator that salvation is taking place in our midst.

Use Qualitative Measures of Community

When evaluating a church, let us go beyond asking questions about the quality of preaching, the worship services, the convenience and usability of children's care services, and the accessibility of restrooms. Let us ask questions in our surveys like this:

When was the last time someone spoke a hard truth into your life? Was it done with love?

When was the last time you confessed sin to someone you felt safe with in this community?

When was the last time you prayed with someone over an issue of needs or discernment in this body?

When was the last time someone in this body visited you in the hospital or brought over a meal when you were sick?

When was the last time a homeless person was brought into this
congregation and made whole?

The questions concerning quality and convenience of services are no
doubt important, although it is still an open question whether it is a
good thing to make church convenient or more "user friendly." These
questions, however, tempt us into thinking that the church's problems
are an issue of right technique, which can be solved through replacing
or improving a few functions up front, while the real problems lie in
teaching our people what it means to be the body of Christ and submitting ourselves to the Word and worship.

So we should ask each other different questions that test the manner of life that we are living in order that we might be used by God as
the body of Christ. As Yoder says, "What needs to be seen is rather that
the primary social structure through which the gospel works to change
other structures is that of the Christian community. Here, within this
community, people are rendered humble and changed in the way they
behave not simply by a proclamation directed to their sense of guilt but
also by genuine social relationships with other persons who ask them
about their obedience; who (in the words of Jesus) 'bind and loose.'"[28]

Let us then turn from only measuring church attendance to measuring
the life being lived in Christ. Are we seeing evidence of his salvation in
our midst? How many marriages have been saved? How much sexual
abuse has been ended? What is the number of times people have come
to another's aid in the congregation financially, how many people in the
church have invited a stranger to the gospel over for dinner, how many
people in the church have reached out to a poor person with the gospel.
Let us measure how many poor have entered the church doors and now
sit made whole in the worship on Sunday, how much giving goes on in
the church, how many people have been restored from alcoholism, social
injustices, promiscuity, or domestic violence. Or is the level of greed,
social victimizing, sexual abuse, depression, divorce the same as or
worse than that outside the church? Then we will be able to tell if being
a Christian makes a difference. We will be able to tell whether what is
going on within these boundaries is really the functioning body of Christ.
In the words of theologian Stanley Hauerwas, "Just as scientific theories
are partially judged by the fruitfulness of the activities they generate, so
narratives can and should be judged by the richness of moral character
and activity they generate."[29] So also our story in the God of Israel and
Jesus Christ will be measured before a watching world by the quality of
life and character it generates.

Measure the Number of New Church Plants, Not the Size of Church Buildings

Let us also turn from measuring the size of buildings to the number of new churches planted. Let us count the number of local congregations each church has formed outside itself instead of the attendance figures on Sunday morning or the increased size of the worship facility. We must ask, Why is it that pastors of large churches are more willing to build bigger buildings than empower a group of forty to fifty people to plant another living body of Christ?[30] If indeed the facts are true that the greatest conversion growth occurs in churches when they grow from fifty to two hundred people,[31] why is it that we insist on building bigger churches after they have reached one thousand?[32] What does it say about our assumptions for church growth when we plant churches that already start with two hundred people?[33] Does it say that a church is not really a "successful" church until it reaches a thousand? But if we accept our new conditions in a post-Christian culture, pastoral success and the success of a church will not be measured by simple numbers alone, but by church plants, the spurring on of missional congregations that can display a witness visibly to the new life in Christ before a watching and lost world. If what we have said above is true, evangelicals should seek a vision of the world that is populated with local bodies of Christ, not megachurch centers.[34] Instead of huge religious arenas for private individuals to come eat, shop, and see a religious production, let us evangelicals pursue a world where one can no sooner go to a Starbucks, a Cineplex movie theater, or a local tavern without also being confronted with an alternative center for life, a life as centered under the lordship of Christ, the visible local body of Christ. If this is what it means to be the physical body of Christ in North America, then the ultimate sign of church success will be "the number of churches you have planted," not how big your church is in terms of attendance, decisions, or church facilities.

> **Why is it that pastors of large churches are more willing to build bigger buildings than empower a group of forty to fifty people to plant another living body of Christ?**

2

Evangelism

Saving Souls beyond Modernity:
How Evangelism Can Save the Church
and Make It "Relevant" Again

But in your hearts set apart Christ as Lord. Always be prepared to give an
answer to everyone who asks you to give the reason for the hope that you
have. But do this with gentleness and respect.

1 Peter 3:15 NIV

But thanks be to God, who always leads us in triumphal procession in
Christ and through us spreads everywhere the fragrance of the knowledge
of him. For we are to God the aroma of Christ among those who are being
saved and those who are perishing. To the one we are the smell of death;
to the other, the fragrance of life. . . . We do not peddle the word of God
for profit. On the contrary, in Christ we speak before God with sincerity,
like men sent from God.

2 Corinthians 2:14–17 NIV

Over the last four years at our church I have encountered several students
from local evangelical seminaries who were seeking to fulfill an assignment for their evangelism class. The assignment, simply put, requires

each student to present the gospel message to five to ten non-Christians and report their results back to the class. They were given various tools in these classes to help them engage these strangers with the gospel, such as various opening lines, the use of surveys, a vigorous apologetic, or a simplified yet well-honed presentation of the need for justification by faith as the entry into a relationship with God through Jesus Christ. The students, however, could not find anyone to talk to. Most of the students had just moved from other parts of the country. They were detached from knowing anyone significantly outside the seminary or church who was a non-Christian. And so they came to me asking where they could meet a stranger to the gospel. They asked if there was anyone in our church they could talk to. Regardless of these difficulties, however, these students were still expected to come up to total strangers and engage them with a credible presentation of the gospel message. After several of these forced engagements, these students repeatedly came to me and reported their total frustration and lack of even a modicum of success in communicating the power of the gospel message to the non-Christians they encountered.

I believe these students reflect much about the current status of evangelism within evangelical churches. First, evangelicals still prize evangelism (i.e., the conversion of individuals to faith in Christ) as the primary task of the church. We seek to convert non-Christians into the Christian faith more boldly than almost any other group or movement within the Christian church. Second, our methods of evangelism reflect a modern confidence in the individual's ability to make a good decision and in the objective truth of the gospel message. We believe any individual can accept salvation in Christ given the right information and a willingness to seek truth. We therefore train our church members to make clear and persuasive presentations of some basic biblical information to a non-Christian from which that person can pray "the sinner's prayer."[1] We teach our congregations how to defend the Bible's authority historically and scientifically so as to overcome false prejudices the hearer might have. Since we depend upon the Holy Spirit and because the truth is the truth, we believe we can do this with complete strangers. And so evangelicals are known for their methods to bring people to conversion such as *The Four Spiritual Laws* booklet, Evangelism Explosion training, and Billy Graham crusades. Yet with all this effort, the results we are getting are much the same as those students were getting. Today, our church attendance has plateaued and our conversion growth is minuscule. Less and less people are listening to and understanding what we are saying about the world's need for salvation in Jesus Christ.[2]

Within our history, many of the evangelistic methods I just described have succeeded in bringing large numbers of people to Christ. But a new generation has arrived and their culture challenges these methods. This new generation is not impacted by the ways evangelicals have traditionally presented truth and defended their faith. They experience and engage truth differently than previous generations. They want to see how truth is lived, not just talked about intellectually as information. And so the traditional evangelical methods of evangelism do not make sense among this new generation. Whether they are postmodern or post-something else,[3] these post-peoples are adept in exposing the evangelical's modernist ways of thinking. In their demand for a living gospel, they expose how much we have separated the truth of salvation from the way we live it.

In response, some evangelicals simply write off postmoderns as relativists and assert more vigorously the value of absolute truth in their evangelism.[4] Others just avoid this "relativism issue" entirely and instead address postmodernism through repackaging the image of their Sunday morning worship services to appeal to the cultural manifestations of postmodernism either in music, media, or other aesthetics.[5] I would argue, however, that in either response we avoid engaging the way postmoderns understand reality and the culture they are living in. We reject the work of intercultural evangelism with these postmoderns we are trying to reach with the gospel all in the name of preserving "absolute truth." Some evangelicals falsely act like "there's just no talking to people who don't believe in absolute truth."

But this is not necessary. There are other ways to talk about truth besides the ways we hold so dear. In fact, once we get past the initial reactions, it becomes apparent that postmodern people may embrace some chaos in their culture but they do not reject truth in its entirety. They might suspect truth known only in words or propositions, but they respect a truth that can be seen and experienced in life. These postmodern people demand a living truth they can participate in, and this can provide the basis for a new evangelism. But all of this challenges the ways evangelicals do evangelism. Indeed, these postmoderns challenge us to live the truth we tell as a body of believers. They seek a living display of truth and in so doing force us to move the church back to the center of the work of evangelism. They reveal how much we evangelicals have given away our evangelism to parachurch organizations and expert techniques and, in the process,

> **Postmoderns challenge us to live the truth we tell as a body of believers. They force us to move the church back to the center of the work of evangelism.**

made the church a sideshow to the work of evangelizing the masses into Christ's salvation.

In this chapter, I describe two of the important shifts in the way post-modern people know truth. I then show why evangelicals need to discard some evangelistic practices because they are married to assumptions and language that no longer exist for postmodern people. I then propose a different basis for sharing the gospel with postmodern people over some understandings of truth we can all embrace. Out of this I then offer some practices for evangelism that make sense for saving souls beyond mo-dernity. The result is an evangelism that requires a shift of Copernican proportions. It requires the display of the truth, not propositions, deeper understandings of salvation, not four-law formulas. And whereas tra-ditionally evangelicals have sent evangelists out from the church with the message of the gospel, this evangelism requires the church itself to become the message. In effect, this evangelism requires that we no longer "give away" the task of evangelism to parachurch organizations or techniques that take place outside of the life of the church community. Instead, "postmodern evangelism" requires the evangelical church to take its own salvation as seriously as it does others' and, in the process, make its own way of life impossible to ignore as the standard-bearer for what is real and relevant in a fragmented and seeking world.

From Modernity to Postmodernity: The Shift

What has changed about truth in postmodernity? At the risk of over-simplifying, I propose that there are two shifts to the way people ex-perience knowledge in postmodernity. These two shifts are part of the new structure of the way people know, which is engulfing wide sectors of our culture, especially those educated after the 1980s. The origins of this structure are the academic institutions of the West, but the effects of this structure are widening throughout Western culture.

One of these shifts is the way postmoderns experience modern sci-ence. As opposed to most modern people, postmoderns no longer naïvely accept modern science as the central authority for their lives. From its birth with Isaac Newton until the present, modern science proved its abil-ity to bring about material improvements in the way we live, travel, deal with disease, and communicate. Scientific method consistently yielded "hard" findings that were verifiable, dependable, and useful in improv-ing human life. People of modernity therefore tend to trust in the hard sciences' ability to deliver truth and progress. They believe in science as the objective source of truth totally free of prejudice. This, however, is no longer true for postmoderns.

Contrary to modernity, philosophers such as Karl Popper, Thomas Kuhn, and W. V. O. Quine articulate how science is a theory-laden, faith-requiring enterprise.[6] They argue that from Copernicus to Newton, Einstein to quantum physics, scientific theories have changed several times, each time changing the "paradigms" for the way we understand the world. This was not because the objective world changed. It was because science constructed better theories to understand the world for certain purposes. Consequently, a "molecule" is a theory now, not a representation of the way things are. "Molecules" are part of a paradigm that helps us understand how certain things work, not a representational fact about the world. Science, in other words, is not objective. It is a purveyor of webs of belief that we believe in for their heuristic value. As a result, science is just one more way of depicting the world that has pluses and minuses. And modern science has limits. As a result, it may yield powerful results regarding the manipulation of the physical world, but it cannot explain a lot of human behavior and is stumped when speaking about the moral and religious issues of human life.

In addition, science and historiography reveal themselves to be open to interpretation and a power agenda. As French philosopher Jean-François Lyotard contends, modern science is a form of discourse that excludes all other discourse. Yet science itself relies on nonscientific discourse for its own legitimization. Science therefore only masquerades as an objective discourse and can be manipulated and used for power interests as much as any other language game.[7] Modern science regularly partners with power interests within politics, democracy, and capitalism. Witness the use of science to undergird both the legitimization of the homosexual lifestyle on the one hand and the moral inferiority of the homosexual lifestyle on the other, using either genetic or statistical data.[8] Witness the use of the scientific method to argue both for evolution (Darwinism) and creation (intelligent design) as theories of life's origin in the universe. Science, it seems, is as prejudiced and perspectival as any other realm of knowledge. In postmodernity, people recognize that science is limited, sometimes given to a narrow understanding of the world, and often prone to an agenda of power.

This postmodern critique of science disturbs some evangelicals because they believe it necessarily leads to truth being relative. Such relativism, however, is not the only option.[9] A more powerful option is carried out by Alasdair MacIntyre and his followers, who argue for the inherent repository for proven truth in the progression of tradi-

Postmodernity deposes science as the indisputable arbiter of all truth in modernity. In point of fact, science limits reality.

tions.[10] Whatever the options, postmodernity deposes science as the indisputable arbiter of all truth in modernity. In point of fact, science limits reality. And it must take its place alongside other traditions as a historical tradition to be examined and appreciated within its limits. In the process, traditions can become the central enclave for the testing and proving of truth.[11]

A second shift in the perception of reality is the way postmoderns doubt that objective truth is accessible to the critical individual mind. Most modern people trust unabashedly in the powers of the individual mind to arrive at basic truths. Originating in the seventeenth century (according to modernity's story), thinkers struggled for a certainty that would stand above the violence and tyranny they were experiencing in the European religious traditions. They mistrusted truth handed down in traditions because it caused wars and other abuse. To avoid religious wars, thinkers like Descartes and Kant exalted the reasoning powers of the individual as the source of objective truth.[12] The individual self could stand above and detached from traditions and make free judgments on truth based on one's reason. This has formed how modern people see reality and understand truth. It lies behind the way modern people defend the individual's rights to make up one's own mind and trust one's own heart in searching for truth.[13]

Postmodern hermeneutics, however, undermines this confidence. German philosopher Martin Heidegger exposed how determined our understandings of God are via the linguistic structures of Western metaphysics we have been caught in.[14] Jacques Derrida, Michel Foucault, Hans-George Gadamer, and Paul Ricouer expose the ways the human self is interwoven within texts, narratives, and cultures. They examine the individual quest for truth in the written text and show how cultural and ideological forces shape what lies within each text and indeed each mind. And so for Derrida, there is no stable metaphysics, and language is always moving. There can be no secure meaning coinciding with the text.[15] Authorship is ellusive and there is no self so autonomous that it can exist above or outside the text. Selfhood is the product of intersubjectivities. Under these influences, postmodernity sees all knowledge as determined within language and culture caught up in power structures. It requires "deconstruction." The bottom line is that objective knowledge does not exist because the modernist objective knower does not exist as moderns are used to thinking about it. In this way, there is no such thing as objective truth.

Some evangelicals fret over this demise of objective truth. Yet the postmodern critique of objective truth does not necessarily require the demise of truth.[16] And postmodernism correctly reveals the powerful ways the self is formed out of cultures and how knowledge is bound to cultural histories.[17] The question then is threefold: who can know truth, how can we know truth, and within what limits should we approach truth? At the very least, we evangelicals can appreciate the postmodern push to examine the limits to the ways in which we know within our human condition and the nature of our personal formation.

In summary, the culture of postmoderns undermines two main assumptions of modernity, which are that scientific truth is objective and objective truth is available to the powers of an individual's reasoning. Any attempts to evangelize postmoderns based upon these assumptions will likely fail.

The Waning Effectiveness of Evidentiary Apologetics and Seeker Services

If the above is accurate, evangelicalism's methods of evangelism will prove ineffective among postmodern peoples. In the face of the postmodern shift, the effectiveness of our traditional methods of evangelicalism will wane because they are (mostly) grounded in modern assumptions whose perceived value and formerly prevalent influence in culture are also waning. To understand how and why this is so, let us examine two examples: evidentiary apologetics and "seeker services."

The first practice of evidentiary apologetics uses modern science to defend Christianity. Authors using this strategy typically build a scientific case for the veracity of Scripture and the resurrection using historical and scientific evidence. The popular *New Evidence That Demands a Verdict* by Josh McDowell and *The Case for Christ* by Lee Strobel are just two prominent examples of this strategy.[18] Creationist science and the "inerrancy" defense of Scripture are other examples. All such authors and their strategies depend upon the hearer believing in the authority and objectivity of modern science. But that belief has waned within postmodernity. Hence, in postmodernity, evidentiary apologetics comes off sounding like an agenda-ridden manipulation of scientific methods. Scientific defenses of the Bible fail to carry weight because the "inerrancy" defense assumes that there is an objective scientific basis for "what is an error." As the German historical critical method has revised its so-called objective conclusions regarding Scripture again and again, it has revealed itself again and again to be as subjective and "agenda ridden" as any premodern tradition.[19] Consequently, efforts like these make less and less sense to the postmodern when they are based in scientific method and modernist terms like "inerrant." In postmodernity, the power of evidentiary apologetics wanes and the authority of scientific defenses fades.

A bigger postmodern problem, however, is the way evidentiary apologetics undermines Christian authority in a person's conversion. In the earliest stages of a person's evangelism, evidentiary apologetics endorses the authority of science. The logic goes like this: if I can prove it scientifically, then Scripture must be true. In the earliest moments of one's conversion, science and historiography are set up as final arbiters of truth, not the Scriptures, the Holy Spirit, or the church. Postmodern cultural psychology therefore exposes how the initiation process shapes authority and ways of seeing in the initiate for a lifetime. Evidentiary apologetics shapes the new believer to forever look over one's shoulder at science as the authenticating truth test rather than Holy Scripture and the Holy Spirit working in his people. Consequently, evidentiary apologetics falls short and fails in postmodernity because it tacitly trains the new initiate to depend upon science as a higher source of truth than the Scriptures given in Jesus Christ. It teaches the new believer to trust science more than the Scriptures of the church, both of which are considered historical traditions in light of postmodernity.

> Evidentiary apologetics falls short and fails in postmodernity because it tacitly trains the new initiate to depend upon science as a higher source of truth than the Scriptures given in Jesus Christ.

The second practice of "seeker services" assumes objective truth is available to the rational powers of the isolated individual. Churches using seeker services therefore seek to craft the presentation to be as appealing as possible to draw in the individual so he or she will eventually hear the message. All that matters is that the individual hears the simple message. The seeker service strategy therefore works to draw seekers into a large anonymous setting where they can view a professionally produced, entertaining presentation of the gospel that attempts to be contemporary and appeal to "felt needs."[20] "Seeker service" strategies do not shy away from marketing to an audience, using psychology and other forms of self-fulfillment to interpret the gospel.[21] Seeker services have faith that people, upon hearing a well-packaged message, can use their individual mind to make up their own mind for the gospel.

Postmoderns, however, suspect the machinations of consumer-oriented messages to have power over them to make "buying" decisions. Instead, postmoderns recognize truth most where it is lived day-to-day one with another. The postmodern is convinced of truth through participation, not consumer appeals; through wholly lived display, not merely by well-reasoned arguments. Seeker services will still work for the boomers and those raised in modernity whether by age or immersion in the evangelical subculture. These people of modernity were taught to trust only their individual minds or experiences. Postmoderns, however, know their minds or experiences can be manipulated. Modernist boomers are suspicious of tradition in the true Enlightenment sense. They are the ultimate feeling generation, self-indulgent, and focused on their own "felt needs." Postmodernity, however, finds a generation that suspects the blatant consumer-oriented persuasion of the dominant media. Their "felt needs" have an ever-shortening, MTV-like life span. Some of this next generation sees marketing and advertising as capitalist intrusions with an agenda into forming people certain ways so as to benefit certain economic power interests.[22] They respect truth that is lived. The postmodern generation may enjoy the show for a short while. But they are looking for a home, a community wherein a belonging can take root and the moral fabric of truth can be borne out. If postmodern culture is for real, seeker services are running out of time. The next generation seeks community over anonymity and is overdosed on consumer appeals to felt needs. Postmoderns desire something bigger to be transformed into.

Yet more problematic for seeker services than waning effectiveness is the postmodern revelation that seeker services initiate converts into a Christianity that forms them to be self-seeking. Seeker services often present salvation as self-fulfillment, as the answer to "felt needs."[23] They present the gospel as attractive, professional, and successful. And despite the emphasis on small groups and community, the seeker strategy initiates the new believer through a portal where most people make isolated decisions in a sea of anonymity, the so-called megachurch setting. Isolated as an individual, the "unchurched Harry" can decide to follow Christ for self-centered reasons, because it is attractive, makes him feel better, or takes care of his needs. The megachurch setting that often develops tends to make the church into a mall where you get saved and then use the church to take care of all the needs a Christian might have. Postmodernity, however, reveals how individualist evangelism trains new Christians to be consumers of Christianity and God.[24] It forms the minds of the seekers so powerfully that it is too much of a "bait and switch" to later ask new believers to then deny themselves and follow Christ. Such an evangelism method does not recognize that making salvation into an individualistic trans-

If postmodern culture is for real, seeker services are running out of time. The next generation seeks community over anonymity and is overdosed on consumer appeals to felt needs.

action between a person and God based solely in that person's desire to escape from hell or meet a felt need may in fact not only fall short of the full intent of Scripture but initiate that person into another form of self-centered existence.

In summary, postmodernity undermines the prototype ways evangelicals have done evangelism based in modernity. Postmodernity jeopardizes evangelistic practices that depend explicitly on the authority of science or the sovereign powers of the isolated individual mind, two assumptions that evangelicalism has relied upon in its past. In addition, however, postmodernity exposes how these same practices may tacitly shape the character of the convert in ways that work against the gospel of Christ taking root in a person's life. Postmodernity reveals that the means of initiation form the character and the mind of the individual as much as a rational decision. Evangelicals therefore are forced to look for a different basis for our evangelism if we are to reach the postmodern era.

A Postmodern Basis for Evangelism

The question then is, How do we make sense of the Christian claim that "Jesus Christ is Lord" in a postmodern world where old ways to truth have broken down? The answer is we display what these words mean in the way we live and worship so that its reality, once displayed, cannot be denied, only rejected or entered into. We will persuade through living displays of truth, not rational one-on-one arguments. We will orient salvation away from an individually centered transaction to a salvation based in God's cosmic activity in Christ and the invitation to participate in something bigger than one's self in the kingdom of God. The church then becomes the postmodern portal to truth. It becomes the basis for evangelism. And as a result, both truth and salvation will look different from our previous modern ways.

Our notion of truth will look different in an increasingly postmodern environment. Instead of a spoken proposition to be communicated rationally from an objective vantage point, truth will now be known through entering into it and personally participating in it. Postmoderns will be saved through "osmosis" as opposed to one-on-one persuasion.[25] Postmoderns therefore will learn the truth by coming into the community of Christ, inhabiting it, living within it, and gradually learning the language by which we speak. The words of Christian truth start to make sense as they are spoken and used among a people. Within the community, postmoderns can taste truth, test it, recognize its fruit, and see that it is good (Ps. 34:8; Luke 6:43–44). This view of truth might limit the possibility for objective truth for isolated minds, but it does not sacrifice truth. Instead, it situates truth in location. It forces the messenger to live truth, not just talk or argue about it. In this way, postmodern evangelism happens amidst living truth. Evangelists therefore must have a place to embody truth before they can speak it. This means the onus is on the church to become the center of living truth. Christian claims will only make sense amidst postmodernity when they are lived and participated in among a body.

Such a view of truth will invigorate the importance of historical traditions as carriers of living truth.[26] As postmoderns enter the community's life, the richness of all Christian history becomes an apologetic with weight. In traditions, Christians become witnesses to a specific reality of Jesus Christ lived in their history, not advocates of an argument that has universal appeal. Historical traditions carry truth, prove it by living it and testing it out in people's lives. Traditions only rationalize the truth as they embody it. They have a depth that cannot be denied. The power of Scripture as centuries-old narratives carries more weight than a rational argument for inerrancy. Scripture that is lived into by a body of believers comes alive in new stories. And postmoderns gather around stories. Postmodernism therefore returns truth to the work of traditions.

For postmodern evangelism, this means that truth is best communicated as it is lived in the life of a body of Christ out of its (his)story and its stories, not one-on-one combat via evidentiary apologetics. Instead, the church itself becomes the apologetic.[27] As the truth of the gospel is worked out in the real lives of people living together in community, its veracity cannot be debated or individualized; its reality is something into which we may simply invite others to "come and see," and the church thereby becomes the center for evangelism. Evangelicals often preach that what the culture needs is absolute truth, but what the culture needs is a church that believes the truth so absolutely it actually lives it out. Living traditions of depth that tell stories of wonder provide the basis for Christian claims of Christ's lordship to make sense in the postmodern world.

As a result, evangelism among postmoderns takes on the character of witness as opposed to coercive evangelism. The witness reports on particular events seen or heard. A witness rejects coercion and refuses the role of prosecuting attorney and instead gives testimony. The good news cannot be received as good news if it comes to the stranger by means of coercion.[28] Conversion is the sovereign work of the Holy Spirit, never the human work of manipulation or salesmanship. Amidst postmodernity, people live out of different worlds, making sense of their lives within narratives that coexist side by side. In this context, the task of the witness is not to argue or contend for universal meta-proofs but to live truth so deeply and sufficiently that it throws alternative worlds into "epistemic crisis" and leaves open the door to those in that crisis for conversion and entrance into the kingdom of the God of Israel and Jesus Christ. The power of our own narrative, the compelling display of our life in Christ reveals gaping holes in the others' narrative, leaving them asking questions and searching for a more coherent and meaningful life. Once they see our lives, they come asking us questions. We are then ready to give an "account for the hope that is in [us]." We are to do so "with gentleness," with no coercion, and with "reverence," knowing that Jesus is Lord and sovereign over all things including the converting of the world to Christ (1 Peter 3:15–16 RSV).[29]

> The task of the witness is not to argue or contend for universal meta-proofs but to live truth so deeply and sufficiently that it throws alternative worlds into "epistemic crisis."

In addition to our notion of truth looking different, our notion of salvation will look different from our previous modern ways as well. Among postmoderns, our notion of salvation must take on additional historical depth. The Christian account of salvation in Christ alone will only make sense in postmodernity when that salvation takes shape in real lives. And if it truly is a gift, this salvation must be bigger than our own selves. Salvation must be more than an intellectual transaction where the individual receives forgiveness of sins in exchange for faith, salvation from God's wrath, and a justified legal status before God based upon some intellectual assent. Postmoderns recognize the folly of an isolated individual coming to truth via another isolated individual. And they recognize the folly of isolated individualism and its inability to be freed from cultural formation. Without a corresponding way of life, individualized salvation looks like cognitive consumerist manipulation for the postmodern. There must be something larger to be invited into. Evangelicals therefore must preach and embody the reality that salvation is much more cosmic in scope than a transaction to take care of an individual's legal guilt before God. Evangelical churches must recapture the cosmic scope of the classical *Christus Victor* model of the atonement in the ancient church. We must preach that although salvation begins with an individual's trust in Christ for forgiveness of sin, the new believer is invited into the social territory of his lordship where one can live the victory over sin and death that Christ accomplished on the cross and through his resurrection.

In our doctrine of salvation then, evangelicals must avoid commoditizing salvation into an individualist consumerist transaction, something we have been prone to. There is a reason why it sounds intrusive to ask a stranger the question "Do you know Jesus Christ as personal savior?" We have privatized the relationship with Jesus so as to make him into a gnosticized faith that seems isolated from everyday life. We must un-privatize our faith in Christ and reconnect our relationship with God through Christ to a way of life that we can invite people into and a movement of God in history. Then we can ask, "Do you have a place where you can ask your questions about life?" "Do you know a story that can make sense of your life?" When we do this, we focus away from scaring people out of hell to inviting people into a compelling way of life. We realize that making salvation about being saved from hell irrespective of being saved to new life cheapens it into a piece of individualist knowledge, bordering on Gnosticism, that does not take root in embodied lives.[30]

In postmodernity, truth is about character. Religious truth can no longer be relegated to the realm of private feeling or preference. This is because modern science, which pushed it there originally, no longer reigns supreme. Truth is in the living. Any evangelism therefore that separates one's renewed legal status before God from the new life we have in Christ strips the gospel of its power for a postmodern evangelism. For the postmodern world, justification cannot be separated from sanctification and sanctification cannot be separated from a living people of God. The basis for a compelling Christian account of salvation in postmodernity is a changed life among a living community of Christ.

> **The basis for a compelling Christian account of salvation in postmodernity is a changed life among a living community of Christ.**

Postmodernity therefore forces evangelicals to base evangelism in a living body of Christ that lives the truth and possesses the salvation of a cosmic Lord. It forces our churches to be relevant again. This is not to say the goal of the church is to be relevant to the wider culture. Instead, the relevance we seek is that the church becomes relevant to its own message of God's salvation in Christ and thus relevant to evangelicals again. In other words, the church becomes so real and authentic in its own living of the gospel that in effect evangelicals quit proving the truth of the gospel rationally or scientifically and let its power speak for itself. It is an evangelism where our churches can quit selling "escape from hell" because we actually believe our life in Christ is superior to the life in the world. A whole new mind-set of evangelistic practices can then be built around this.

Practices That Restore the Church to the Center of Evangelism

What will such evangelistic practices look like?

Practice Hospitality

First, the challenge of postmoderns requires that evangelicals invigorate the practice of hospitality in our churches as the means to invite the stranger into our homes (Rom. 12:13; Heb. 13:2; 1 Peter 4:9). Simply put, evangelical Christians must consistently invite our neighbors into our homes for dinner, sitting around laughing, talking, listening, and asking good questions of one another. The home is where we live, where we converse and settle conflict, where we raise children. We arrange our furniture and set forth our priorities in the home. We pray for each other there. We share hospitality out of God's blessings there. In our homes is where strangers get full view of the message of our life. Inviting someone into our home for dinner says, "Here, take a look. I am taking a risk and inviting you into my life." By inviting strangers over for dinner, we resist the fragmenting isolating forces of late capitalism in America. The time-honored practice of hospitality is so exceedingly rare today that just doing it at all speaks volumes about what it means to be a Christian in a world of strangers.

> In our homes is where strangers get full view of the message of our life.

Furthermore, inviting a stranger into one's home alongside another church friend shares and immerses that person in some of the bounty of fellowship and commonality Christians share. We do not need to say anything we would not ordinarily say. We do not need a method or a conniving plan to convince them of Christ. That is the Holy Spirit's work. We just live until this person asks what is different about the way we live (1 Peter 3:15–16) or comes to us asking, "My wife and I are getting a divorce. What would you do in my situation?" And then we pray for them. We consistently reach out to our neighbors by praying for them, ministering to a need, or offering some hospitality to someone suffering physically, financially, or spiritually (Matt. 10:7–8; 25:34–40). Postmodern evangelism incubates in the climates of hospitality, in the places of conversation, posing questions and listening to the strangers in our midst. In the process, we Christians grow when the stranger challenges us in ways we have not been confronted yet. And when they finally do ask, "Who is this God that enables you to live the way you do?" we take the opportunity to tell them our story or to invite them to our worship together to see this God we worship as Lord who has invited them into a fellowship with himself that makes life beyond compare. Hospitality as a way of evangelism may be as old as the Celts.[31] Yet inviting a stranger into my home for dinner is an evangelistic practice that in itself must become a way of life for the evangelical church.

Reinvigorate the Ministry of Prayer, Mercy, and Justice

Second, evangelicals must reinvigorate the practice of sharing mercy and justice with the stranger. Certainly Protestant mainline churches make this practice central to their understanding of evangelism. Likewise, evangelicals have taken on the task of justice and mercy in the world. But too often, Protestant mainline and evangelical churches have done the works of mercy and justice detached from the local church. We have sent teams to the inner city or we outsource justice ministry so that victims of sin in a fallen world rarely enter into our congregation to be loved, healed, and redeemed.[32] Instead, we must actually minister to the hurts and injustices of the stranger next door, the sicknesses and the brokenness of actual neighbors in order to challenge their self-sufficient narratives of capitalism. By actually ministering mercy and prayer, we embody the message of the gospel instead of arguing for it. We actually see all people as persons Christ died for, whether they be homeless or rich, immigrant or native, hurting or secure (Matt. 25:31–46). But when we separate them from the congregation, we shortchange the work of salvation, for the new life can only be learned by participating in it. So after prayer, mercy, and justice, there must come the moment to invite the victim or victimizer into the fellowship of redemption and renewal. So, unlike certain classic Protestant liberal approaches to justice, our justice must be an extension of the church body and the bridge into the church body. Then we will no longer have congregations that look homogeneous in race, economic sector, and age.

Evangelical pastors therefore need to teach our congregations how to show mercy, pray for the sick, and do justice to those we meet every day at work, in the neighborhood, or on the local news. We need to teach parishioners how to pray with the stranger, minister helps to the newly divorced, pray for healing over the sick who has nowhere else to turn, and love the unlovable crank who has isolated himself from the neighborhood. When

> **When the church reaches out to actually minister justice or mercy to a victim of sin and pray for the victimizer, it witnesses to the gospel in ways words can never do.**

we do so, we break the determinations put upon us by capitalism and democracy that keep us "to ourselves." When the church reaches out to actually minister justice or mercy to a victim of sin and pray for the victimizer, it witnesses to the gospel in ways words can never do. The sign of a lost stranger sitting in worship as one of the redeemed is the ultimate testimony to the new life we have been invited into in Christ Jesus. The ministry of justice and mercy then is inextricably linked to the congregation and is a key strategy for evangelism in postmodernity.

Be a Community

Third, evangelicals must recover the true practice of community if they are to evangelize in the new environment of postmodernity.[33] As an evangelistic strategy, evangelicals should teach Christians how to journey together in groups of twenty to thirty people who meet together regularly to share fellowship and discernment. Postmodern evangelism is about living truth, and this happens among Christians and their communities of friendship. Here we share our joys and our sorrows (Rom. 12:15). We share barbecues and games of croquet, bocci ball, or whatever social rituals make sense. And when one of us gets sick, there is a time of discernment of sin and faith, and the elders pour oil and lay on hands (James 5:14–16). When someone moves to another city, we discern, lay hands, and "send them out" (Acts 13:3–4). When someone seeks marriage, we counsel, discern, post the bans, read letters of affirmation, stand beside, and bless the marriage. In the rhythms of life we give witness to who we are and the power of God's salvation in Jesus Christ set loose in our midst. These gatherings are petri dishes for postmodern evangelism. Christians invite strangers to these places, and there we love strangers and display the manner of life we have in Christ Jesus. In these groups, we can truly listen to our neighbor's questions and trust the Spirit will lead us into all truth. In these communities of conversation we share the journey of life's most sacred moments and are witnesses mutually to the activity of God in each other's lives. Here is the perfect social manifestation of truth postmoderns require to be compelled to the gospel.

These communities can also function as more specific communities of conversation, baptizing the pagan into the meanings for the ways we raise children, grieve loss, support the elderly, and form Christian marriages. These communities go beyond typical twelve-step recovery groups or singles groups. They are communities formed to foster instruction and formation into various Christian tasks and healings. They can be a seven-week instructional community of marriage formation to a twelve-week gathering on the task of being single for the kingdom of God. Out of these places, the strangers sit among us, participate in the meanings of the gospel, and postmodern evangelism takes place.

At our church, we structure house gatherings to happen on Friday or Saturday nights (sometimes Sunday afternoons as well). They begin at 5:30 or 6:00 p.m. People bring food to share. We fellowship, talk, and sometimes play a game that tells people more about each other. We often have a provocative question to pose to one another to start conversation. Questions or fill-in-the-blanks such as: "The hardest thing to believe about God is _____?" Then at every house gathering, at approximately 8:00 p.m., we wind the evening down with a time of corporate prayer for each other's struggles and the furtherance of God's kingdom in our midst. If someone is sick, we have a healing service; if someone is moving, a sending out takes place; and if someone gets engaged, we gather to affirm the marriage. Every evening at the house gathering 8:00 p.m. signals that strangers are welcome but always given an easy out. No stranger to the gospel leaves, however, without knowing where in the neighborhood they can go when they are in crisis or need. At 8:30 to 9:00 p.m. we depart refreshed, having made this home a lighthouse for the inbreaking salvation of God in Christ.

John and Sue were a couple who lived next door to some friends of mine for many years. My friends tried to invite them to church, but they were never interested. They were busy, successful professionals who had it all. And so no tracts, no interesting presentations, no Alpha group could interest them. My friends just had nothing to say that could ever interest John and Sue in the gospel, and they were very discouraged. Nevertheless, my friends continued to invite them over for dinner, get to know them, have wonderful times of fellowship, and offer them prayer. John and Sue, however, would always slip out before the prayers could begin. One night, however, after knowing this couple for five years, and never receiving any indication they were interested in Christian faith, John and Sue came to my friends and asked if they could talk. They said, "We've tried everything to have a baby and we have been denied. We're at the end of our road. We have no place to turn. Could you please pray for us?" My friends were floored. That night was a glorious night of ministry, talking, and crying. From that encounter, the couple started coming to church. The steady witness of hospitality became the portal from which this couple began their journey toward Christ. These kinds of hospitality gatherings have brought many non-Christians to our own church.

Create Room for "Third Space" Evangelism

Evangelicals need also to create new spaces for connecting to the stranger if we are to evangelize postmoderns. For even if we do make our homes and churches open for community and relationships, many strangers will still reject these spaces for meeting other people. Hypermodern society spatializes its citizens into individuals, alienates us from one another in subtle "me-versus-you" relationships, walls us off in subdivisions where neighbors rarely know each other, and shapes us into being consumers of virtually everything in life—including relationships. Our churches must find ways to resist these forces if relationships in community are to be the basis for postmodern evangelism. We must find "third spaces" that are neutral yet conducive to creating these relationships.

Starbucks has often seen itself as the social third space for American society alongside the home and workplace. Postmodernity longs for such third spaces as meeting places for connecting with other people. Some might suggest that the church become this third space. Although I do not propose that the church become a third space alongside the family and work as though the individual could then balance his or her own investment in each one, third spaces can nonetheless be essential as a connecting place where Christians and strangers to the gospel can meet. Surely we must not forsake the home as the welcoming place for strangers, but in a society drowning in its hyperindividualism, there will be many strangers who resist being invited to another person's home for dinner. It is too threatening. Third spaces can germinate the kind of relationships necessary for postmodern evangelism to take place because strangers can come there on their own terms under other pretenses (like buying something) and relationships will be formed.

Churches can, for example, set up not-for-profit businesses that provide services such as coffeehouses, which provide places to study, interact, and drink coffee. Churches can organize community centers that provide socializing and fitness programs for the community at large. Churches can sponsor art galleries or theater companies. These sites are not on church property. They are safe yet social. They provide the opportunity for strangers to interact one-on-one with Christians from the church on other terms.[34]

My own denomination has provided seed money to begin coffeehouses and community centers with this goal in mind. Such endeavors become self-sufficient, not-for-profit businesses that provide places for Christians and others to meet. In Hamilton, Ontario, Pernell Goodyear's church, The Freeway, has purchased a storefront in a downtown area to set up a coffeehouse as well as provide computer Wi-Fi services for the community, plus computer classes for the elderly. Places like these perform services to the community yet also provide neutral space for Christians to meet and talk with those outside the salvation of Jesus Christ. The church must remain the central place from which all other life flows from and to God. Yet these third spaces provide the bridge place for the church to connect relationally with the community at large. They create the safe spaces for strangers to come in and engage the life of Christ witnessed relationally in community together. Such third spaces are the launching pads for relationships that naturally allow us to invite people into our homes and our churches from whence the gospel can be seen from the vantage point of hospitality and worship.

Worship

In postmodernity, evangelism should happen in fully embodied Christian worship.[35] In worship, Christians present salvation, not in a rationalized, cognitive word only, but in the rich display of mighty acts in symbol and art. Worship does not divide the scientific from the religious, the material from the spiritual. As with postmodernity, worship embraces mystery, body, soul, and spirit. It springs forth out of the depths of its traditions and brings the ancient into the future. It therefore cannot be denied because it is real. It cannot be argued with, only embraced or rejected. In this way, Christian worship is the ultimate postmodern evangelistic act.

In worship, the church becomes the center for evangelism. As will be discussed in chapter 4, however, evangelicals must recover practices of worship that display the reality of his lordship sufficient to reveal the shallowness of the reality as the surrounding world sees it. Using the arts, as well as the skills of the Word, Christians re-present the story of who God is in song and dance, visual art, and drama. He becomes present in a real way in the mystery and power of the Lord's Supper, services of healing, and the power of joint praise in song. Christians convey the depth and history of our God through the sacred times of renewal and formation we have in the church's calendar. In all of this, the Christian bows before his lordship in the display of his glory. Christian worship therefore is a good place for postmoderns to meet God because worship is where they can stand before the depth and wonder of what God has done down through the ages and understand themselves in light of that. Such worship need not be "seeker sensitive." A stranger entering worship may not and should not receive of the Lord's Supper. But in the Eucharist an outsider can witness the renewal and transformation of a people firsthand. And as the outsider evidently did in 1 Corinthians 14:24–25, the unbeliever may end up bowing before God and declaring, "God is really among you!" because one cannot help but be confronted body, soul, and mind with the God of Jesus Christ in worship.

Reinvigorate the Rite of Baptism

If evangelicals are to do evangelism in the post-cultures, we need to reinvigorate the practice of baptism in our congregations. The practice of initiation and baptism is the vortex that funnels strangers walking around in our midst into the full salvation of Jesus Christ. At our church we have developed a version of the third-century Hyppolytus practice of initiation with the help of Robert Webber's book *Journey to Jesus*.[36] At our church, strangers to the gospel have come among our congregation via one of the avenues described under the previous practice. They will meander around taking part in worship, house gatherings, and even triad confessional groups. There will come a time, however, when they are challenged to make a decision and follow Christ. This usually happens at the end of the fall season, the end of ordinary time in the church calendar when those who have never been baptized or seek a reconsecration of their baptisms are encouraged by the church to join the "Journey into Christ" instructional community, which meets for an hour and a half before each church service every Sunday morning.

The "Journey into Christ" instructional community follows the third-century practice of Hyppolytus of initiating new converts into full participation into faith in Jesus Christ. It takes the believer through four stages. In the version we have developed, the first stage is conversion. We gather, learn about repentance from sin, receiving of forgiveness, and turning toward Christ. We work through with the class what it means to cross the line of conversion to faith in Jesus Christ and talk this through with each new believer in the class. We call this the seeker stage. The next four weeks we review the basic doctrines of the Christian faith as summarized in the Apostles' Creed and the Lord's Prayer. We work through with the class what it means to assent to these articles of faith and how we must grow into them the rest of our lives. We call this the hearer stage. At this point we ask everyone to announce his or her intention to be baptized. Those who commit to baptism are then taken before the congregation at Communion hour and presented for preparation and support for baptism. Their names are symbolically written in a large book symbolizing the Book of Life. The next several weeks, coinciding with Lent, the students learn of the commitments to live the moral life that God calls us to in Christ. We enter a time of examination with the class. At the end of this time, we pronounce them ready for baptism. On Easter Sunday morning, very early, at sunrise, at the break of the vigil, we baptize all who have prepared and celebrate renewal of baptism with the rest of the church as we gather for Easter Sunrise celebration. The next weeks before Pentecost we teach the class the tools for walking the Christian life and then send them out on Pentecost to be witnesses to the gospel as members of Christ's body. In this way, we seek to reinvigorate the practice of baptism in our church. The call to baptism becomes the means of sealing one's decision to follow Christ and enter into his life through baptism. These baptismal practices become the vortex from which the wandering strangers in our midst get funneled into becoming full participants in the salvation of Christ and his body.

Summary

All of these places—the home, the community, third spaces, the sacred space of worship—serve to make the church the postmodern space for evangelism. They speak to an evangelism that invites one in to see the message before one hears the message in words. They speak to an evangelism that is willing to save via subtle osmosis versus immediate rational persuasion. It is an evangelism that meets postmoderns who do not trust individual arguments, slick presentations, or scientific proofs. They want to come, see, and be confronted by the reality of Jesus Christ. The practices of postmodern evangelism therefore must converge in the living, breathing spaces of the local body of Christ.

From Crusades to Church Planting, from "Just As I Am" to Baptism

If we accept postmodernity's challenge to our modernist ways, evangelicals will no longer give away evangelism to places outside the church. Instead, amidst postmoderns, we will make the church, the living body, the vortex of evangelism. We will no longer impart universal truths to individual minds outside the church. We will live truth together so as to compel the lost to come and see his lordship in full display in a worship service. Salvation is more than a matter of one's individual status before God. It is the victory of Christ over sin and death into which Christians invite strangers via the forgiveness of sin and the infilling of the Holy Spirit. Our evangelism then strives not to make the gospel relevant to the categories of the post-Christian generation outside the church. It strives to embody the gospel in the church so that all else becomes irrelevant to the stranger who walks in. In a world where the truth that "Jesus is Lord" is viewed as irrelevant, the task of evangelism is not to somehow make his lordship relevant to that world but to live his lordship so truthfully that it makes it impossible for alternative worlds to ignore. In this way, the church becomes supremely relevant to Christians in the work of evangelism.

Such an evangelism beckons evangelicals to leave several of our modernist habits behind. In modernity, the goal of evangelism was personal decisions for Christ by individuals, and the church could afford to be a sideshow. It was enough for the church to provide support and services to new converts. Hence in modernity, evangelism was often a parachurch endeavor, carried on more ably by specialist organizations outside the church like the Billy Graham Evangelistic Association, Campus Crusade, and the like.[37] With the arrival of postmodernity, the mode of communicating the truth of the gospel shifts from a one-on-one encounter to a one-on-church encounter, from one-on-one well-reasoned arguments and slick presentations to the vivid display of its message in the lives and worship of its people. Such a shift makes evangelism impossible separated from the church. The rise of postmodernity in Western culture forces us into a Copernican shift where the church becomes the center of its evangelism. "Outsourcing" evangelism to outside groups or techniques becomes impossible.

All of this is not to suggest that personal decisions for Christ are no longer important. In the postmodern world, however, personal decisions will die without a social context in which they are lived out.[38] Personal decisions will die if there is no story into which they make sense. Maybe in the past, individuals were afforded time to find a home after they decided for Christ at a crusade because there was an existing powerful ethos of national Protestantism. In the new fragmented culture of consumerism devoid of Christian ethos, a decision for Christ, if separated from the church and left alone in the sea of self-oriented democratic culture, will deteriorate into another consumer choice, a transaction for a benefit, the escape out of hell. We evangelicals must see that true evangelism invites people out of the consumerist ethos of the world and into the alternative world where Jesus is Lord. This must happen if the decisions are to "stick." Evangelism therefore depends upon the existence of living communities of Christ.

> **Church planting is the ultimate form of postmodern evangelism.**

Church planting then is the ultimate form of postmodern evangelism.[39] When we go from an Enlightenment-based epistemology (viewing the work of evangelism as primarily a communication from one mind to another) to a postmodern reality (where truth is understood as it is lived and displayed), when we go from modernist evangelism (primarily passing out salvation one decision at a time) to the gospel as (his)story (whose viability and power is best delivered as it is lived in a social embodiment), the first course of business is to found communities in that story. Only then will we be able to show people what we mean when we say "ye must be born again." Church planting is the necessary prerequisite to "saving souls" in postmodernity.

The focus of our evangelism will shift from decisions for Christ to baptisms or (in non–Free Church traditions) confirmations. The chronology of our evangelism will expand from everything that leads up to the personal conversion decision to include everything that happens from that initial decision all the way to baptism (or confirmation). Salvation is something bigger than a self and its decision; it is what that self is invited into in Christ. Evangelism's defining moment therefore moves from the crisis decision of faith to the initiatory rite of baptism (or confirmation). Salvation is no longer an individual transaction that takes place in the head, it is the participation in the work of Christ, something greater than one's own self-absorption.

Evangelism therefore requires that evangelicals retrieve the significance and power of baptism and/or confirmation as an initiatory rite. It requires that our churches develop processes that link "making a decision for Christ" with a process of baptism (or confirmation) and all that lies in between.[40] For Free Church evangelicals, baptism will signify more than a "public declaration" of a decision already made, it will signify the entrance—mind, body, and soul—into the resurrection of Christ and his rule in his body (Rom. 6:4). And whereas evangelism used to end with the ritual of the candidate walking down the aisle to "Just As I Am," now such an experience marks one of many moments in that person's participation in the salvation process of the Holy Spirit. And churches engage these moments as character-forming processes that take one to the place of baptism (and/or confirmation) into the life of Christ. Our evangelism should embrace as its work the entire journey from the decision for Christ all the way to baptism (or other initiatory rites of established church traditions), because it is the entry into the world of his lordship that marks a disciple in postmodernity.

In summary, when evangelizing postmoderns, evangelical churches cannot do evangelism within churches that act as franchises selling goods and services of Christ. Our evangelism cannot separate from the living body and sell his wares. Evangelizing postmoderns requires a colony of the King, full of his culture and life into which the Christian can invite those starved for life and meaning. As if it were an outpost, the church inhabits space amidst a fragmented and decaying world and lives a reality whose fullness lies just ahead (Phil. 3:20). Its evangelism is therefore not a debate. It is not a consumer appeal. It is a carnival in the village, a boisterous parade that marches through town. It displays Christ with marching bands, beautiful floats, vivid symbols, and a way of living so powerful that it threatens the surrounding principalities and powers. It is the march of victory over sin and death begun in Christ to be consummated in his return. It both celebrates and invites those around to take a look and participate in this wondrous manner of life made possible in Jesus Christ. It is more than a word, more than sight. It is a full-bodied fragrance that cannot be denied, only entered or rejected. It is sweet fulfillment to those who join in; it is bitterness to those who have already chosen death. As a living vibrant people, Christians do not sell, they just live; they do not peddle, but do speak sincerely; they do not debate, they witness to his presence in worship and invite people into this great victory over sin and death we have in Christ's death and resurrection. In this way, our evangelism will be faithful to the apostle's description in 2 Corinthians 2:14–17 (NIV):

> But thanks be to God, who always leads us in triumphal procession in Christ and through us spreads everywhere the fragrance of the knowledge of him. For we are to God the aroma of Christ among those who are being saved and those who are perishing. To the one we are the smell of death; to the other, the fragrance of life. And who is equal to such a task? Unlike so many, we do not peddle the word of God for profit. On the contrary, in Christ we speak before God with sincerity, like men sent from God.

3

Leadership

When Evangelical Pastors End Up in Moral Failure:
The Missing Link between the Pastorate and the Virtues

You know that among the Gentiles those whom they recognize as their
rulers lord it over them, and their great ones are tyrants over them. But
it is not so among you; but whoever wishes to become great among you
must be your servant, and whoever wishes to be first among you must
be slave of all. Because the Son of Man did not come to be served but to
serve, and to give his life a ransom for many.

Mark 10:42–45 NRSV

Over the last ten years, I have served on conflict resolution teams among
evangelical churches. I have also observed conflicts within evangelical
churches as an outside pastoral observer. Tragically, in the course of these
conflicts, pastors are often exposed in the midst of significant moral failure. What is surprising, however, is not that the moral failures happen,
but the persistent manner in which these evangelical pastors defend their
failures in terms of the effectiveness of their churches. In one case, for
instance, a pastor hid an affair that his wife had with another leader in
the church for the express purpose of "protecting the church's ministry"
in the local community. In another case, a pastor continued to hide his

indiscretion from the elders because it would be bad for the future of the church. Once a pastor excused his anger and physical abuse toward a staff member as being the only way to get maximum performance from the employee for the success of the church. One time a pastor sat in an elders' meeting month after month while continuing an affair with one of the elders' wives. In this case, the pastor had defended the lack of fellowship among the elders and himself as necessary for the success of the church. A pastor, he said, should not divide a church by becoming too close friends with any one person or group of persons in the church. In each of these cases, there was the sense among these evangelical pastors that the integrity of the body of Christ was subordinate to the success and effectiveness of the church. In the case of marital infidelity, there was even a sense that one should be faithful to his spouse solely for the sake of the success of the church. The calling to live faithfully in Christian marriage as unto the Lord was somehow secondary.

Perhaps the above episodes are anecdotal. Nonetheless, they illustrate how a pastor's construal of his or her vocation and mission impacts the direction of one's character. If pastors view their vocation in terms of success and view the church as a corporate entity, their pastoral character will be formed toward those ends. Success will be the goal of their character and not faithfulness in life and mission. And so when evangelicalism trains a pastor to view the pastorate more in terms of leadership models taken from American business as opposed to those received with the callings and gifts given to us in Jesus Christ, we should expect corresponding changes in moral character, plus moral failures of the same kind. We can expect, for instance, that many evangelical pastors might handle conflict via the terms of a top-down organizational chart as opposed to a patient discernment of a body of people guided by the Spirit. We can expect that many evangelical pastors will not be able to confess their struggles and vulnerabilities within a congregation for fear of putting their own position as moral leader in jeopardy. And in all of this, we can likely expect that the quality of the pastor's moral fitness becomes more an issue of pastoral success than the pursuit of holiness in his own life as a glory unto God. As a result, we might expect to see more of the immoral behavior we see in American business taking place among our church pastors, things like bitter conflicts, hostile takeovers, isolation, CEO-style decisions, and personal moral failures.

This chapter describes the way American business has influenced the shape of evangelical church organizations and the character of pastors. Evangelicals commit the modernist faux pas: we assume that what works in one sociological arena must have the same cause-effect relationship in another. We therefore rely on techniques that enable us to forsake Christ's model of servant leadership for a corporate notion of leadership.

In essence, evangelicals "give away" our calling as pastors to become corporate-like leaders. In the midst of modernity's demise, however, with the rationale for such a leadership undercut, the opportunity exists for evangelicals to reinvigorate practices for the faithful training and formation of ordained pastors as faithful servants of Christ and as participants in communal life, not mere leaders of corporate success.

The Evangelical Fascination with Leadership American Style

The idea of "leadership" has captivated evangelicals in the last twenty years. During this time, leadership conferences have proliferated among evangelicals, along with leadership books and consultantships. These conferences train pastors how to manage staff, inspire volunteers, cast visions for growth, and generally lead churches as effective organizations. These conferences along with publications teach concepts learned in American business schools like "branding," marketing your church, casting a vision, how to write a mission statement, how to motivate volunteers, and other subjects derived from schools of business or organizational behavior. All of this has led to the meteoric rise of CEO-style "pastor-leadership" among evangelicals.

This rise of the "CEO-leader-pastor" is recent. Indeed, one must search hard to find the word *leadership* among American church vocabulary prior to World War II. Behind this rise of the CEO "pastor-leader" in evangelicalism have been several developments. For instance, many local evangelical churches since the 1980s have migrated from the model of the local parish pastor to the notion of the megachurch CEO–leader–public speaker. As more small evangelical churches close and more megachurches arise in North America, today's evangelical church boards seek pastors who can lead, motivate, and manage large groups of employees and volunteers. Becoming a megachurch has become the goal of many evangelical churches despite the relatively small percentage of churches over one thousand members in evangelicalism. Furthermore, as multiple staff churches become the norm in North America, even moderate-sized churches demand senior pastors with managerial and vision-casting skills. Whereas the average evangelical congregation in the 1960s had a single pastor and a church secretary for a church of five hundred members, the same church today would have a multiple staff, with expectations to grow bigger. These developments create demands for the leader-pastor-CEO. In the meantime, evangelical denominations extol the virtues of the megachurch pastors, have these pastors speak at their general councils, and send their young pastors to the megachurch leadership conferences. Because of all these developments, the leader–public speaker–pastor–CEO has become the preferred model of evangelical pastoral leadership.

The end result of the developments that have promoted the CEO-leader-pastor has been the redefining of leadership according to evangelicals. The defining mark of this change is the way evangelicals look to American business to understand leadership. Stunningly, much of the leadership conferences and publications draw extensively from the American corporation and business community for their definition and understanding of leadership. Professors of American business schools write many of the Christian leadership books. Business schools themselves do case studies on evangelical megachurches as examples of excellent business leadership.[1] And in return, case studies are extracted from situations in American business or government and used to teach churches at leadership conferences. Many of the speakers at these conferences are leaders from American business or American government. The most high-profile speakers, for instance, at megachurch Willow Creek's Leadership Summit (Barrington, Illinois) have been business/government leaders such as Warren Bennis, Kenneth Blanchard, Peter Drucker, and not least of all, President Bill Clinton. John Maxwell's Injoy Ministries, popular among evangelicals, openly advertises his leadership seminar as a seminar for bringing non-Christian business leaders into the church by educating on "The Qualities of a Leader" using presenters who are major business leaders of Fortune 500 corporations (or successful sports coaches). These leadership-training resources occupy numerous shelves in evangelical seminary bookstores. Few would disagree, when it comes to understanding leadership and the management "operation" of the local church, evangelicals are fascinated with American business.

> When it comes to understanding leadership, evangelicals are fascinated with American business.

Evangelicals, American Business, and Modernity Gone Awry

How do evangelicals justify going to American business, universities, and government as sources to understand leadership in the church?

In this regard, evangelical leadership teachers contend that the principles of leadership and organizational behavior are universal and traverse all socioethnic and religious boundaries. It only makes sense then for Christians to draw leadership wisdom from American business leaders. Megachurch pastors Bill Hybels, Ken Blanchard, and Phil Hodges can say therefore in their preface to *Leadership by the Book: Tools to Transform Your Workplace*: "In this book we invite students of leadership of all faiths, culture and experience to take another look at the leadership genius of Jesus Christ."[2] Jesus becomes a leadership principle applicable across all working environments. Leadership does not change from one cultural context to another, and that includes the church. Former evangelical pastor turned leadership expert John Maxwell articulates this same premise in the introduction to his book *The 21 Irrefutable Laws of Leadership*:

> One of the most important truths I've learned over the years is this: Leadership is leadership, no matter where you go or what you do. Times change. Technology marches forward. Cultures vary from place to place. But the true principles of leadership are constant—whether you are looking at the citizens of ancient Greece, the Hebrews of the OT, the armies of the last two hundred years, the rulers of modern Europe, the pastors in local churches, or the business people in today's global economy. Leadership principles stand the test of time. They are irrefutable.[3]

The implicit bottom-line understanding here is that leadership principles are not determined in specific ways by the person and work of Jesus Christ that demand allegiance to him in order to make sense. Instead, leadership principles apply universally. Therefore, there should be no conflict if we invite Bill Clinton, president of the United States, to speak at the Willow Creek Leadership Summit for pastors because "who is better qualified than the president of the United States to talk about leadership"?[4] We are inviting him here because somehow what leadership principles work in governing the United States executive branch will also work in leading the body of Christ. There is no direct link between character formed in Christ and what it means to pastor and lead his church. The workings of "leadership" stand above historical contingency and the specifics of living as the historical people of God in Jesus Christ.

Behind these evangelical notions of leadership stand the assumptions of modernity. Modernity subscribes to the notion of scientific objectivity even when classifying sociological behavior. It is the modern habit to forever seek to grasp predictable principles of sociological behavior that stand above historical contingencies and call it science.[5] Evangelical experts on leadership fall into line with these modern assumptions when they seek out timeless principles that will make every leader effective and predict positive outcomes.[6] Though it is unspoken, evangelical leadership teachers assume modernity's confidence in the authority of the organizational disciplines at the secular universities in their writing and speaking. In addition, modernity subscribes to the notion that efficiency is good, that it is possible, and that it merits authority. Originating with

Modernity subscribes to the notion that efficiency is good, that it is possible, and that it merits authority.

Max Weber's justification for bureaucracy, managerial effectiveness is assumed as a good that justifies much of how we live modern-day life.[7] This modern quest for efficiency lurks behind many of the evangelical leadership books and conferences. We seek faster growth, efficient programs, and measurable discipleship. Evangelicals seek effective leadership that inherently underwrites controlled outcomes and the development of techniques to increase efficiency. These are the assumptions of modernity, and evangelicals, like fish in water or birds in air, are willing to endorse these assumptions, yet they are unaware such notions need articulation and defense. And so in these ways, evangelicals allow our commitments to modernism to underwrite the "giveaway" of how we define leadership in the church of Jesus Christ to the forces of American effectiveness.

Evangelical Leadership at the End of Modernity

But outside evangelicalism's world, modernity is breaking down. Postmoderns question the so-called objective sources that give power to leaders. This is especially so with American business, where "leadership" principles come under suspicion for what lies behind them: manipulation and abuse of power for ulterior capitalist gain.[8] Critics of modernity reveal the subjectivity and the historical contingencies from which the social sciences cannot be liberated.[9] Therefore, sociological science hardly serves to mitigate the suspicion surrounding the business world's and evangelical church's grand objectification of leadership as a category of study that can transcend cultural contingencies. Efficiency and leadership that "gets it done" smacks of control, manipulation, and the disguise of oppressive human power.[10] So the postmodern populations carry the modern suspicions toward authority and tradition and look with disgust upon the evangelical church. They are looking for places of community with leaders of humility, not the massive organizations with the leaders of technique and control.

As modernity fades, evangelicals therefore seek "effective" leadership at their own peril. Indeed, the very word *efficiency* poses theological problems. As Alasdair MacIntyre contends: "Managers themselves and most writers about management conceive of themselves as morally neutral characters whose skills enable them to devise the most efficient means of achieving whatever end is proposed. Whether a given manager is effective or not is on the dominant view a quite different question from that of the morality of the ends which his effectiveness serves or fails to serve. Nonetheless there are strong grounds for rejecting the claim that effectiveness is a morally neutral value."[11] The advocates of evangelical leadership write about leadership as if effectiveness is the criteria of a good manager, ignoring the question as to whether effectiveness may not be a good thing. However, the postmodern asks, who can be trusted to manipulate and control outcomes assumed behind the guise of effectiveness? While evangelical leadership gurus underwrite the notion that a leader can have dominion over events given the exercise of a good leader's skills and understandings, the postmodern asks, Who gives this kind of power and control to a leader in the church? Wherein lies accountability and the Holy Spirit in relation to this kind of authority, the governing of events, and their outcomes in the body of Christ? What role should a leader have in governing the events of a church that claims to be his body and the arena of his Holy Spirit? And should such authority be concentrated in a leader (or group of leaders) through organizational techniques? When it comes to asking these questions, evangelical leadership instructors are deftly silent.

In the face of MacIntyre's deathblow to efficiency, Scripture points us in another direction. Putting aside questions of church order and whether a church should be governed through a congregational, eldership, or hierarchical rule, the church of Jesus Christ is pictured as the body of Christ, of which Jesus Christ is the Head (Eph. 4:7–16). The body of Christ is indeed the arena of the Spirit where "Jesus is Lord"(1 Corinthians 12 and 14). It is debatable then whether such leadership should be so construed as to achieve predetermined results. Any results among the body should be the Lord's under his sovereignty. It is debatable then whether a technique-driven leadership style is appropriate to the church. Such leaders should serve the church faithfully within the role that God has given to each one (Rom. 12:3) under the lordship of Christ. The results should not be a matter of sociologically manipulated technique. In the words of John Howard Yoder:

> If we claim to justify the actions we take by the effects they promise, we shall be led to pride in the abuse of power in those cases when it seems that we can reach our goals by the means of our own disposal. . . . We are drawn into the twofold pride of thinking that we, more than others, see things as they really are and of claiming the duty and the power to coerce others in order to move history aright. If our faithfulness is to be guided by the kind of man Jesus was it must cease to be guided by the quest to have dominion over the course of events. We cannot sight down the line of our obedience to the attainment of the ends we seek.[12]

In other words, Yoder advocates that effectiveness is not a good thing if determined by secular sociological reason. Instead, faithfulness will be rewarded with the results wrought by the hand of a sovereign God in history. To engage in any other type of leadership produces inevitable coercion and pride if one's own goals actually are achieved for the benefit of God. Evangelicals therefore, amidst the end of modernity, would do well to reject "efficiency" and "technique" in their search for faithful leadership.

A second aspect to this end of modernity is the way that postmodern insights undermine the modern assumption that we can acquire truth irrespective of particular cultures and historical contingency. Postmodern writers continually contest universal claims for principles that ignore the culture and history from which they were formed.[13] They give evangelicals reason to pause when we ignore our history in Christ when developing leadership principles from other places. British theologian John Milbank rightly contests that the work of theology and the church must start first from who we are as the people of God in Christ and work out from there. Only thereafter can we take principles exterior to the people of God and see which ones have symmetry with being the body of Christ. Evangelicalism, in its leadership approach, follows modernity's social strategy in seeking out universal principles of sociology and then applying them to the body of Christ. But as Milbank has stated, "Theology has frequently sought to borrow from elsewhere a fundamentalist account of society or history, and then to see what theological insights will cohere with it. But it has been shown that no such fundamental account, in the sense of something neutral, rational, and universal is readily available. It is theology itself that will have to provide its own account of the final causes at work in human history, on the basis of its own particular, and historically specific, faith."[14] In other words, evangelicals naïvely believe that sociology or business can somehow help us because it is objective. But this is an objectivity and a definition of truth born out of the disciplines of American business. By deferring to the history of American business to teach us how to lead, evangelicals "give away" the "leadership" bequeathed to us specifically in Christ and exchange it for the ones given by capitalism and modernist sociology. But in fact, each social history carries its own historical agenda, and this is just as true for business and the Western university as it is for the church. Thus, why would Christians not start with who we are and where we came from in history

> **Why would Christians not start with who we are and where we came from in history to determine how we should lead?**

to determine how we should lead? The postmodern writers reveal the perils of placing our confidence in business-school-type generalizations to teach us about leadership for the body of Christ.

In the face of modernity's fading influence, it is therefore presumptuous to assume that "leadership is leadership" wherever we might find it. One's understanding of leadership is born out of one's history. Because leadership is imbued with purposes, it has a cosmology that assumes things about the way the world works. Christians have a different purpose (*telos*) for and a different understanding about the way the world works (cosmology), which fundamentally alters our understanding of what it means to be a leader. For Christians, Jesus is the Lord and the Spirit makes possible a different reality that supersedes sociology's laws of "cause and effect." Human effectiveness is not what we seek. The kingdom of God is not ours to control. Some things can be learned from American business, government, and what it means to be human. But the direction of the learning must go from finding who we are in Christ as his body to seeing if there is anything we can learn in American business and government that we can then bring into the captivity of the lordship of Christ. It is only in the enlightenment of his Spirit through his Word among his people that we can then see what is worthy of God outside the church. In Yoder's words, "Not everything that is happening [in the world] is the work of God. Instead of asking, What is God doing in the world? the church should ask, How can we distinguish, in the midst of all the things that are going on in the world, where and how God is at work? The answer to this question will not be found by reading on the surface of daily history but by the Spirit-guided understanding of the discerning community."[15] As with Yoder then, evangelicals should seek to first discover the leadership we have been given in Christ before we seek its reality in the world. If we do anything else, we risk "giving away" the leadership given in Christ and exchanging it for American business because of our unexposed confidences in the myths of modernity.

Leadership according to Scripture

Having said all of this, and to be fair, many evangelical leadership teachers advocate that Scripture and the life of Christ argue for their specific leadership concepts. For example, evangelical pastor and leadership guru Bill Hybels enlists Scripture to support various leadership categories such as building a team ("building a kingdom dream team"), managing resources, and finding and developing a leadership style.[16] Don Soderquist of Wal-Mart uses Scripture to argue for the leadership "concept of innovation" and taking risks.[17] Hybels and other evangelical leadership teachers ascribe modern leadership concepts directly to Jesus himself. Hybels, for example, suggests Jesus "had a three year strategic plan."[18] Kenneth Blanchard uses Jesus as the primary model for the now universally recognized concept of "servant leadership," popularized by Blanchard and founded by secular leadership guru Robert Greenleaf.[19] Evangelical leadership writers show little hesitation in enlisting Jesus Christ as the model CEO.[20]

We have reasons, however, to suspect these uses of Scripture. Evangelicals may not appreciate postmodern hermeneutics, but in regard to the above-mentioned uses of Scripture, can anyone ignore the question of whether in our interpretation, we have imposed meanings from the business culture upon the text? In the evangelical world especially, there resides a belief that Scripture is a collection of propositions whose meaning we can get to through divining the original author's intent. This often leads to casual prooftexting. Putting aside whether these assumptions are valid, the reality is that there just is little exegesis or hermeneutical engagement found in evangelical leadership books when they use scriptural texts. To say Jesus had a three-year strategic plan, or displayed leadership principles in his life, requires that we question which culture is driving this interpretation of Jesus and for what purposes. But because such a deconstruction is not within the scope of this chapter, let us simply ask, Is there another understanding of the Scriptures regarding pastoral authority and leadership that finds its origins in the church, which should then govern the interpretation of Scripture as we seek to engage the world and the demands of leadership in the church amidst capitalism?

In this regard, we should note that the word *leader* in the New Testament is generally avoided in the New Testament context of the church.[21] The apostle Paul avoided elevating himself over other workers, consistently using *brethren* and words with the preface *co-* (co-laborers, co-workers) to describe those working in the churches with him (1 Cor. 3:9; Phil. 2:25; 4:3; 1 Thess. 3:2; Philem. 24). Likewise, the New Testament writers generally avoid using secular or Old Testament (LXX) titles for authoritative office.[22] The New Testament instead uses the term *diakonia* ("servant" or "service") to label people in leadership, far more times than any other term.[23] The New Testament writers therefore used a word to describe leadership in the church, which contrasted violently with the current secular notions of office. Roman Catholic theologian Hans Küng outlines how the New Testament writers saw that any words that suggest a relationship of rulers and the ruled were unusable in the new community context.[24] The New Testament on this reading appears to carefully avoid the models of authority available in surrounding society for defining leadership in the church.

Why was the New Testament so careful? Most certainly it is because the New Testament church carried the consciousness of Christ's words, "If anyone wants to be first, he shall be last of all, and servant of all" (Mark 9:35 NIV). "You know that among the Gentiles those whom they recognize as their rulers lord it over them, and their great ones are tyrants over them. But it is not so among you; but whoever wishes to become great among you must be your servant, and whoever wishes to be first among you must be slave of all. For the Son of Man did not come to be served but to serve, and to give his life a ransom for many"(Mark 10:42–45 NRSV par. Luke 22:25–27). The New Testament church bears the image of Christ modeling "leadership" as the ultimate act of servanthood when he washed his disciples' feet (John 13:13–17). They remember his words from Matthew 23:8–11: "But do not be called Rabbi, for One is your Teacher, and you are all brothers. Do not call anyone on earth your father, for One is your Father, He who is in heaven. Do not be called leaders; for One is your Leader, that is, Christ. But the greatest among you shall be your servant. Whoever exalts himself will be humbled; and whoever humbles himself shall be exalted"(NASB). Jesus commands his disciples to refuse any titles of the secular authorities, including religious (Rabbi), family (father), or group style leadership (leader).[25] Though we may disagree how to implement Jesus's commands regarding authority and leadership within the church, we can surely conclude that Jesus instructs the church to resist modeling its own leadership in any way on the secular notions of leadership that exist outside of the church. With Yoder, evangelicals should seek to discover first what it means to follow Christ in our leadership as a people under his lordship and only then look to American business and sociology and seek to distinguish which leadership practices we must reject as Christians in the world.

The Moral Character of the Effective Evangelical Pastor

What are the costs to the evangelical church from modeling leadership on sources outside the church? CEO-style leadership may grow churches larger and more efficient, but what toll does this take on the character of our pastors and the quality of Christlike community taking place in the churches? Within evangelicalism, there exist significant percentages of pastors who deal with depression, burnout, and fall into moral failure.[26] The number of church splits and pastors asked to leave remains a chronic problem among evangelical churches.[27] The Southern Baptist Convention reports a rise in the 1990s in forced terminations due to "control issues, poor people skills, and pastoral leadership style perceived as too strong."[28] Is there any link between the ways we teach leadership and the character of our pastors?

There is no evidence available that links pastoral moral failures to effective leadership training. Nevertheless, the question remains, how are evangelicals shaping character in our pastors when we train them to be "effective leaders" along the lines of American corporations? Character is a person's orientation to the world. As Stanley Hauerwas delineates, character is based in "the general orientation his life acquires because of the way he insists on understanding and describing the world."[29] "Effective leadership" instructors describe a world where technique and skill can control the outcome of organizations. Effective leadership pictures churches as organizations to be run for goals that determine success of some kind. Effective leadership subtly trains pastors to act and behave as if they are in control of the church. These CEO-pastor-leaders do not serve, they lead; they do not submit to the community and the mutual gifts of the Spirit, they direct the organization; they do not see the church as an alive organism in which the Spirit moves to discern the future, they discern the future. This is the new language of church leadership, and it cannot help but shape the way pastors are oriented toward their churches and themselves. Such pastors' character cannot help but become more controlling, authoritarian, and bottom-line oriented.

When you take such pastors, formed as they are into effective leaders and trained into a scientific understanding of Scripture, you have a double recipe for heavy-handed despotism and future church splits. Many evangelicals already have a scientific-historical critical approach to interpreting Scripture. Such evangelicals believe that the pastor, with good skill, can arrive at the single right interpretation of the Scripture. No community need be involved. And since no conciliar process for doctrinal disputations in evangelicalism exists, conflict is inevitable.

So when the pastor, elders, and congregation come together over a conflict in the church, they naturally proceed to arguing over who is right. They do not come together as members of the same body pursuing the same purposes in Christ to pore over Scripture in the unity of the Holy Spirit to discern the next way to go (Acts 15). They do not come together as a community respecting authoritative gifts in the body to test the unity of the Spirit. At the time of conflict, evangelicals instead come together as individuals maneuvering to determine who was right and who was wrong. Put this together with many pastors' understanding of effective leading, and the pastor-leader will naturally impose solutions and hand down decisions in the manner of a dictator. The pastor may seek to influence key people to see what he or she sees, because this is what effective leaders do. But when push comes to shove, the leader must take the lead and enforce a solution. Leaders are either right or they are wrong and their leadership is threatened when their interpretation of Scripture is challenged.

Conflict leads to problems because the body cannot meet together to discern what the Scripture means and where the Spirit is leading in regard to the conflict at hand.[30] Whereas the pastor could have offered a scriptural admonition to be tested in the community, he or she now offers Scripture for his or her own agenda and everyone else is wrong. What could have been a community discerning in the Spirit becomes a stratified community of individuals taking sides. Church splits are inevitable. It is the modernist way. More regrettably, it is too often the evangelical way.

In addition, the pastor-formed-into-effective-leader acquires character prone to moral failure, because the effective pastor-leader's desires are shaped toward success in ministry not personal faithfulness to Christ. Effectiveness is derived from setting goals and outcomes. Carefully couched in the language of piety, pastors seek effectiveness in bringing "souls to Christ." But subtly, perhaps even unwittingly, moral behavior for the effective leader becomes a subset of whatever is necessary to be a successful leader in the church marketplace. The pastor-leader now wants to be morally faithful to his or her spouse not because God has called both husband and wife into redeemed Christian marriage with all the purposes for which he created it, but because a moral failure would ruin their ministry. As a result, pastors fail because they have character molded for success more than character for following Christ in marriage, work, ministry, and every other calling in life. And because their character is trained toward effectiveness, effective pastor-leaders are prone to deep emotional lows and emotional egotistical ecstasies with each failure or success because their emotions are formed in relation to success not faithfulness. So-called effective pastors are therefore prone to depression, fatigue, and mental breakdown, and are not given to long-term faithfulness of following Christ amidst the many obstacles in the course of ministry. Effective pastors inevitably become prone to emotional and moral failures. Their character therefore has been mis-trained by "effective leadership," and their pastoral desires have not been shaped in a way sufficient to sustain them through what they must endure irrespective of immediate effectiveness.

Character problems like the ones described above are always a danger to the evangelical church regardless of time and place in history. But the missing link between the pastorate and the character of the pastor who can shepherd and truly serve a congregation comes at an especially inopportune time because our splintered, postmodern society notices truth only when it is lived and listens to the messenger only when he or she speaks authentically. The compartmentalizing tendency of modernism is what allows technique to be separated from truth, and truth from character. But we must not put spiritual disciplines and moral character at the utility of effectiveness and thus subordinate them.[31] Ministry can only flow out of one's life and character. In the end, moral failures are not the worst of the problem: the worst is when leaders give off the air that they are doing things in order to be effective instead of doing things out of faithfulness to Christ and who they already are in him because of what he has already done.

The Social Structure of the Pastorate That Forms Failure

When an evangelical pastor morally fails, one question rarely considered is, How did the training and the social structure of the evangelical pastorate foster such moral failure in the pastor's personal life? We have already described how pastor-leaders are formed for character failure by evangelical "effective leadership" training. But there are ways in which the very structure of the evangelical pastorate works against the moral character needed to shepherd a body of Christ.

> **The worst is when leaders give off the air that they are doing things in order to be effective instead of out of faithfulness to Christ.**

For instance, many evangelical pastors are set up as leaders if not virtual CEOs over a board of elders that oversees the congregation. This often is more the product of the church culture than the church polity itself. In most cases pastors are given authority by the church or denomination based upon a licensing and ordination process by which they carry a job description to lead the church. Pastors are expected, as part of that job description, to possess a sufficient moral maturity so as to back up their words and leadership with a life well lived. When a moral failure occurs, pastors inevitably must proceed through a process of reconciliation that will eventually restore them to their moral position as leaders of the church. This structure is necessary and provides the means to authenticate, empower, and guide the pastoral leadership of the church. Yet underlying these structures is the assumption that pastors are expected to maintain their own moral character all on their own. There are no regular accountability structures or confessional processes available to evangelical pastors as part of everyday life. After all, it would be too dangerous for a pastor to admit even the slightest moral deviation to the congregation because a pastor's authority depends on being morally fit. Intervention therefore happens most often when it is already too late. Some evangelical pastors still maintain they are above challenge by the congregation and elders. Oddly, they adopt the Old Testament maxim voiced by David regarding Saul that one should not "lay a hand on the Lord's anointed" (1 Sam. 26:23). The character of our pastors therefore is isolated from and put above the rest of their engagement with the congregation because if moral issues are revealed, pastors compromise their jobs.

Underwriting this understanding of pastoral character is an individualist theology of sanctification. It says one's character and growth is a product of one's individual relationship with Christ. Evangelicals have no theology of character and virtue where we view one's growth in Christ as a product of one's worship and communal practices in a community governed by the Holy Spirit. Postmodern writers reveal the myriad of ways social worlds construct "selves," postmodern theologians help us see that in the liturgical participation of worship we find our subjectivity in Christ, and postsecular writers help us realize that we can only see the truth about ourselves in the community of Christ. In stark contrast, we evangelicals want to remain cloistered unto ourselves, working out our "sin issues" in the privacy of our closets. Because character and virtue have been previously associated with a theology of works, à la Roman Catholicism, we reject sanctification that comes from engaging our lives in the skills of confession, repentance, discernment, and speaking truth in love.

Given this moral milieu, effective leaders reveal their character problems to anyone in the church at great peril, effectively placing their job and ministerial status on the line. Such transparency would harm their ability to effectively lead. This state of affairs is why most pastors have no accountability groups, and when they do, the groups are composed of members outside their church who neither see them in leadership nor know their week-to-week life among the church. It is inevitable therefore that the effective leader/evangelical pastor is isolated from the very body that the Spirit uses to help one grow and overcome moral deficits, which surely exist in all pastors until death.[32]

In regard to the sanctification of our pastors, they then are left to themselves. Their character flaws are revealed at great personal peril. Worse, they have no place to work out their own salvation with fellow believers. In evangelicalism, the eerie unspoken assumption persists that somehow pastors are living the already-perfected Christian life. But moral failures of many kinds are certainly regular events in pastors' lives. Whether it be moral depression, pornographic wanderings, personal pride, or obesity, pastors have times of moral struggle. The Christian life requires struggling through these times in one's life, yet strangely, pastor-leaders are exempt: they have no place to struggle and no one to struggle with. So instead, they stay morally stuck in whatever troubles they came into the church with because they have no place to work out their growth in Christ. For many evangelical pastors, there simply is no community that together pursues its mutual edification until we all come to "the unity of the faith . . . to the measure of the full stature of Christ" (Eph. 5:12–16 NRSV).

Tragically, the evangelical structure of the pastorate isolates pastors from the very community that can help them grow. Christian growth over sin does happen among a living community of Christ. This kind of growth comes through regular confession (James 5:16), being spoken truth to in love (Eph. 4:15), edification (Eph. 4:16), and discernment (Matt. 18:15–20), all of which should be parts of regular church life. These activities define the growing body of Christ. These activities are important for the pastor's Christian growth and mental stability just as they are for the rest of the church body. But the pastor as effective leader is closed off from these activities in the body because to reveal weakness is to somehow jeopardize one's moral authority as an effective leader. Neither can the pastor model these practices, so the body itself suffers from a lack of good models. Any admission to sin is a point of lost leadership because somehow leadership is qualified by distance from the congregation as some sort of perfected person. The body suffers and the pastor is isolated to him(her)self to govern his own moral growth or else he cannot lead others in Christian growth.

> **Tragically, the evangelical structure of the pastorate isolates pastors from the very community that can help them grow.**

Evangelicalism's individualism is part of its modernist inheritance. We have built it into the very structure of our pastoral office. There is no sense of God's wider cosmic work of salvation into which we are all invited to participate and by which we all are formed and shaped into holiness. The pastor's moral character is to be worked out between him and God. This individualized nature of evangelicalism undercuts our leadership's potential to grow in character. We do not see formation and progress in character within a community as an essential part of what it means to live the Christian life. Therefore our pastors are exempt from these practices. There is no place for them to work through their sin. As such, the evangelical pastorate is formed and shaped for moral failure not for moral growth.

Returning to the Concept of the Servant

As evangelicalism faces this leadership crisis, many seek to revive leadership with more conferences, books, and new leadership concepts. Still others provide retreat centers, places of renewal, and counseling centers specifically for the emotional needs of pastors. The above analysis suggests, however, that the structure of our pastorate needs to change. We must revise the foundation upon which we locate, affirm, and support leaders to recapture the essence of pastoral leadership in Christ versus leadership borrowed from outside worlds.

The New Testament church viewed Christ as modeling leadership after the servant. Repeating the discussion above, the New Testament used the word for servant (*diakonos*) above all other words to describe leadership in the church. It is this word alone that most captures the meaning given to us by Christ, the apostles, and the New Testament church for understanding leadership. To avoid succumbing to other discourses of leadership honed and developed within the worlds of late capitalism, the evangelical church should reject all other starting points for understanding how we are to pastor Christ's church. We must return to the language of "servant" to define our leadership.

Evangelicals, however, should avoid the temptation to make "servant-hood" the tool of effectiveness. Our definitions must be carefully derived from Jesus Christ and Scripture rather than adopted from whatever current leadership trends are popular. For example, we should distinguish our definitions of servant-shepherd leadership from the popular efforts of leadership gurus such as Robert Greenleaf. Greenleaf was the originator of the concept of "servant leadership" among leadership studies in the secular world. Although Greenleaf has numerous insights into the dynamics of servanthood that ensure good leadership, he cannot seem to avoid the modernist temptation to make these servant dynamics into a technique to be employed to achieve a desired outcome. He therefore can characterize servant leaders in the following terms: "A mark of leaders, an attribute that puts them in a position to show the way for others, is that they are better than most at pointing the direction. . . . It may be a goal derived from a consensus, or the leader, acting on inspiration, may simply have said, 'Let's go this way.' But the leader always knows what it is and can articulate it for any who are unsure."[33] Yet what Greenleaf evidently fails to realize is that the nature of servant leadership changes when it is looked upon as a technique to achieve different goals. Indeed, one's very character as a servant depends upon being able to submit to the ultimacy of a higher source of authority. Indeed, and more to the point, servanthood in the New Testament always accedes the outcomes of one's service to the lordship of Christ. A servant always serves a master whose goals and purposes are inscrutable to a certain extent (John 15:15). Therefore, it changes the nature of the way we are called to be servants to God when we put "servanthood" to the service of the goals and outcomes we presume to already know.

As opposed to making servanthood a leadership technique, let "servanthood" redefine the very character of the pastor as one who faithfully serves Christ's body on behalf of the Master. This means the servant-pastor does not lead by being out front telling everyone where to go (Mark 9:35). Rather, such pastors serve the congregation in humility with their gifts, which have been tested, marked, and affirmed within the congregation and church structures.[34] A servant-pastor does not lead as one over the congregation but as one who uses his or her gifts within the limits given within the body (Rom. 12:3). This leader does not usurp authority over the congregation when there is a conflict (Mark 10:42–45). Instead, as with all members, the servant-pastor serves in mutual submission to the congregation (Eph. 5:21). As far as goals and outcomes are concerned, the servant-leader certainly carries broad vision and goals as part of his or her life. But ultimately the future of this church is God's, the head of this body is Christ, and he will do what he will do. We will therefore care more for faithfulness than for effectiveness. Stated goals are still there, but faithfulness takes priority over success. We still care about qualifications for ministry and the affirmation of gifts. But this affirmation is tested among a people where growth in the church as Christ's body matters as much as if not more so than growth in numbers.

Servant pastorship in the local church should be collegial, positioned in relation to a body of believers, and affirmed within a community. Servant pastors should not arrive from nowhere but arise within the body as their gifts are recognized and bear forth fruit. This should not diminish ordination but rather should make ordination the proper authorizing sacrament or ordinance upon those God has chosen out of a people to minister God's gifts faithfully manifested and properly stewarded within the body of Christ. Ordination, however, does not mean CEO. It means authority has been given that depends constantly upon God, stays in relation to the community that has affirmed it, and sustains the teaching of the Scriptures as handed down to us.

When disputes arise, a leader will not serve over the congregation but as part of the congregation in mutual submission one to another. What is there to lose for the pastor if he or she simply submits to the accusations of the congregant? The worst that can happen is that he or she

> As opposed to making servanthood a leadership technique, let "servanthood" redefine the very character of the pastor as one who faithfully serves Christ's body on behalf of the Master.

might have to confess sin. But it is only in the CEO world where power depends upon one's invincibility that this can be a bad thing. In the body of Christ, this is just another opportunity for the pastor to grow and for the congregation to grow in Christ and in mutual fellowship one with another. If the pastor is exposed in a grievous sin, the pastor is brought to restoration through a process lovingly in grace. The pastor will be stronger having gone through such a restoration. More than likely, however, with such a leadership, future defects in the pastor's character will be dealt with much earlier, before it can be allowed to bloom into full-blown grievous failure. Therefore, following the instructions of Matthew 18, the servant-pastor should welcome the conflict and accusations as an opportunity for the Spirit to discern the way forward. There is no need to be perfect when we are all one in the body serving one another out of love in faithfulness. If it is an issue of Scripture, we do not argue between ourselves. We call all the interested parties around the table to study and submit to one another as to how best to discern the Scripture's meaning for this time in our place in the history of this church. Teaching gifts will be recognized. An Acts 15 occasion is fostered, and the church discerns together the way it should go.

Such leadership models, however, make little sense in the megachurch. But as we move beyond modernity, the evangelical church has a chance to reinvigorate a model of leadership that fits the smaller local congregation. Such leadership that works locally and serves the congregation and the world in Christ has the social substance sufficient to subvert the world's suspicions of all leadership as corrupt, duplicitous, and coercive to meet its own personal goals. Such a leadership has the potential to undo the televangelist's status as well as the corporate CEO's status in America after Enron. Such a leadership can truly witness to another way, in a world where violence and coercion rules.

Practices for Restoring the Link between the Pastorate and the Virtues

What sort of practices might nurture such a leadership among our churches?

Reinvigorate Ordination into the Service of Christ's Church: Dealing with the Problem of Rogue Ordinations

Most ordinations among evangelical denominations generally carry tests for doctrinal competency and qualifying character. Yet too often, ordination has taken on the function of a professional credential given much like other professional credentials at the end of graduate school with a degree in hand and a passing grade on certain exams. Ordination should be the affirmation of one as a faithful bearer of what has been handed down (2 Tim. 2:2). It should be the recognition of one's submission to the ministry of servanthood to Christ's church. Too often evangelicals have ordained its ministers based upon biblical competency measured by whether or not one possesses a seminary degree. Too often evangelicals have ordained its ministers based upon character fitness as measured by some form of psychological testing that measures aptitudes and screens for character deficiencies as defined by psychological methods. There is no process by which our ordinands are shaped into servants of Christ and tested for their calling within an ongoing community that knows them. Seminaries need to become centers of spiritual formation, communities of mutual knowing, that birth people shaped for servanthood. Churches should take responsibility to nurture emerging leadership into the ways of servanthood and support (or at least assist) them financially for their educational needs. Our new pastors should be ordained to serve Christ and the continuing community of Christ. We must resist ordination as a professional credential.

The diminishment of ordination has been aggravated by the proliferation of independent evangelical churches that become ordaining bodies unto themselves. Without processes in place, ordination becomes nothing more than the recognition of a pastor who has shown effectiveness to "do the job." In this case, ordination becomes recognition of entrepreneurial success. When one is successful in starting a church, at gathering sufficient people around him or her to pay for the church building, this person is then deemed ripe for ordination. Ordaining to the ministry on the basis of entrepreneurial success defeats the role of ordination as the sign of one's formation into lifelong servanthood and the carrying on of what has been handed on through the church, the gospel, and the doctrines of Christ. All in all, the proliferation of rogue ordinations among evangelicals is cause for concern if we are to reinvigorate a biblical servant leadership for the continuing of Christ's kingdom within evangelical Christianity.

Evangelicals then must renovate ordination as a rite of succession in the servanthood of Christ. We should seek to structure pastoral ministry so that it is not just one more entrepreneurial occupation. We should structure seminary for spiritual formation, not just professional competencies. We should ritualize the pastorate so that the ministry requires giving up attachments to this world, including worldly success. The pastor becomes the servant of the church as opposed to the church becoming a job or business enterprise in the service of his or her personal support. In this regard, evangelicals could learn some things from the older Christian traditions including Roman Catholicism. The wisdom behind the vows of poverty, celibacy, the rites of succession, and other aspects of the clergy vocation in the older traditions should not be ignored by evangelicals in the face of our own leadership crisis. We need not advocate celibacy or apostolic succession excluding all other gifts in order to learn from them some steps toward reinvigorating ordination as the means to train our pastors into the servanthood of Christ and his church.

See Seminaries as Places of Servant Formation

More and more seminaries today require spiritual formation as necessary to the curriculum for a master of divinity (M.Div.) degree, the academic degree for ministry. Yet seminaries can go beyond the testing for personal competencies and the gauging of one's moral maturity upon graduation. Seminaries can look to the older monastic orders for some guidance in these respects. The daily praying of the office (especially morning and evening), cooperative living arrangements, cooprative farming, sharing of chores and childcare, the regular sharing of meals, and the communal service to the poor all shape the future pastor in the ways of servanthood. Regular formative worship, confessional groups, and teaching of the disciplines all focus the gaze of the soul toward God, his glory, and his sovereignty and away from one's personal ego and success. Many of these things Protestants have left behind as we professionalized the clergy and their education alongside all other secular vocations. But if we seek to place effectiveness and management of the church within their proper context, seminarians must be immersed into the One who is in control of all outcomes, and who can be their source through the ups and downs of ministry. This must become primary in the formation of our pastors for ministry.

Form Confessional Groups for Pastors

More pastors now seek some regular accountability in their lives than in the past. They meet regularly to confess sin, talk about difficulties, seek counsel, and mutually encourage one another. Yet these meetings often occur with people who do not attend the church of the pastor seeking accountability. Often these people are other pastors themselves. Certainly these meetings achieve certain benefits to pastors as opposed to nothing. But pastors remain essentially isolated from their congregation and their lives remain isolated from the very people who worship with them and observe them in everyday life. These kinds of confessionals do not promote spiritual growth for the pastors in their weaknesses because such weaknesses can be hidden in a society of professionals. Pastors

Evangelicals must seek structures for pastors where they can confess sin, deal with deficiencies in their character, and seek discernment in regular fashion with people who know them.

still remain somehow above the congregation in the living of their everyday life.

Evangelicals must seek structures for pastors where they can confess sin, deal with deficiencies in their character, and seek discernment in regular fashion with people who know them. Certainly there are limitations for the pastor regarding whom he can be vulnerable to. The pastor should avoid confessing sin to weaker brothers or sisters in the congregation who do not yet have the maturity to support leaders in their struggle or to antagonistic parishioners who have not yet learned to avoid the ills of gossip. There should be guidelines for such a group, including confidentiality and a recognition that there is a difference between patterns of sin that require restoring a pastor to his leadership as opposed to one-time sin, which requires confession and immediate repair. For example, in our church, as pastor I meet regularly with a group of men who all are regular participants in the church life and have all known me for more than a year, all of whom I have personally tested as to their ability to know and engage in issues with a pastor's life. We have promised confidentiality and support to each other. And we all acknowledge that the pastor is not perfect.

Nurture Emerging Leaders and Bi-vocational Clergy

The clergy was the first vocation to be professionalized in Western society via educational rites. Several hundred years later, professionalization is now a hazard because of the temptation to separate character from skills in professional occupations. Today, the professional has skills gained from one's education and training and is able to carry out tasks to which one's character is irrelevant. In this very way, however, the pastoral ministry is not a profession. In the pastorate, one's character is always inseparable from one's competencies.[35]

Ministry therefore should not be just another vocational choice. Ministry is not my doing; it is God's. It is not the pursuit of success but the calling of service. It is in some way a calling out of professionalism into a life of service. There should then be the means to properly test and allow such callings to mature in the congregation. Our own church encourages bi-vocational ministry in the church as the means to test, train, and affirm future pastors, out of which further training and ordination will apply. Ministers therefore can be chastened from pursuing the ministry as another pursuit of competitive success or professionalization because ministry originates in bi-vocationalism and the local congregation. In our church, every person on staff began as a bi-vocational minister, including myself. Over time, as ministry flourishes, and God manifests his calling among the body, we elevate a current bi-vocational person to full-time ministry.

Establish Multiple Leadership

One possible way to avoid the CEO-pastor syndrome is to institute multiple recognized leadership in the church pastorate. The idea of multiple-leader ministry is not new to the church. Anabaptist writer John Yoder claims it existed in the early church well into the days of the medieval church. The theoretical sevenfold ministry of the medieval church, according to Yoder, atrophied from disuse so that other recognized ministries in the church, such as exorcist and lector, simply disappeared and collapsed in one priestly office.[36] The current state of leadership in the evangelical church mirrors these medieval developments. We should counter the proclivity in evangelical churches to pay and isolate specialists over against equipping the laity to do the work of the ministry by encouraging the rise of multiple leaders and respective tasks within the church. By this I do not refer to simply another form of multiple staff ministry. Instead, perhaps there should be no senior pastor at all. Rather, multiple co-pastors may act as a college of leadership for each church. There should be no single teaching pastor but a team of preachers. This would take the focus off one pastor's preaching style to the Scripture itself. It would practice the congregation in the art of submitting to Scripture no matter who is preaching that day. The Brethren churches have much to teach us in this regard. We could then begin to see the teaching role of the church as not about charisma, personality, or buzz but about the faithful delivering of the Word every Sunday. There should never be one superman (or superwoman) pastor. No doubt, a multiple clergy presents hurdles for ordinations, salaries, and church resources. However, if we adopt bi-vocational ministry, perhaps pastors could function as a unit in complementary roles. This could then become a means to promote biblical servant leadership and a church trained to be the church instead of the follower of one charismatic leader.

Grow Authentic Leaders

The word *authentic* is overused in the current evangelical culture. Nonetheless, as modern society breeds suspicion toward leaders and hostility toward authority, as modern leadership implodes from "spin," negative campaigning, and abuses of status in regard to sexual offenses or corporate malfeasance, the church of Jesus Christ can witness to another form of leader. This leader acts out of obedience to Christ not personal gain, in servanthood to his church not vocational success, and in submission to God's sovereignty over his people, not personal goals and visions.

This calls for evangelicals to recover practices for training leadership into models of servanthood, humility, and grace as exemplified by Christ. It calls for critical engagement of leadership training that separates leadership patterns from Christian character and virtue. It calls for models of Christian maturity that require community, the regular confession of sin, and the notion of growth into virtue and character. In the end, the evangelical church must reject secular patterns of leadership and return to the body of Christ as the training ground for virtue, maturity, and leadership.

4

The Production of Experience

Why Worship Takes Practice: Toward a Worship
That Forms Truthful Minds and Faithful Experience
(Not Merely Reinforces the Ones We Walked In With)

> But you have come to Mount Zion, to the heavenly Jerusalem, the city of
> the living God. You have come to thousands upon thousands of angels in
> joyful assembly, to the ["called out ones"] of the firstborn.
>
> Hebrews 12:22–23 NIV

How do you know good worship when you see it? Our church's worship
leaders were talking about this question one night in my office. And I
asked, Whom would you point to in the congregation as a good worshiper? The director of music pointed to two men in the congregation,
John Smith and George Riley (not their real names). These two men
were both visceral worshipers. By visceral I mean they were both prone
to raising their hands, and expressing regular tears during the singing
times of the service. When I asked why this revealed good worship, the
best answer we could come up with was that these people were "into"
worshiping God. Not ironically (I contend), both of these men were prone
in their everyday lives to huge mood swings and abusive behaviors. And

it seemed their commitment to the local body of Christ was as stable as the local weather forecast. Both men were gone from the church one year later. It seemed from external appearances at least that there was little correlation between what constitutes a good worshiper and the consistent living of the Christian life.

This episode seems to typify the problem of worship for evangelicals. We just do not think in terms of defining good worship by the way that it forms people into good Christians. Instead, we look to the level of the worshiper's emotional involvement as a sign that we have worshiped God well. So when we plan our worship, we end up pursuing the arousal of emotions and the "worship experience" as an end in itself, which inevitably turns narcissistic. I do not mean to suggest that emotions or experience are not an important element in Christian worship. Rather, I wish to suggest that our worship services should be ordered so as to form our emotions and our experience into emotions and experiences that are faithful to God. We do this by allowing our imaginations and orientations to be shaped toward the glory of God through the reading of Scripture, liturgy, singing praises, preaching, and partaking of the Lord's Table. Out of this ordering, faithful experience of God will follow. Christian emotions will be produced.

> **When we plan our worship, we end up pursuing the arousal of emotions and the "worship experience" as an end in itself, which inevitably turns narcissistic.**

Evangelicals, however, rarely take the forming of emotions, experience, and imagination seriously. In modernist fashion, we assume these to be givens. So we structure the worship service around listening to a forty-five-minute preaching lecture that appeals to the individual mind, not one's imagination. Or we structure the worship service around singing praise and worship choruses for extended periods of time, appealing to one's stirred up emotions, not a reordering of one's emotions toward God. In either case, the worship service can only reinforce what we already believe or feel. It cannot reshape us out of pagan experiences and emotions into the glory of God.

The following chapter examines this problem in relation to the two dominant approaches to evangelical worship.[1] We examine the traditional evangelical worship centered upon the sermon and then the charismatic contemporary worship with its emphasis upon praise and worship musical expression.[2] Traditional evangelicals criticize contemporary charismatic worship for producing indulgent emotional experiences or a feel-good pep rally at the expense of orienting one's mind toward sound doctrine. And contemporary charismatics often criticize traditional evangelical worship for producing a lecture hall–type experience that presents God as dry intellectual information, not the living God of Scripture.[3] In both cases, each side reveals to the other how our worship fails to form our experience into God.

Beneath both of these criticisms, however, lies the more troubling concern about evangelical worship: we may be giving away the formation of our minds and imaginations to cultures foreign to the gospel. Because traditional evangelical worship services focus on the rational and leave the worshiper detached from engaging God, parishioners leave unaffected. Their minds and imaginations are formed elsewhere by default at places where there is a bodily-emotional engagement available, such as the local movie Cineplex, art galleries, concert halls, or sports arenas. Likewise, because our "charismatic" worship services encourage emotional experiences instead of challenging and shaping them, worshipers basically stay unchallenged in emotions and ways of life that reflect the movies or the places of sin that formed these emotions in the first place. Contemporary worship does not form these emotions into the holiness of God in Jesus Christ. With either approach to worship therefore we end up capitulating to more powerful formative forces in the surrounding culture. We end up giving away the production of experience to foreign powers. As a result, our doctrines may be right when it comes to worship, but our experiences, emotions, and imaginations remain pagan.

The following chapter argues that evangelicals must refocus their worship services. As postmodernity reveals the interpreted nature of all experience, our worship must provide our worshipers a grammar in which to interpret the world so as to receive a faithful experience of Jesus as Lord. As postmodernity reveals the powers of culture to form our imaginations, our worship must become a culture capable of forming our worshipers' imaginations faithfully toward the lordship of Jesus Christ. We must go beyond the focus of right doctrine to being shaped into it. We must go further than expressing existing emotions to being shaped into new emotions that are born out of the world of "Jesus is Lord." We must order our worship to form truthful minds and faithful experience in our worshipers instead of only reinforcing the ones they walked in with.

Traditional Evangelical Worship: The Lecture Hall

Traditional evangelicals design worship services for teaching sound doctrine. The orientation of the worship service is toward the sermon. The goal is maintaining orthodox scriptural doctrine. On a typical Sunday morning, the worship service proceeds with an invocation, a hymn, a prayer, the collection of tithes and offerings, some more hymns and special music—all this intentionally coordinated toward the culmination of this worship service: the pastor's sermon. The climactic moment arrives with the pastor delivering a sermon that lasts as long as if not longer than the entire preceding service. The entire service is organized for the purpose of hearing the Bible being preached and exposited in an acceptably orthodox manner by the exegetically skilled pastor. Some traditional evangelicals may use contemporary music or a vivid sermon illustration in their worship service, but the design is still the same. The sermon remains the focal point of the service.

Evangelicals inherit this focus on the sermon from certain allegiances to the Protestant Reformation. John Calvin and other Reformers emphasized the pure preaching of the Word in contrast to the Roman medieval mass. To these Reformers the mass had become an ornate ceremonial rite in a foreign language. By the sixteenth century some European parishes were abusing the mass, claiming its magical powers were enough to save even those who could not be present but could pay for a mass to be said for them. The Reformers reacted against abuses of the sacraments, icons, and the authority of the pope within the Roman Church. As a result, the Reformers exalted the authority of the Scriptures over the church. This was the means to call the church back to faithfulness. Zwingli and other radical Reformers made the hearing of the Word central to all worship services over the practice of the "Lord's Supper" and other elements he perceived to be distractions.[4] The Eucharist was reduced to a quarterly more peripheral occurrence in worship. The preaching of Scripture became primary in the service. Evangelicals continue on in this historical trajectory when we make the sermon the focus of the church's worship service.

In addition, the Lutheran doctrine of "justification through faith" made the human relationship with God more individualistic and less communal, thereby instilling a more individual-centered worship. Salvation turned subjective, becoming more personal and private. Personal faith occurred through the individual hearing of the Word. As a result, the value of the sermon rose in importance. The new inwardness of faith led to the rejection of any earthly visual "figures" in the worship service. Reformers removed all images from the church and anything visible that would distract from the hearing of the Word and the interior moment of faith.[5] For evangelicals, these influences endure also. External art and symbol have little place in our worship. Preaching claims the central place in our services. And worship is the act of individually hearing the instructed Word and applying it by faith to our lives.

There is another reason that evangelicals are so sermon-centric in worship. We focus upon sermons because we most commonly think about truth in terms of words, propositions, and reason. We inherit this from modernity. We think of truth as contained in statements that are factual and correspond one-to-one to reality. Above all, each individual mind has the ability to reason and to determine the truth of these statements all on its own with the Holy Spirit's guidance and enlightenment. So evangelicals inherently emphasize the rationally digested instruction of Scripture. Truth can just as easily be delivered via a lecture hall, books, or sound and video recordings as it can in the sanctuary. With such confidence in the autonomous mind to arrive at truth, traditional evangelicals make the intellectual presentation and application of the scriptural truth the vortex of worship by which Christians grow and orient themselves toward God. Salvation and sanctification occur as well through the rational intake of biblical instruction as applied internally by the Holy Spirit. When you add this rationalist influence to all of the other historical influences upon evangelicals, it is no wonder evangelical worship naturally crescendos to the sermon.

This all worked for evangelicals when the dominant culture complied with the Christian church. Evangelicalism was formed out of the American fundamentalist battles with Protestant liberalism of the 1920s.[6] These battles resulted in a liberal-conservative split in North American Protestantism but left a largely supportive Christianized culture still amply intact. Alongside this friendly/neutral culture, cognitive-oriented worship sustained Christian life and belief. The sermons defined and sustained Christian life in a culture that at least did not subvert Christian living.[7] The Sunday sermons reinforced and defined on Sunday the doctrines that were unspoken in the cultural moral consensus at large. But North American culture has changed in two key ways that evangelicals depended upon to live and worship.

First, North American culture's growing postmodernity undercuts modernity's confidence in individual human reason to arrive at truth through words. Today, the typical American under thirty-five doesn't learn simply through isolated, rationally delivered propositions via the lecture hall. In fact, they are even suspicious of it. They react with questions such as, "Why are you so interested in convincing me of this?" People now swim in the culture's assessment that truth is not a rational objective argument. They migrate now to truth that is found in ways of life and displays of beauty. The ascendancy of visual technology and the cyber flow of information have changed the way we live amidst time and space, truth and goodness. Still, evangelicals assume truth is primarily rational. As a result, traditional evangelical worship appears isolated and on the defensive to postmoderns. And when postmodern strangers to the gospel enter our sanctuaries, they do so as disinterested students entering large lecture halls, and they are unaffected. They want to know the truth through seeing, participating in, and living it, not merely by hearing it in words alone.[8]

Second, North American culture turned hostile to forming Christians. Certainly it is up for debate as to whether American culture ever was friendly toward being a Christian. But in today's late modernity, more than in the 1950s, the American culture industries have ascended to become powerful shapers of souls into capitalism, consumerism, materialism, and hedonism.[9] In the midst of such cultural shaping, the isolated traditional evangelical church service offers words to the detached rational mind on Sunday morning. It is no match for the onslaught of American culture. Beginning at least with the 1960s, Hollywood, public schooling, secular universities, and American media now imbue its citizens away from Christian purposes for moral life, marriage, justice, and money.[10] The public schools and universities order social life and curriculum to create productive citizens for (i.e., people capable of living in) American democratic capitalist society.[11] The media pummels the psyches of Americans with a consumerist ethos. Justice and mercy is a government program detached from the church of God's mercy. With the cultural powers now turned hostile toward Christianity, the lecture hall of traditional evangelical worship has increasingly become an island unto itself, explicating truth in disembodied words. Parishioners listen passively to sermons in church, while their minds and character are being shaped by other cultures they can see, feel, and participate in.

> Parishioners listen passively to sermons in church, while their minds and character are being shaped by other cultures they can see, feel, and participate in.

So traditional evangelical worship gives away the forming of Christian experience. Devoid of art, images, or liturgy, we ask the parishioners to sit and take notes on sermons every Sunday morning. Meanwhile their souls, character, and imaginations are being formed by the culture technologies of the Cineplex, the television, the university, or the local Starbucks.[12] We assume that the Cartesian autonomous minds of each individual sitting in the pew can intellectually assent and apply information sufficient to grow in Christ.[13] But while parishioners sitting in the pews are agreeing with the doctrines intellectually, their so-called autonomous minds are being compromised before they even come to church. They can no longer hear the preacher's words alone apart from the ways of seeing that have formed in their imaginations elsewhere.

Evangelicals naïvely believe culture is neutral and all we need to do is present apologetic defenses of the faith that any "reasonable" human being would think are right. So we wonder why our young people started wanting things that older ones in the church had not wanted before. And the young of our church start experiencing work and career, money and security, love and friendship differently. Their minds and emotions were being shaped out of the compelling images of a consumer culture and not the world of Scripture. We were "giving away" the production of our experience, desires, and visions to the culture producers of America.

In summary, traditional evangelical worship fails to form character or produce experience that is oriented toward God because it keeps the individual isolated in the pew, taking notes on a sermon. But by the time the person makes it to the pew, a post-Christian culture already forms him or her six days a week, and so the person has already been formed to hear what he or she will hear. There can be no confrontation, because in a post-Christian culture, the words the preacher says will simply have no credibility without the context of life and symbol by which people can make sense of them. In essence therefore, lecture hall worship gives away the production of Christian experience to the post-Christian world of twenty-first-century North America.

Contemporary "Charismatic" Evangelical Worship: The Rock Concert and the Feel-Good Pep Rally

The other evangelical approach to worship is labeled "charismatic" worship because of its emphasis on an "experience." It is also called "contemporary" worship.[14] Its goal is self-expression. Whereas traditional evangelicals orient their worship services toward the sermon, contemporary evangelicals orient their worship services toward simple praise and worship choruses that invite and nurture personal expression. Here a worship leader typically engages in a time of singing contemporary "praise and worship" songs that can extend to as much as forty-five minutes or longer. The "praise and worship" songs often use "I" in the lyrics to promote personal involvement.[15] Choruses are repeated several times, not just once. Often this "worship time" is separated from the sermon or teaching time. Much like a rock concert, the worship leaders encourage self-expression through handclapping, lifting of hands, dancing, and even on occasion, speaking in tongues.[16] In this way the worship resembles a pep rally aimed at fostering good feelings of intimacy with God. The worship service nurtures spontaneity, emotion, and the freedom of the worshiper's self-expression to God. This kind of worship achieves its goal when there is a feel-good emotional experience of one's direct relationship with God. Achieving such spiritual euphoria is the signpost of "the worship experience."[17]

Evangelicals inherit this also from our religious past. Our traditions in the American frontier revivals emphasized the importance of personal experience. From the various Holiness revivals of the turn of the century, to the "anxious bench" technique of Charles Finney, to even the Puritan search for inner confirmation of their divine election, personal "experience" pulsates through our historical blood.[18] "It is not enough to believe," say the evangelists we have been raised with, "you must have a personal experience." Contemporary evangelical worship is a mere extension of this historical emphasis on personal, inner experience.

> Achieving such spiritual euphoria is the signpost of "the worship experience."

Yet evangelicals also inherit their emphasis on "experience" from modernity as well. It is modernity that says innate human experience is to be trusted inside every individual. By "experience," I mean that which is supposedly available to any individual immediately in perhaps marveling at the Grand Canyon or in seeing something take place directly in front of one's face. True experience is unmediated and freed from any social interpretations, so the modern person says. The modern seeks to bracket prejudices and social encumbrances in order to secure the untainted core human experience. In this way, "personal experience" equals truth for modernity. We therefore must experience God for ourselves. From Schleiermacher to Emerson and Thoreau, modern thinkers rejected the passing down of truth in traditions and instead they preached that we must look inward to immediate autonomous experience for truth. Even Baconian science contributed to this notion with its appeal to immediate experimentation and inductive methods of investigation. Rousseau trumpeted the need to be freed from society altogether so that its citizens could be free to develop and express the purity of their unencumbered inherent natures.[19] Schleiermacher trumpeted the feeling of ultimate dependence as the experience of God which all moderns could trust. Down through modernity, therefore, experience is the foundation for religious truth. This is the modern edifice upon which religious knowledge was constructed by the "enlightened" ones after the demise of medieval Christendom.

Evangelicals epitomize this modern prejudice that puts stock in inner experiences first and "passed-down truth" last. Although liberal Protestantism led the way theologically along these lines, the "evangelical" revivalists were the real practitioners. This same confidence in experience bloomed further among the 1960s culture revolution of "free love" and experiential movements of that period. During these times the charismatic renewals of the '60s (as well as the Jesus People Movement) brought contemporary forms of rock music to Christian concerts and introduced the expressive happenings of the rock concert to the life of the Christian church.[20] Although unspoken, these forces accepted the experiential assumptions of the modern edifice. Contemporary evangelical worship carries these influences to this day. Contemporary evangelical worship works under the modernist assumptions that personal self-expression, freedom in the Spirit, and personal experience are the basis for authentic engagement with God.

But today, cracks are appearing in the modern edifice. Postmodernity undermines the unquestioned veracity of emotions and immediate experience. In postmodernity, there is no innate human experience and emotions are interpreted experiences. The forces of the culture industries act as technologies of desire, forming and shaping us into desires that then must be satiated by the market. Global economic forces order the cities into the production of desire and ways to satiate it.[21] Even experimental psychology reveals the complexity of human emotions that form in relation to appraisals of reality.[22] Different emotions are formed deep within alternative interpretations of reality.[23] Postmodern writers question whether psychological notions of well-being are not really the disguised constructions of the marketplace or society for effective adaptation to consumer life. According to all of these thinkers, the ways in which the self and its emotions are constructed socially are out of power interests residing in a given culture.[24] In short, any illusion that we can trust our experience as innately given has been undermined by postmodernity. Our experiences and emotions are being formed by the cultures and histories we find ourselves in.

This demise of modernity sounds the alarm for contemporary worship leaders because they can no longer count on self-expression alone to produce a truthful experience of God in worship. We can no longer safely assume that truthful emotions and experiences will automatically be awakened when we sing "praise and worship" songs long enough for an emotional catharsis in Christian worship. Many worshipers after all come into worship having been shaped by a post-Christian culture. Perhaps in the past, congregants came to worship with a repertoire of emotions and experiences already formed in the church or Christian cultural influences. In the past, worship leaders could awaken or even revive emotions that were already formed in the congregation.[25] But today, many worshipers enter the sanctuary with emotions and experience formed in another world. In the post-Christian cultures, we can no longer assume that our people's emotions and experiences have been formed out of a righteous past or a culture that recognizes Jesus is Lord (such as an early catechesis experience).

We cannot gauge worship by the presence of simple emotion or a positive experience. In fact, if "rock concert" worship is focused upon cheerleading an experience, worship leaders may in effect be doing the opposite of worship: giving the worshiper a "short-term high" sufficient to enable the worshiper to continue in a way of life that runs contrary to the Christian life. A worshiper might be getting positive feelings of encouragement that God will provide or sustain him or her when in fact the worshiper may need to repent of sin, submit to the Word, or be "stung" by the Spirit's transformation. In a post-Christian culture then, contemporary evangelical worship leaders may be leading the opposite of Christian worship, inflaming emotions that run contrary to the glory of Christ instead of directing the whole worshiper to his glory.

I argue therefore that contemporary worship, just like traditional evangelical worship, by default "gives away" the production of experience to the post-Christian cultures of North America. We give away the entering of the experience of "Jesus is Lord" by choosing to nurture whatever is immediately available to the worshiper instead of forming it anew. In postmodernity, people pursue experiences of all kinds. For them, emotions and experience can and should be manipulated. The question then for contemporary worship leaders in a postmodern context is, In what fashion am I leading worship that forms people into an experience directed toward and formed out of the holiness of the God of Israel and the Lord Jesus Christ?

In the last twenty years, virtue theologians have revived the Thomistic notions that the body, mind, and soul need to be shaped and formed toward the truthful purposes of God. In other words, Christians require character shaped by communities of faith and habits of truth in order to experience truth.[26] These folk teach us that Christian worship must lead persons into this transformation of emotions and experience into the lordship of Christ. A feel-good pep rally fails to suffice as a model for Christian worship because it only awakens emotions; it does not form them. For this reason, worship cannot aim for an "intimacy-with-God experience" as the primary goal of worship. Instead, true worship leads worshipers into the orientation of God's glory, out of which true experience is birthed, which then produces lives as well as experiences and emotions that are faithful to who we are called to be in Jesus Christ.

Immersive Worship: The Alive Body

The problem with evangelical worship therefore is that it fails to form experience in a people that is faithful to the reality of God in Jesus Christ. As a result, evangelical worship gives away the production of experience by default to the culture industries inherent in American life. And so our emotions are formed and our desires are shaped under the culture technologies of secular America, not through worship on Sunday mornings. Evangelicals go to church on Sunday yet are unaffected because we either sit passively in a lecture hall taking lecture notes for later use or we indulge in a rock concert/pep rally that titillates our emotions but leaves little to order our selves into the glory of God. Neither traditional nor charismatic forms of evangelical worship are sufficient to orient persons into God's glory amidst the secular cultures of desire.

Evangelical worshipers therefore have need for more than a lecture hall or a feel-good pep rally. We unconsciously hunger for an alive body of Christ we can be immersed into, an encultured organism that orders our desires, orients our vision, and livens our words through art, symbol, prayers, mutual exchanges, participatory rituals, readings of the Word, and the Eucharist every Sunday morning. Only through immersion can our "selves" be ordered doxologically so as to experience God as he is and live the Christian life in the world.

Such an immersive worship would immerse our individuated selves into something bigger than our selves in order to form our selves into that reality. This is necessary because only when the self is immersed can it be shaped into a reality beyond itself. For Christians, that reality must be the God of Israel and our Lord Jesus Christ. Yet there can be no immersion of our "selves" if our worship puts our "selves" at the center of it. There can be no immersion if our selves remain in charge, thwarting the immersion.

Both traditional and charismatic forms of evangelical worship thwart the immersion because they put the worshiping self at the center of worship. Traditional evangelical worship targets the mind of each individual as the center from which each worshiper digests teaching and makes decisions as to what he or she agrees with concerning the pastor's sermon. In the same way, contemporary worship targets the individual's emotions and experience as the center from which God engages and meets the worshiper in the service. In both cases the Holy Spirit's involvement with this process is assumed. Yet in both cases, the worship service isolates the self at the center of worship in relationship to God. Sitting in the pew, the self is separate from God and is essentially still in control. Therefore, our worship cannot form the self into the work and glory of God without our granting permission. And so the worshiper's character cannot be formed, the worshiper's gaze cannot be redirected, and the worshiper's experience cannot be produced in any way other than the way the worshiper is already predisposed. The worshiper cannot grow beyond himself or herself. The worshiper's immersion is thwarted.

In the case of sermon-centric worship, the worship service targets the autonomous reasonable mind of modernity, sitting in the pew while intellectually digesting the expository sermon based in the scriptural text. Within this structure of worship, Scripture is delivered as information, rhetoric that is rational, persuasive, and easy to understand and apply. Yet the listening subject cannot help but be separated from God. God is made into an object delivered to each mind via propositional sentences which are trusted as true because of their direct deduction from Scripture (expository preaching). This scenario fancies the worshiper as the subject, firmly in control and approaching God as the object. But as postmodernity uncovers, the modernist preacher must depend on each autonomous intellect in each believer to individually decipher and apply the sermon to oneself. In this way, the evangelical service places the Cartesian mind of the believer firmly in charge of the believer's word-ship. But one's mind when firmly in charge cannot transform itself. Such a mind can only reinforce the ways it already thinks in interpreting the sermon for itself. Surely the Holy Spirit can overcome the limits of modernity. But the structure of the evangelical lecture hall discourages such transformation because the worshiper's subjectivity is located at the center of worship, firmly in control. Individuals enter worship and use the sermons and songs totally unaware of the fact that they are but furthering their own schemes, which are already in place. Instead, we need a worship where out of our participation we are changed and formed into the scheme of God's glory for becoming new people. In short, if orientation is to occur, we need a worship that is constitutive of the worshiper's subjectivity, not the product of it. Our worship requires immersion.

> The "erotics" we emote in worship have little to form them if our hymnody is not thick with the realities of the Christian story.

Likewise, in the case of contemporary rock concert worship, the worship service targets the emotional and experiencing person singing in the pew. Because the goal of such worship is the eliciting of positive emotions and experience, the experiencing self is again placed squarely at the center of worship. It should not surprise us then when the words of the "praise and worship" hymnody are dominated by the repetitive personal pronoun "I." The goal is self-expression not orientation. But there is no uninterpreted experience to express. And so the "erotics" we emote in worship have little to form them if our hymnody is not thick with the realities of the Christian story.[27] We merely reinforce the emotions we walked into the Sunday service with. If there is no art, no images faithful to Christ, no eucharistic rituals to submit our bodies to, no communal discourse to enter into, or hymns rich in substantive doctrine, the "subjectivity" of the self is driven inward, and the emotional formation that is already enclosed is what will be expressed and reinforced. Therefore, contemporary Christian worship turns inevitably to self-indulgence based in whatever it is we bring to worship that day. If orientation is to occur, we need a worship that is constitutive of the worshiper's experience and emotions, not merely the product of the emotions we walked in with. Our worship requires immersion.

What does such immersive worship require for its services?

1. *Immersive Worship Removes the Self from the Center of Worship: The Liturgical Necessity*

First, immersive worship requires liturgical form. In the history of Christian worship, the self has been decentered and the worshiper's mind and emotions have been constituted through liturgical worship. This is because liturgy by definition is immersive. In liturgy, the individual does not approach the Word as object to analyze it and accept or reject it based upon the limits of one's individual rational subjective mind. He or she submits to the Word, participates in it, and out of that relation understands it and is determined by it. In liturgy, the songs sung or the words spoken are given in response to God as he has first been presented in all his narrative scriptural depth, artistic symbol, and eucharistic presence. Songs are not sung as self-expression of whatever one is feeling that day.

Liturgical participation prevents the self from becoming self-governing by inviting each person to participate into the life of God through the Scriptures and the Table. Liturgical worship invites the worshiper into a worship that was going on before the worshiper arrived and that will continue after he or she is gone (Heb. 12:22–23). Liturgy therefore cannot be self-generated, only participated in. Through liturgical participation in the very work of God through the Word and Lord's Table, the individual is invited to become part of a people and participate in the life of God through the Scriptures. Through submission to the Word (not analysis of the Word), the believer avoids being separated from God in order to know him. In other words, the worshiper is not left in his or her modern subjectivity to make an intellectual decision as to whether he or she "got something" from the sermon. Likewise, through submission to God and response to him in liturgy, the worshiper's emotions are given appraisal and a directional gaze out of which his or her experience is interpreted and elicited toward God. Through liturgy, a true immersion occurs out of which flows a transformed subjectivity, a faithful experience of God, and the gift of (a stable) self in Christ. British theologian Catherine Pickstock wonderfully summarizes all of the above when she describes liturgy:

> This performance of faith, which does not operate according to the worshipping subject's full command of his action, but, rather, his submission to a narrative mode of knowledge which disallows the isolation of empirical or intellectual essences, subordinates that which the worshipper knows and does to what passes through him, beyond his analytic grasp. This willing subordination to the surprise of what arrives alone genuinely liberates him from the de-constitutive assumptions of autonomy, epistemological certainty, and self-presence of secular existence. By committing himself actively to becoming the conduit of the event of the Trinity, that is, by confessing his faith, the worshipper's subjectivity is enacted and fulfilled.[28]

For these reasons, if evangelicals are to practice a worship that immerses the self, constitutes the self, and births faithful experience, we must return to the practice of liturgical form and historically based liturgy. If we hope to overcome the sterile impotence of lecture hall worship and the vapidity of self-expressive worship at the end of modernity, we will have to restore the liturgical to our worship.

2. *Immersive Worship Requires Art: Toward Truth as Beauty*

Second, if immersion is to take place, truth must be entered into physically and visually as well as (but not only) intellectually. Immersive worship therefore requires art. Apart from the physical encounter with art, propositional sentences delivered in the pulpit can be interiorized by the worshiper for his or her own agenda and lost in the rational constructs that predetermine one's mind. If there is no uniform culture of meaning beforehand, truth as words falls flat, deconstructed of their meaning and distrusted for their agenda before communication can even take place. In the world of postmodernity, logocentric truth unravels in the lecture hall worship of traditional evangelicalism. Untested and unlived, propositional meaning proves too unstable as it is interpreted and reinterpreted by the fragmented grids of individual minds. Truth therefore must be more than propositions given in sentences that correspond one-to-one to an external reality. Truth must live in a people, displayed boldly in its physicality. In postmodernity, spoken truth only has currency as it is inextricably related to its manifestation as beauty and lived goodness among a people. In this way, art provides the context by which words take on flesh in people's lives and displays of beauty.

Immersive worship moves evangelicals beyond a modernist version of truth that is propositional, factual, scientific, or rational. It reclaims beauty as a category of truth from premodern orthodoxy. Through art, we embrace that knowing God is more than an intellectual engagement. To know God is also to see his beauty. Until we embrace this notion of truth, art will always be an illustration that merely sets up the sermon. Art will not serve to immerse the believer or confront the unbeliever. It will be reduced to a benign illustration or a cheap commercial.

Radical Orthodoxy theologians argue for such a version of truth. They describe a medieval (Thomistic) understanding of truth, which depends on the medieval transcendentals of the one, the true, the good, and the beautiful. Medievals (especially Aquinas) once believed that to know something as true is inseparable from knowing it also as good, whole, and beautiful. In Thomistic theology, something was true because it participated in the Being of God. The one (whole), the true, the good, and the beautiful were all transcendental conditions of pure Being.[29] Since God *is* pure Being, anything that participates in God would also participate in his beauty. One could not know something was true without recognizing its beauty through its participation in form and proportion. Veracity and truth were revealed in harmony, proportion, and form.[30] These were conditions of being that flowed from God. Radical Orthodoxy theologians argue that such an understanding of truth overcomes the nihilism inherent in the postmodern deconstruction of meaning.[31] Such a view of truth overcomes the Cartesian modern requirement that we as selves must doubt in order to know. Such a view of truth removes the self from the center of worship. If evangelicals desire an immersive experience of the Holy (whole) that overcomes the modernist fracturing of intellectual logocentrism, we too must recover this sense of truth for our life and worship.

To know God is also to see his beauty. Until we embrace this notion of truth, art will always be an illustration that merely sets up the sermon.

Armed with this understanding of the truth, evangelicals must open sanctuaries to be places for the Holy Spirit to reorder our imaginations and shape our characters into his holiness. This is truly immersion. We can use art not merely to entertain, or to illustrate words, or to be the preamble to an expository sermon.[32] Rather, art points us through a visible piece of art to a reality that transcends it. It calls us out of ourselves to a world that is much bigger than us.[33] Art is iconic in that it points us beyond the image to a glimpse of his holiness.[34] It submerges our lostness into the full-orbed reality of Christ that consists of more than just words. In so doing, art and symbol no longer distract from the spoken Word but unfold it into a world where we can be immersed, shaped, and formed into it. The reality we then display will not only be truthful but sufficiently compelling to witness to the shallowness of the foreign shapers of experience. We receive back the production of faithful experience from the secular producers of culture through worship.

Art in the sanctuary also witnesses powerfully against the implosions of nihilism and subjectivism that inhabit the growing society of postmodernity. Because all reason has power interests, the postmodern world rejects reason yet remains fascinated with the sublime.[35] Postmoderns don't argue with art, they just stand before its reality and note its beauty. The church, however, embraces the beautiful as more than postmodern fascination; it is the participation in the truth of God. Our worship therefore both proclaims and witnesses Christ through the arts in a way postmoderns can be invited into. As the Hebrew Scriptures declare, "Ascribe to the LORD the glory due his name, bring an offering and come before him; Worship the LORD in the beauty of his holiness" (1 Chron. 16:29 NIV; cf. 2 Chron. 20:21; Ps. 27:4; 29:2; 96:6–9; and Eccles. 3:11). Art in worship provides the visible witness which the unbeliever cannot argue against, only reject or be drawn into.

As modernity passes, evangelicals must relate to God's glory in more than just words or propositions. We cannot simply say "Jesus is Lord." We must embody the truth and reality that "Jesus is Lord." We must display "Jesus is Lord" through art, rituals, and symbols that submerge the worshiper's mind, body, and soul into the world that is Scripture. When we do this, the worshiper goes beyond the lecture hall from intellectually engaging the concept "Jesus is Lord" to being immersed into the world where Jesus *is* Lord. Such worship produces a culture of experience that parades his lordship unapologetically in contrast to the defensive attempts to promulgate Christ on the fragile terms of modernity's suspicious well-reasoned arguments.

3. *Immersive Worship Is Formative: Worship as* Lex Orandi, Lex Credendi

Third, immersive worship requires that we turn from our modernist naïveté that believes in a core internal religious experience universal to all humans.[36] We are modernist siblings to Protestant liberalism in this regard. I contend this misinformed credulity lies at the heart of charismatic worship. In light of postmodernity, however, we have no experience that has not already been formed out of culture and language. What we say and do precedes what we experience and feel. Therefore, if experience is not being formed at church, it will be formed elsewhere.

Charismatic worship then cannot escape the question, How does our worship form experience in our worshipers?

For postmodernity, religious impulses and experience are not innate. Desire is created by lack, by seeing what I don't have, and by imitating others who do.[37] We cannot escape just how much capitalism aggressively seeks to form desires in people to make us good consumers. Therapy, politics, culture and media industries, and even modern sports all seek to form the emotions and character of Americans. Experience is not innate therefore; it is formed out of all these seeming benign linguistic structures and cultural forms we inhabit. In Yale theologian George Lindbeck's terms, there are no precritical, inner experiences universally common to which our words merely refer. Instead, it is necessary to have the linguistic or symbolic means to express and ritualize such an experience first in order to have the experience. Experience is the product of our linguistic and symbolic worlds. It does not exist prior to them.[38] Experience therefore by definition requires immersion.

Immersive worship leads the worshiper into participating in God's already preexisting reality through language, ritual, and symbol as revealed in history through Scripture. By so doing, immersive worship births true experience of God that can only come at the behest of God as an ex post facto development when we have been faithful in our worship. It then enables the expression of our emotions to God or the seeking of an immediate experience of God. Such worship cannot, however, pursue "experience" as an end in itself because we cannot assume a truthful experience without first being shaped by God in worship (1 Cor. 12:1–11).[39] Yet it does not deny the expression of emotions in worship. Being immersed in worship makes it possible to experience joy, sadness, celebration, and hope birthed out of who God is and what he has done. Immersive worship produces faithful experience of God and the full range of emotional expression out of submission to, confession before, and participation in the truth of God.

The critique of the modern category of experience therefore returns us to the necessity of liturgy in faithful worship. Christian liturgy is the means by which the linguistic structures, symbolic gestures, and artistic presentations are practiced in a manner that immerses us into truthful experience of God via the Holy Spirit. Christian liturgy structures experience so that it is always God initiating and the people of God responding.[40] The presenting, remembering, and re-presenting of God through the Word and the Table comes first to the congregation, which then in turn responds. As opposed to contemporary worship, which often begins by coming to God with our self-expressions, liturgy demands that we first be confronted by God and then respond. Christian liturgy prevents self-indulgence and self-reference by its very structure because it always begins at the initiation of God to which we then respond. Through that response we are invited into God's reality as structured by Scripture and the history of God in Christ. We are formed into God and not vice versa. Immersive worship is always structured as "call and response."

The feel-good pep rally format is not sufficient to generate faithful experience because it elevates self-expression unto itself. Christian liturgy demands that music either present God's revelation or lead the congregation into a faithful response to it. Self-expression alone is not worship. Contemporary music therefore can and must take on liturgical form if we are to make good use of it in our worship. It must be a celebratory response when this response is in order, and it must be penitent when this response is in order. Contemporary music liturgically participates in all the emotions but in a transforming way. Because through liturgy, we are invited out of our old emotions to new ones, out of old experiences to new experiences as all things are made new.

> **Christian liturgy demands that music either present God's revelation or lead the congregation into a faithful response to it. Self-expression alone is not worship.**

And so immersive worship grounds the believer in the verbal, bodily, and visual participation in the historic work of God in Jesus Christ. Christian liturgy provides a check against the isolated worshiper self-expressing a catharsis that might be encouraging sin. Through liturgical practice, worship recaptures the substance of the ancient doctrine *lex orandi, lex credendi* (the law of prayer, the law of belief), which teaches us that often one must first learn to pray in the way of Christ to fully comprehend and experience belief in the way of Christ.[41] In other words, worship takes practice. It requires ritual and the learning of a language. And such practice forms an orientation. And orientation shapes a new experience.[42] Liturgical participation makes possible the grounding of a true experience of God in worship through immersion.

This is all strange to most North American evangelicals because for most of us, liturgy is the sign that your worship is dead, superstitious, and impersonal. But in postmodernity, the evangelical emphasis on personal subjective experience has become the source of deadness in that it always has a "short shelf life," which leads us to further despair. Postmodernity reveals that evangelical contemporary worship can be as self-indulgent as any other secular cultural preoccupation, and we must resist that (1 Cor. 14:20–26). Evangelicals can resist through liturgical worship.

4. *Immersive Worship Is What Happens via the Alive Body, Not a Lecture Hall or a Pep Rally: Worship according to Lindbeck*

Thus the occasion of the demise of modernity reveals the inadequacies of evangelical worship. Traditional evangelicals rightly assert the need for orthodox truth in our worship. And charismatic evangelicals rightly plead for experience.[43] But, as we have learned, we cannot naïvely perceive that truth can be communicated in word propositions alone. Nor can we assume that pure experience exists inside every human heart that somehow just needs to be awakened. The demise of modernity renders the lecture hall as well as the feel-good pep rally unfit for true worship. Instead, for true worship, we require an alive body that we can be immersed into. Only the church as an alive body that carries on an organic life in language, symbol, art, and ritual can sufficiently produce a faithful experience of the God of Jesus Christ.

George Lindbeck's typology of doctrine explains how this can be so. Lindbeck states that in the church, doctrine functions in one of three ways: as propositions, as expressive-experiential articulation, or as cultural-linguistic grammars.[44] The lecture hall views doctrines as verifiable propositions while the feel-good pep rally sees doctrines as the articulations of experiences. The former locates truth in spoken or written propositions while the latter locates truth in immediate experience. In the cultural-linguistic mode, however, doctrines of God function as "comprehensive interpretive schemes, usually embodied in myths or narratives and heavily ritualized, which structure human experience and understanding of self and world."[45] Immersive worship correlates with this third mode. Here in immersive worship, the coalescence of language, music, art, ritual, and symbol enable the faithful to participate in the truth, thereby enabling the worshiper to fully experience it and know it as truth.[46] Because in postmodernity, experiencing the truth depends upon participating in an alive social organism with all its parts living and interacting in the language and ways of Jesus Christ. Lindbeck's cultural-linguistic model argues for designing worship as an enculturated living place of God where our personal character is formed into the specific culture of Christ in order to truthfully know and experience God in worship.

According to Lindbeck's "cultural-linguistic model" then, truthful worship requires that the worshiper learn to use language, engage his or her body, see through symbols, and submit to faithful constructions of reality in order that he or she will be shaped and formed into an experience of God. Indeed, worshipers of Christ are invited into a worship that is already going on in heaven in liturgies that have been spoken for hundreds of years (Heb. 12:22–23). True propositions and experience remain important to good worship. But doctrinal truth is embodied in the way we live, praise God, and speak to one another. Experience follows likewise after language and ritual forms our souls into Christ's lordship. This is a picture of immersive worship and its dependence upon the "alive body" of Christ. In Lindbeck's terms, good worship is more than a propositional or experiential exercise; it is a culture speaking its given language, producing art, symbols, and truthful experience in an intratextual integrity with the person of Jesus Christ (as passed on historically in the Scriptures and the church).[47] True worship shapes us mind, body, and soul toward the glory of God in a community and thereby enables experiences hitherto unknown by the pagan soul. It requires the alive body of Christ.

> True worship shapes us mind, body, and soul toward the glory of God in a community and thereby enables experiences hitherto unknown by the pagan soul.

In summary, immersive worship goes beyond the doctrinal orthodoxy of traditional evangelical worship or the emotional experience of contemporary charismatic worship. It makes both of these possible. Immersive worship forms us into an alive body from which we can know and experience enlivened truth. It displays the God of history with art, symbol, and beauty, not just propositions. It rehearses the drama of God in Christ liturgically and invites us into this drama to participate in it, not just express ourselves cathartically. Immersive worship is not new, it is merely forgotten among evangelicals. Immersive worship does not compromise truth nor give away experience; it reclaims the place of the church as the center for all truth and faithful experience.

No More "Giveaway"

The postmodern criticizers of propositions and experience expose how evangelicals give away the production of experience to secular culture by virtue of our worship practices. And for that we should be thankful. For postmodernity affords evangelicalism the opportunity to receive back worship practices that can form God's people into the faithful experience of God by the Holy Spirit. By reordering our worship liturgically, embodying it through art and symbol, and re-sacralizing the mysteries of the Word and Eucharist, we can recapture the shaping of our people's imaginations for the lordship of Christ. Such a worship may take practice and therefore require patience because we have been so addicted to appeasing our "selves" in worship as opposed to shaping our "selves." Nonetheless, by faithful practice we can receive an immersive worship that "absorbs" us into God's world, the world of Scripture and his kingdom.[48] By so doing, we become an alive body of Christ that refuses to "give away" the production of our experience to the foreign producers of culture alien to Christ.

Such an immersive worship changes what we look for in identifying what constitutes good worship. For when worship refuses to "give away" the production of our experience but instead seeks to form the experience of God in the lives of his people, we no longer point to John or George crying tears or raising hands in the pews as the sign of good worship. Instead, it will be their lives lived out in the body and in the world that validates those emotions as good. Simply put, faithful worship reveals itself in the shape of the lives it produces. Immersive worship does not deny that robust emotions often coincide with the faithful worship of God, but we will know the faithfulness of those emotions from the quality of our life together.

In this way, immersive worship restores the church to be the center for the production of true experience for the believer. Once our evangelical churches no longer give away the production of experience to Hollywood, Disney, Starbucks, Las Vegas, Broadway, and the professional sports venues, our churches become the center for experience that is thick with the meaning of God's kingdom. From here, all other experience separated from God is exposed for what it is: a cheap veneer that cannot sustain life. Amidst America's cities of endless repeatable desire, the church becomes the center for true and ordered desire, transformed experience, and the display of the true, the good, and the beautiful.[49] Because our worship is faithful and subverts all other images as either faithful participants in God or simulacrum, the church becomes a producing center for experience, placing all other competition in its orbit. The church becomes that which enables the believer to locate all other truthful experience in society.

> **Immersive worship does not deny that robust emotions often coincide with the faithful worship of God, but we will know the faithfulness of those emotions from the quality of our life together.**

Such worship recalls the reports given about Byzantine worship to the grand prince Vladimir, in tenth-century Ukraine. Vladimir had sent ambassadors to Byzantium in search of truth, goodness, and beauty when he was planning to introduce his people into the civilized world. They came back to him reporting that the Byzantine liturgy was so beautiful that we "did not know if we were in heaven or on earth, for on earth there is no such beauty. . . . One thing do we know, that God was living there with men, and . . . we cannot forget this beauty."[50] Likewise today, through the church's worship, the body of Christ can become visible again, a compelling witness before the world to the beauty that is Jesus Christ our Lord. And Christians can engage that world because through worship they know that all true beauty points to God, both inside the church and out.

Practices for Finding Our Way Back to Liturgy and Art in Christian Worship

For worship like this, we evangelicals are in need of new practices. By practices, I mean skills of worshiping that take practice yet afterward enable deep and substantive experiences to take root in our lives.[51] Worship requires practice because it enables a reorientation toward God, out of which life with God flows. But the goods we seek from worship will not be instantaneous. The goods of life in Christ through worship will become evident only after we are formed into this orientation through practice so that we can indeed see them and therefore experience them in Christ.[52]

But these practices present significant challenges for evangelicals. Immersive worship requires that we learn new languages, different symbols, and a sense for mystery that we rejected under the old regimes of modernity. But we can expect nothing less in a post-Christian world. For we are no longer born into Christian language and symbol. We are imbedded in the overwhelming symbols of consumerism and the structures of late capitalist desire. The worshiper therefore must learn ways of speaking, seeing symbols, history, and art that enable him or her to enter into the drama of God, not just study it as a textbook. Only modernity pretends that the richness of God is accessible to everyone's immediate consciousness. With the end of modernity, many have discovered that the old spontaneity in worship was an illusion. To the post-Christian society's uninitiated, worship will take practice, and self-expression is not sufficient alone to experience God. I offer the following suggestions for renewing some necessary practices for immersive worship in the American evangelical church.

Restore Liturgy to the Church and Make It Accessible

Evangelicals should restore liturgy to our churches. Evangelicals should return to liturgical forms in their worship such as the practice of the church calendar and the various elements in the Lord's Day service. We should make the Eucharist central to the rest of what goes on Sunday morning. But we must do all this in a manner that makes it accessible not only to evangelicals but to strangers coming into our midst. Making things accessible to strangers has always been one of our strengths. We should put this strength to work in bringing liturgical form back to our services.

Evangelicals should admit liturgical elements into our services, and as we do, we should translate liturgy into contemporary languages, enliven liturgy with graphic arts, and initiate the stranger with user-friendly instructions. Liturgical elements and phrases such as "The peace of Christ," "The Lord be with you," and "The Word of the Lord" can all be revived and fashioned so that their rich historical meaning can be brought to bear upon the worshiper while at the same time made accessible to the new worshiper.

Some may argue that accessible liturgy is an oxymoron. Indeed, to make liturgy user-friendly may compromise what liturgy is in the first place. But translating liturgy, with explanations, current language, and art, merely extends the practices that have always gone on within the historical development of liturgy. We must ennoble this history and translate it anew with contemporary graphic arts and technology. Failing to do this, we risk debasing the church into an antiquated museum for only the already initiated.[53] At our church, we publish an insert that explains the history of each liturgical part of the service and invites the congregation to participate. Bishop Thomas Cranmer famously rewrote the liturgies for the Church of England hoping to make possible the centering of every English person into the life of God. Thus came the *Book of Common Prayer*.[54] Evangelicals, if we are to move forward at the end of modernity, must become the Thomas Cranmers of our day, rewriting and developing the sacred liturgies of the Christian church in order that we might invite the lost generations into the participation of the life of God in Jesus Christ.

> **Sometimes we must explain where these words came from and why we do them.**

To do so, however, evangelicals must practice historical continuity alongside accessibility. To stay frozen in history is to make liturgy inaccessible to most strangers and evangelicals. Sometimes we must explain where these words came from and why we do them. On the other hand, to ignore history and "make up" ritual is to endanger the worship service with triteness and manipulation. The liturgist, in making liturgy accessible, must not detach the liturgy from history and Scripture. Each liturgical part of the service has language grounded in Scripture and an integrity all its own worked out over hundreds of years. Thus we must treat the meaning and depth of these liturgies with great care. Their purposes and history should not be overridden. Instead, they should be continued and carried on in ways that make them accessible. Liturgy invites us into the narrative of God in Scripture. To break continuity with the scriptural basis or historical form of the liturgy risks making the liturgy arbitrary and the parishioner feel manipulated. The liturgy must be bigger than the parishioner in order to invite him or her into it. It must have the depth of historical continuity and the scriptural power. Evangelicals therefore should approach extending the liturgy with the same practice they approach extending the Scriptures through preaching. It requires the care of an exegesis that seeks historical continuity within the texts.

Pattern Worship after Call and Response

Worship is basically call and response.[55] It is God's Word coming to us and our response. It is the re-presentation of the Christ's presence in the Lord's Table along with our acquiescence and participation. It is the display of his beauty and our awed reception. It is the declaration of who he is, and our uniform agreement. It is call and response. This is the pattern of all the great worship texts of the Old Testament.[56] It is the pattern of the great worship texts of Revelation (chapters 4–5). Evangelical worship must move from a structure of service that isolates either self-expression or the hearing of the Word as an entity unto its own in the service. If we are to go beyond the sermon-centric or the self-absorbed, cathartic worship services of our time, we evangelicals must structure all of our worship in the "call and response" rhythms of historical worship. In so doing, we create the great drama that is Sunday morning where God not only comes to us, but his people respond. And we are shaped by that.

We may keep our contemporary music, especially if it is theologically strong. But we must place it into patterns that structure the worshiper into a rhythm of God's call and our response. Likewise, the reading of the Word should be read dramatically as the Word of the Lord and the congregation should be led in a response to it either through singing or shouting the words "Thanks be to God!" The service in its entirety must embody the rhythm of "call and response." At our church, the singing of praise and thanksgiving follows the hearing of the Word and sermon.

Revive the Church Calendar

We must reinvigorate the church calendar. The Christian sense of time reorders our whole lives toward the rhythms of Christ and removes us from the world's attempts to mold us into consumers.[57] The use of the church calendar is essential at the crucial times from Advent through Christmas to Epiphany and then again from Lent to Holy Week to Pentecost. The lectionaries can be used skillfully to produce descriptive sermons of the central understandings of the drama of salvation. By so doing, it is the Word of God and the story of Christ that is shaping us, and not vice versa.

At our church we follow the lectionary closely from Advent to Pentecost, highlighting different sections of Scripture each year. We read four readings each Sunday performatively, yet preach consistently each week from the same section of the Bible such as the exilic prophets or the Gospels. Evangelicals appreciate this consistency while still rehearsing the major doctrinal themes of the calendar each year: the second coming and incarnation at Advent, God's revealing during Epiphany, the doctrines of conversion, repentance, atonement, and sanctification during Lent, and the doctrines of new life, discipleship, and Holy Spirit after Easter and leading up to Pentecost.

By engaging the whole of Scripture in the lectionary to teach the repeated biblical themes of the church calendar, we are drawn in to the drama of God's consistent character unfolded across the whole traverse of Scripture. Our church uses ordinary time for certain teaching needs, evangelistic outreaches, and emphases the church has need of. Yet even these ordinary times have a yearly rhythm. For example, every September we preach on "the call to be the church" for the whole month as the community returns from the slowness of the summer to the work of being the church.

Reinvigorate the Eucharist

There is no more sacred and basic practice in the church than the Lord's Supper. It is the ultimate coalescence of the Word, embodied symbol, and the redemptive narrative of God in Christ. Immersive worship therefore is centered in the mystery and practice of the Eucharist, the celebration and great thanksgiving of God's great gift to us in Jesus Christ. If evangelicals seek immersive worship, we must reinvigorate the Lord's Table for our churches. We must go beyond the intellectualist, reductionist approaches we have learned from our modernist heritage. We must (a) practice it more regularly, preferably every Sunday, (b) revive its mystery and the healing powers set free through it by the Holy Spirit, and (c) elevate its significance as a body-forming practice in all its historical richness.

To do this, however, will be a challenge. And to simply adopt an Anglo-Catholic liturgy will not suffice. Indeed, we evangelicals will require more to train us out of the old habits of modernity. We will need specific teaching so that we go beyond "remembering" as a modernist intellectual exercise to truly participating in the partaking of the Lord's body at the Table. We may require longer times around the Table than ten or fifteen minutes at the end of the service of the Word to truly receive it as a gift. We must learn to take in (*anamnēsis*; 1 Cor. 11:24–25) his forgiveness and new life, open our selves and our life happenings to being formed out of this reality without the paranoia that somehow we have succumbed to "re-sacrificing" Christ as older Protestant accusations toward the Roman Church assumed.

At our church, we come to the Table only after each person has considered his or her relation with God and in turn, with each other in the community. Then and only then does the parishioner enter the sanctuary, receive a candle to signify the special presence, and say, "The peace of Christ be with you." We all light the candles around the Table, signifying his heightened presence, and then we sit for an extended period of time before the Table. We instruct out of Scripture for five minutes. We hear a prayer of confession, throw our burdens onto the cross, sing a eucharistic prayer of thanks, sing the Sanctus, hear the words of institution, and invoke the Holy Spirit's blessing on the elements. We then pass the bread and the cup, saying each person's name: "John, this is Christ's body broken for you," and later "John, this is the new covenant life in Christ's blood shed for you." At the end we pledge our financial commitments for one another in a benevolent offering. This eucharistic practice produces a profound experience of the forgiveness, new life, and oneness in which we participate in Christ. And in this practice we are truly changed through the Holy Spirit.

> **We evangelicals should visualize and ritualize our worship around tangible symbols that invite us out of our heads into the existence of God.**

Use Candles and Other Tactile Symbols

We evangelicals should visualize and ritualize our worship around tangible symbols that invite us out of our heads into the existence of God. We need to symbolize mystery and recognize his transcendence in ways science and modernity won't let us. We need to touch, see, and remember the cross because it was and is real. We need to be invited into his drama with real things. Candles historically have been symbols of the Holy Spirit and his presence. At our church, not unlike other churches, we visualize his presence at the invocation with symbols of candles. We light a candle often when our confessional groups meet to confess sin and speak into each other's lives. We teach and use candles to help us become aware of his ever-abiding presence through the Holy Spirit.

Use the Visual Arts

At our church, almost every Sunday morning the liturgist uses the visual arts to transform a part of the liturgy into a compelling, commanding reality, which the congregation is then invited to submit to, participate in, respond to, and enter into. The liturgist skillfully uses art not to entertain, not to manipulate, but to present the narrative of God in Scripture, which provides the context for the assent to the creed, or the communal prayer to our Father, or the corporate confession of sin. It could be a painting, it could be a dance. It could be a skillful piece of graphic art projected on the screen. It is often simple. Yet other times it requires the honed skill of a graphic artist in the congregation. And although many liturgical purists reject such arts in the liturgy, these arts nonetheless can play a role similar to the wondrous works of art in many a medieval cathedral. When properly discerned, they provide the visual context that invites the congregants into the great drama of God. They are aids for our discipleship similar to the depictions of the stages of the cross, the marvelous stained glass windows, or the great ceilings in the cathedrals of old.

Sing Substantive Music

The singing of praise, thanksgiving, exaltation, and attribution to God has always been part of the church's worship (1 Cor. 14:26). Music and song enable us to give over our selves to God beyond ourselves in voice, words, and body. It is mind, body, and soul oriented toward him in truth.

We should therefore not sing only for emotional catharsis. We must sing to recognize his glory and greatness to which we bow and are shaped. We should avoid singing that is only "about me." Music and lyrics should be more than self-expression. They should present who God is. If we are to recover immersive worship, we need practices of songwriting that make the songs about God and his drama.[58] Our singing should display the doctrines of God and invite us to participate in them. We therefore need practices to recapture the historical breadth of Christian lyrics and translate them for the musical language of the current congregations. When we revive and connect to ancient music we help the worshiper to participate in something that is bigger than life itself: God's movement down through the ages. We can mine old hymns, revive ancient Celtic music, or even translate sacred prayers of the past as sources for songs that will unite us with all the saints and shape us powerfully toward the God of all the ages. And then when we do write worship music, its content will be informed by God's work through the ages.

Our singing times must reject performances by worship leaders that promote passive entertainment. Worship leaders instead must be instruments to draw the souls of congregations into the story of God in Christ so as to be shaped by it. If we are to go beyond self-expression and emotional catharsis in our worship, we need practitioners that lead worship singing so as to guide the worshiper's focus upon God, not upon the styles and exploits of the musician. There is a time for the musical performance as the delivering of the beauty of God and who he is before a congregation. This would be the "call." But congregational singing is the "response" to what we have just heard, seen, and experienced about God, and the two functions should remain separate in order for the "call and response" rhythm of worship to be preserved.

At our church we sing in congregational praise for as much as twenty minutes or more following the hearing of the readings of the Word and the proclamation of the Word in the sermon. The worship leader begins the praise and worship time by saying, "We have just heard . . . Let us respond with . . ." Sometimes this time of congregational praise approaches the quality of a rock concert, a rock concert of people performing for God as the audience.

See the Sanctuary as an Art Gallery

The sanctuary is the sacred space. Since all things come from him and participate in his beauty, Sunday worship should turn the sanctuary into a display of that beauty. We display art to demonstrate that beauty and to bring us into the world where the divine Jesus dwells as Lord. With art that is iconic, liturgical, historical, and contemporary, artists lead the worshiper to engage God throughout the Christian times of year. The sanctuary visually and spatially guides the gaze of the worshiper toward God, who he is, what he has done, and where he is taking us. At our church, when you walk in, you see the altar at the center of the gathering, draped with color and symbols of church time, with the cross prominent upon it. The altar leads us to put our lives before the altar to be formed into the work of the cross. We transform the sanctuary into an art gallery inviting the worshiper into the experiences of God in the church calendar. Art points us toward his glory. At our church, during the church's ordinary time, we take special doctrines and unfold them scripturally and artistically as well. Art draws us out of ourselves and pulls our imaginations into his lordship and the experience of the world as it is where he is Lord. And during the great liturgical march of time from Advent to Epiphany, Lent, Holy Week, and Pentecost, art enlivens the reality of the history by which we have been formed. Historical art and color drapes our sanctuary. During Pentecost, for instance, the great paintings of that historical event center our consciousness while more recent art points us toward a reality where the Holy Spirit is always working in those who call Jesus Lord. At our church, we often have fifteen-minute art gallery tours before the beginning of the service. The artist briefly describes certain features of the art and guides the worshipers into a time of response, meditation, and prayer in the midst of artwork that points toward God. As in medieval times, the church becomes the center for the formation of our imaginations. If we are to take back the formation of our experience in post-Christian worlds, evangelicals need to train curators for the outfitting of our sanctuaries for his glory.

If we are to take back the formation of our experience in post-Christian worlds, evangelicals need to train curators for the outfitting of our sanctuaries for his glory.

Summary: Does This Mean We Must Become Catholic?

Practicing worship as described above may mean for some evangelicals that we are simply becoming Roman Catholic. This is a legitimate question. To some evangelicals, this chapter risks turning worship into a rote and dry exercise devoid of experience, the "everyman's critique" of High Church liturgy. To others who are liturgical purists, this chapter risks corrupting the liturgy. I hope I have articulated sufficiently that I intend to do neither. I believe we evangelicals have much to learn from our Roman brethren. At the same time, I believe there are things the High Church folks can learn from evangelicalism, mainly our resolve to reach out to those in our midst who are strangers to the gospel. But that is truly a statement which cannot be defended here. The challenge, however, lies in between these two positions. For truly we can no longer do without liturgical processes in our worship in this post-Christian time. But neither can we carry on with a liturgy that is frozen in a former time. Liturgy should not be rejected but rather developed to both keep its historical integrity and yet have some point of contact with the foreign world within which it seeks to live. This is perhaps the kind of liturgical renewal that the "younger evangelicals"[59] can take up as we seek to minister in the new post-Christian cultures of the Western world.

In making liturgy evangelical, however, we evangelicals need criteria to guard the faithfulness of liturgical practice. I have neither the space in this chapter nor the expertise to offer such criteria. I simply contend to all those who seek to bring liturgy into previously evangelical contexts (here the emergent church comes to mind) that the church's liturgy must have sufficient continuity with historical form, sufficient memory of those who have gone before, sufficient faithfulness to Scripture, sufficient catholicity to join in with the church universal, and sufficient repeatability to emboss truth so that it will be possible for the church to reclaim its citizens from their captivity to capitalism and consumerism into the glorious story of Christ. Somehow the basic worship orders of gathering, reading and proclaiming the Word, responding through confession, singing and the Eucharist, and sending out to serve Christ in the world must all take place on Sunday morning. And we must revive these practices as liturgy and not as modernist techniques the people in the pew can use to achieve personal goals or to just plain feel better.

Evangelicals have some specific hurdles to overcome in this process. We have inherited iconoclastic views of art that derive from the Radical Reformation of the sixteenth century. Given our propositionalism, we have not been accustomed to treating beauty as a category of truth. In addition, our commitment rests with the goal of conversion, saving pagan lost souls. Therefore, we cannot sponsor a church service inaccessible to the "man or woman on the street." Liturgy will not come easy. So as evangelicals, we must recover liturgy and the arts without losing the strength of evangelicalism: its concern to communicate the gospel in a form that is understandable to the stranger. We must recover liturgy in our services, but we must do so in a manner that maintains a bridge to the lost souls within capitalism and democracy and yet does not compromise the integrity of the liturgy, both of form and content, in relation to both history and Scripture.

In so doing our worship opens the church as portal to the world for all to come to the One who lives as mysterious and transcendent. Our worship prevents the God of Israel and Jesus Christ from being subsumed by a scientific culture that discredits a God who reveals himself for all time in the drama of history. Our worship subverts the trivialization of God into thirty-second sound bites. Our worship puts a check on those who would make it an orgy of emotions for self-absorption, not the formation of the self into Christ. Our worship then truly invites believers into submission, participation, and immersion into the reality that Jesus is Lord. And in so doing, our worship produces an experience of God by the Holy Spirit that is faithful to Jesus Christ as Lord. In essence we no longer give away the production of our experience but recapture it for Christ and his kingdom.

In March of 2003, a production company decided to invite people to the Palace theater in Chicago to watch the 1939 classic *The Wizard of Oz*, starring Judy Garland. They did more, however. They invited the guests to participate in a costume contest, an "audience fun pack," and a sing-along of the famous classic Oz tunes. Instead of investing in a multi-million-dollar stage production, typical of most Broadway shows, the producers showed the movie inviting all in attendance to participate. A huge success resulted. I believe this illustrates a lesson for worship. Christian worship also retells a classic story, except that its story is true and all-encompassing, and its members are then invited to participate in that story and be immersed into it, because this is the story into which any and all other stories have any validity. It is Christ's "triumphal procession" which gives life to all who would join into it (2 Cor. 2:15). Through the Eucharist, the liturgy, art, music of substance, and the everliving Word, we can be faithful to the apostle's vision of worship. This is not a new way to worship. Rather this is the reinvigoration of the old ways for the challenges that face us in these post-Christian times that are so new to us evangelicals.

5

The Preaching of the Word

The Myth of Expository Preaching: Why We Must Do More Than Wear Scrolls on Our Foreheads

Beloved, do not believe every spirit, but test the spirits to see whether they are of God.

1 John 4:1 RSV

And we impart this in words not taught by human wisdom but taught by the Spirit, interpreting spiritual truths to those who are spiritual.

1 Corinthians 2:13 ESV

When John and Sue moved to the suburbs and started to look for a church, they came and visited our church. They talked to me since I was the pastor and they described what they were looking for in a church with the words, "We're looking for a church that preaches the Word." So I asked them what they meant by a church that preaches the Word and they said, "You know, a church that preaches sermons right out of the text of Scripture, word for word, sentence for sentence." "Anything else is man's opinion," Sue said. "We just want to study the Word," John said. This conversation seems to encapsulate what many evangelicals look for in preaching. Evangelical Christians love expository preaching because this is how we recognize that a particular church truly "preaches the Word." Because expository preaching follows the text, sentence by sentence, sometimes word for word, it stays true to the "preaching of the Word." And so for many evangelicals, expository preaching is the means by which we secure the Word for ourselves over against contamination from sources outside the Word. It is how we know a church is serious about the Word.

In New Testament times, Jews who were serious about their devotion to God often wore scrolls on their foreheads. The Torah had commanded the wearing of such scrolls (Exod. 13:9, 16; Deut. 6:8; 11:18). It was a means to remind the Jews of God's covenantal faithfulness with the nation of Israel. Wearing scrolls on one's forehead focused one's vision toward the ways of God represented in the Law. In evangelical terms, these people were serious about "the Word." Jesus, however, accused the Pharisees of wearing these scrolls for show and power (Matt. 23:5–7). In some way, the scrolls had become the means for the Pharisees to secure the knowledge of God for themselves and to manipulate the power that came from that. For those confident of their knowledge, the "scrolls" ensured who the orthodox were, that is, themselves. I contend that expository preaching can play this same role of "wearing scrolls on our foreheads" among evangelicals. For many evangelicals, expository preaching marks off who is serious about the Bible and who is not. For serious folk, expository preaching is the means of securing the Word. Often then, expository preaching cannot help but become the means to control the power associated with the authority of Scripture for evangelical preachers and pastor-leaders.

> For many evangelicals, expository preaching marks off who is serious about the Bible and who is not.

In the following chapter, we examine the assumptions behind evangelical expository preaching. Can we or should we be this secure in our knowledge of God's Word in the manner described by John and Sue? Does expository preaching really guarantee "the preaching of the Word" as promised? Postmodern hermeneutics reveals a world where what the scriptural author wrote, what the preacher says, and what the listener hears are hardly a stable matter. What are we to do with preaching in such a world? In this chapter, I seek to dispel some myths that evangelicals attach to expository preaching given their modernist pretext. But I also seek to reveal how expository preaching can accommodate scriptural interpretation to other agendas, including the pastor's own, without anyone being aware it is happening. In this way, ironically, expository preaching can covertly become the means to "give away" the interpretation of the Word to agendas outside of the body of Christ.

From this analysis of expository preaching, the chapter will then explore how the whole community of Christ in reliance upon the Holy Spirit can be the means for faithful biblical interpretation. We uncover how faithful biblical interpretation requires the Spirit-filled communal practices of the authoritative gifts, liturgical submission to Scripture, intercommunal testing of truth, as well as a chastened historical-critical exegesis. Such interpretive practices may not be as secure as the expository exegetes would have it, but the alternative "wearing of scrolls on our foreheads" offers only the illusion of secure interpretation while it hides potential abuses of power in the name of the Bible. Once uncovered, however, we can see that the secure interpretation of God's Word is one that is governed by "vigilant communities" of the Holy Spirit.[1] We can see how only a community of faithful practicers of Scripture can resist the "giveaway" of our interpretations of Scripture to agendas brought in from foreign places.

Preaching in the Evangelical Church

Within evangelical churches, parishioners and preachers alike debate the merits of expository preaching versus topical preaching. Good preaching, so the debate goes, requires both faithfulness to the biblical text and the relevant application of the biblical text to people's everyday lives. Expository preaching, however, accentuates the text and what it is saying prior to applying it. Topical preaching supposedly accentuates the relevant issue to which Scripture must be applied by the preacher. Within evangelicalism, the debate is usually about which should come first. So we have churches that stress faithfulness to the biblical text and advocate expository preaching. Their churches regularly proceed through books or epistles of the Bible on Sunday mornings, often taking months to get through a book of the Bible. On the other hand, we have churches that stress relevancy in preaching and appreciate topical preaching. Their churches use sermon "series" on Sunday mornings to handle the relevant subject matter for the congregation. Typically, the "Bible church" services emphasize expository preaching and the seeker service megachurches emphasize topical preaching. The "Bible church" parishioners love their church because it "preaches the Word." On the other hand, the seeker church parishioners love their church because it is relevant and they can bring their non-Christian friends.

This current state of affairs has its origins in the modernist-fundamentalist controversies of the 1920s, among other places. During these controversies, many pastors and parishioners of Protestant main-line churches accused their churches of succumbing to the relativizing effects of modernist historical criticism upon scriptural authority. Many of these pastors and parishioners left their Protestant mainline churches to start churches that would believe the whole inerrant Bible. Amidst this struggle, these folk valued highly that the Bible is historically and scientifically accurate over against the "modernists" of the day. One of their main missions in starting new churches was to maintain the Bible before the world as trustworthy for all of life, practice, and worship. Hence they named their churches "ABC Bible church." In their sanctu-aries, they placed the Bible front and center in the sanctuary (following some Reformation churches). Biblical authority was the focus and the closer they could stick to it the better. Expository preaching became the preferred mode of preaching. A large sector of evangelicalism still car-ries this agenda and expository preaching fits the bill for it. Meanwhile, the seeker services arose in the 1970s and '80s as a response to these traditional Bible church services, which supposedly had become "ir-relevant" to the average North American person who didn't speak that language. Thirty years later, the new Bible churches point to the seeker service people and see compromise of the Bible and its agenda for life. Likewise, the seeker service people point to the Bible church people and see encrusted Christians, unconcerned for making the message of Scripture hearable for those outside of Christ.

Today, among evangelicals, expository preaching has emerged as the champion of the pure preaching of the Word. Even seeker service megachurches now make time in the middle of the week for expository "meaty" preaching. Today, evangelical spokespeople decry the lack of biblical preaching and they offer expository preaching as the solution.[2] And like wearing scrolls on our foreheads, expository preaching is for many evangelicals the sign that a church takes the Bible seriously.

Uncovering the Myth

But is expository preaching all it claims to be? Inherent in the name, *expository* is the subtle implication that expository preaching exposits the meaning of the existing text as opposed to interpreting it (or at least that interpretation is subordinate to exposition). Somehow the myth surrounds expository preaching that if we follow the text more closely we shall stay closer to the already existing, stable, perspicuous mean-ing inherent in the text. By following the text closely, the expository method supposedly prevents preachers from allowing external agendas and meanings to drive their interpretation of the text. The Scripture, by implication, remains in control. But does the expository method work this way? In other words, à la Derrida, can there be any repeating of the text without its meaning changing? Isn't significant interpretation unavoidable for even the staunchest of expositors?

There are some assumptions that undergird this evangelical love affair with expository preaching. These unspoken assumptions allow the everyday parishioner to assume that through the expository method, Scripture remains in control of the preaching. For example, most evangelical expository preachers assume a deep trust in the scientific methods of historical exegesis to arrive at the meaning of the biblical text. From their days at seminary, such evangelical preachers are taught to begin sermon preparation with their exegetical work upon the text. Through skillful training in the original languages, grammar, lexicography, and historical backgrounds, expository preachers seek first to uncover "the author's original intended meaning." If preachers but apply these skills well, aided by the Spirit, they can arrive at the singular best meaning of the text. The meaning is then exposited. Interpretation comes second and can only follow the text.

These assumptions concerning expository preaching feed into the modernism of evangelical culture where we are comfortable with hardened notions of propositional truth. Here we know that it is truly the "preaching of the Word" by the way the preacher follows the propositions of the text. Once these propositions have been exposited, the preacher is free to extract this meaning faithfully, taking it across time,[3] and apply it to the concerns and needs of the congregation. The emphasis on scientific exegetical methods, however, feeds the culture of expository preaching that asserts there is a stable propositional meaning to the text that needs to be carefully followed and exposited.

But the premise of such a scientific exegesis proves to be a myth.[4] The consensus interpretation for the biblical texts is located in the history of church doctrine not the scientific exegesis of texts. Historical-critical methods of exegesis have yet to yield a consensus interpretation for any texts in the Scriptures. This is evidenced in the fact that one hundred years of historical-critical exegetical studies have produced thousands of commentaries written on various books of the Bible. Each of these commentaries reports on the historical divergences in interpreting the grammatical minutia within each given text. Most of these scholarly commentaries offer at least two to four options for understanding the grammar and textual data for each verse of Scripture. So instead of producing a consensus interpretation for the Bible, exegesis and historical-critical studies have disseminated multiple interpretations of each biblical text.

The expository preacher therefore is actually arbitrating between exegetical choices as the sermon is developed as opposed to extracting the one meaning of the text. Since evangelical expository preaching assumes that we do not need a church teaching authority to interpret a text, each expository preacher is left on his or her own to make these grammatical choices "objectively" for the edification of the church. The textual meaning then is in fact open for the expository preacher to select which grammatical option best suits one's chosen agenda. There is no "objective" grammatical meaning given the multiple, historical-critical scientific interpretations. And the history of the church's teaching authority provides no immediate arbitration for the evangelical. The result is that there is no one determinate meaning of the text that can be exposited apart from the history of the church and interpretation. Instead, under the guise of "preaching the Word," expository preachers have the final say on what the text shall mean for their listeners.[5] The idea of a single "original intended, propositional meaning" proves to be a myth. And expository preaching thus leaves preachers more on their own to determine meanings for given texts.

> **As any preacher knows who has ever stood in the back, shaking hands on Sunday morning after the service, the parishioner often hears something different than what the preacher said.**

In addition, the evangelical culture of expository preaching assumes that an idea can be communicated from the preacher to the hearer and in the process the idea will mean the same thing to preacher and hearers alike.[6] The goal of expository preaching is providing application points that each parishioner can use to further his or her Christian life. Taking notes is generally encouraged. No additional engagement between preacher, parishioners, and other parishioners is necessary for the preached word to take effect. Yet as any preacher knows who has ever stood in the back, shaking hands on Sunday morning after the service, the parishioner often hears something different than what the preacher said. And if indeed the parishioner did hear it right, then once it is repeated it is never the same.[7] As Derrida reminds us, repetition leads to a difference, never to the "same." Each idea, each propositional truth is heard in terms of each hearer's context. The person in the pew takes notes, selects what he or she hears for special notation, and walks away with "the nugget" for the day that can best support his or her current life or context. The hearer hears through the grid he or she walked in with. So even if there were a stable authorial meaning inherent to the text, it still could not be communicated in the ways expository preaching assumes.[8] These assumptions also prove to be a myth.

The culture of evangelical preaching as a whole assumes isolated selves can benefit from hearing the Sunday morning message alone. The sermon consumes the most time in the Sunday service. The parishioner in the pew can hear the sermon, take notes, and go home with what is needed to live the Christian life. The evangelical sermon does not advocate further interaction or testing for it to be valid. In fact, the parishioner can take it home on tape and listen to it in the car to gain more information. In this way, evangelical preaching underwrites the myth that the isolated self can transform its own self through its own rational powers with the help of the Spirit, assuming of course that he or she can take good notes.

Expository preaching enables the person in the pew to remain isolated from further conversation and testing of the Scriptures within the congregation. It carefully dissects the text into three (stereotypical) points and an application which is offered to the parishioner as the means to further one's Christian life. By default, such a sermon cannot help but situate the parishioner so he or she is in control of the Scriptures. Expository preaching operates under the assumption that the congregation (or radio audience) is composed of individual Cartesian selves isolated and separated from each other yet capable of listening and receiving truth as information from the pulpit.[9] And so expository preachers commoditize the Scripture, putting it at the disposal of the user in the pew. They make the text into an object to be dissected, cut up into three points, and distributed in "nuggets" by themselves to be used by parishioners to improve their Christian living or to receive salvation when the gospel is preached. Because parishioners sit isolated, in the pews, analyzing, taking notes, digesting the sermon, rarely giving the Amen, it is the parishioner who decides whether, how, and what to consume in the preaching. Ironically, as expository preachers carefully follow the text in their preaching, the center of control for the meaning of Scripture has shifted from Scripture to the autonomous minds of the listening parishioners. The parishioners' egos remain firmly intact, governing their consumption of the Word as they return home with what they think they heard or wanted to hear. And the preacher seeks comfort that the Holy Spirit works in mysterious and unsuspecting ways, plus his "word shall not return void."

Postmodern hermeneutics, however, reveal the ways in which meaning and truth can only be worked out in the language we speak and the lives we negotiate in communal relation to one another. For Christians, we do this in submission to the reading, hearing, and engaging of the Word of God given to us in Scripture as his body. For Christians, there can be no self apart from submission to his lordship (Mark 8:34–37), and the Spirit will not transform one who does not first submit. The self can only become a Christian self as it is a participant in the world of the texts being preached. And so through preaching and reading, in humility, diligence, and submission to the Spirit, the text is opened. The congregation then submits, engages, tests, discusses, and discerns what the text means for them to go on one more day following Christ. Because the text is language by definition, its interpretation cannot escape the languages, meanings, and social structures of the preacher and the congregation. In fact, these structures are what enable interpretation to occur in a way that lives into and through people. Therefore, scriptural interpretation cannot be separated from the ongoing life of God's people. It is not enough to hear a sermon isolated in the pew. Rather, we submit together to the preached Word, test it, discuss it, engage it, and its truth takes on life in our lives through the Spirit. The Spirit, governing over the community, works faithfulness among his people.

But expository preaching discourages practices like these. The very structure of expository preaching encourages each person in the pew to be an independent thinking person capable of hearing a good sermon and doing something with it. The sermon that focuses on grammatical dissection and multiple points encourages note taking and rational intake yet discourages humility, submission, and communal testing necessary to have a faithful hermeneutic. The "three points and an application" form of expository preaching encourages the parishioner to take an application home to work on in one's life in isolation from the rest of the body. Expository preaching reinforces the idea that meaning can be distributed as one more of the many "goods and services" available to those willing to attend an evangelical Sunday morning worship service. And evangelicals, unaware, do not see how there can be no real hearing of the Word apart from the mutual humility, submission, and testing that takes place within Christ's body. Instead, we believe that each proposition comes to us already scientifically extracted and nicely packaged for us to go home and try to do something with. But all too often, we never get to the doing. "The applications" of the sermons accumulate like an ever-growing stack of self-help books and tapes we can never hope to get to. After many months of this, because we cannot possibly put into practice all of the applications, preaching becomes nothing more than a scroll we wear on

> **Expository preaching reinforces the idea that meaning can be distributed as one more of the many "goods and services" available.**

our foreheads that comforts us in the knowledge that we are the ones who are serious about studying Scripture.

It Requires a Community to Interpret the Word

Some will say all of this discounts the role of the Holy Spirit in the preaching of Scripture. Certainly I do not intend to discount the necessity of the Holy Spirit in the preaching of the Word of God. But for evangelicals the Holy Spirit is most often associated with the inner voice of conviction. The Holy Spirit enlivens the preacher's words and makes possible the inner conviction of each individual's heart. The Holy Spirit's work is an inner individualistic action that aids the isolated Cartesian mind in discerning meaning.

Yet as Stephen Fowl teaches us in his book *Engaging Scripture*, "the Spirit's activity is no more self-interpreting than a passage of Scripture is." In other words, we have all been present in the same room with two people both claiming the Holy Spirit's inspiration over contradictory interpretations of the same Scripture.[10] Fowl then goes on to say, "Understanding and interpreting the Spirit's movement is a matter of communal debate and discernment over time. This debate and discernment is itself often shaped by prior interpretations of Scripture and by traditions of practice and belief."[11] In other words, scriptural interpretation cannot help but be governed by prior orthodox interpretations as carried on within communities over time. My own denomination's interpretation of Romans 6–8, for example, will be governed by its own historical conversations over sanctification in the believer. And these interpretations will be tested over time by its faithful communities (e.g., see 1 Thess. 5:20–21; 1 John 4:1; 1 Cor. 14:16). Such testing will require people properly formed and focused to lead such conversations toward a Spirit-governed interpretation of Scripture for their church and (hopefully) someday the ecumenical discussion of the church at large.

Stephen Fowl argues only those born of humility, the regular confession of sin and repentance, and a "vigilant eye" can truly receive Scripture, discern issues of interpretation, and test the interpretations that are among us. These are virtues born in people out of communal practices together. In the end therefore, the Holy Spirit's work in interpreting Scripture is essential to interpreting Scripture in the life of the believer. But the Holy Spirit functions inextricably within the community of Christ. Immediate revelations born in individuals can be known to be revelation only within a testing community. Indeed, through communities of Christ given the Scriptures, preachers, teachers, discerners, and testers, the Holy Spirit produces and verifies the so-called inner convictions that are immediate in individuals.

The community of Christ therefore is necessarily the place out of which interpretations under the Spirit are worked out. This does not mean we must all meet following every sermon to discuss its merits and Holy Spirit endorsement. In fact, the regular preaching of the Word most often already reflects the existing ongoing consensus of interpretation at work in the church. The pastor reflects that "canon" of interpretation and should be engaged in it and in leading the church through it with the teaching and preaching offered. This is what church conflict pastor Jim Van Yperen refers to as the "interpretive leader."[12] But when there is disagreement regarding an interpretation of Scripture, or something new to be discerned, here the pastor as interpretive leader must stand ready to submit to and engage the church in the communal practice of seeking out God's will for the church over this fork in the road. Out of this process, Christians in communities are not embattled over who is right or wrong, but rather are engaged in asking how shall we be faithful to Scripture, to go forward in Christ. In the process, Scripture not only informs each Christian but shapes and forms the way we live. Stephen Fowl describes this process when he states that "for Christians, Scriptural interpretation should shape and be shaped by the convictions, practices and concerns of Christian communities as part of their ongoing struggle to live and worship faithfully before God."[13]

In this way, the community of Christ is the fertile ground for the interpretation of Scripture. As Hans Frei once described, the community provides the "*communio sanctorum*" for the interpretation of Scripture, properly setting limits upon it and enabling the furtherance of it for the new situations that arise inevitably from time to time in each community. No individual can escape the "interpretive strategies" of some community.[14] No preacher can interpret Matthew 28:3, "His appearance was like lightning," as meaning Christ's resurrected body came from Saturn, without soon having one's district superintendent, bishop, or body of elders being called for a corrective consultation with the pastor.[15] No one, including the expository preacher, can interpret Scripture out of a vacuum. As literary theorist Stanley Fish eloquently states,

> In our postures as seekers, after meaning or after Christ . . . we place ourselves outside a system and presume to make sense of it, to fit its parts together; what we find is that the parts are already together and that we are one of them, living in the meaning we seek—"in him we live and move and have our meaning"—not as its exegetes but as its bearers. We are already where we want to be and our attempts to get there—by writing, by reading, by speaking—can do nothing else but extend through time the "good news" of our predetermined success.[16]

The "system" we are in, where the parts are already together, is the ongoing body of Christ and that stream of interpretation which flows historically through it. This ongoing communal consensus, what Roman Catholics call tradition, is one instrument of the Spirit to guide interpretation. The interpretation of Scripture therefore is inseparable from the community of Christ.

Expository preaching, however, would seem to undercut these interpretive communal processes necessary for the faithful preaching of the Word. As Stephen Fowl argues, faithful interpretation requires vigilant communities that engage in regular practices of truth telling, forgiveness, and reconciliation.[17] These communities must have the skills of engaging one another in humility and listening until the point they can all come together and recognize the Spirit in one another's lives and the fruit of a particular one's interpretation sufficient to say as James did, at the council of Jerusalem, "It seemed good to us having become of one mind" and "it seemed good to the Holy Spirit and to us" (Acts 15:25, 28). But expository preaching relies on the assumption that meaning is self-evident to every individual. Many times in evangelical churches, therefore, disagreement over Scripture automatically signifies, to one side or the other, the other's ignorance or even heresy. The epistemological assumptions of much expository preaching do not allow the space to develop the virtues of humility amidst disagreement in the community sufficient to carry on the communal discerning of the Word. Evangelicalism and its preaching assume meaning is perspicuous and truth is deliverable in propositions. And this leads to the stunting of humility and the cutting off of discussion about meaning. As John H. Yoder describes, "Fundamentalism is most fairly characterized as the denial that there is a hermeneutic task. . . . The words of the biblical text are held to be univocal, to such an extent that anyone's doubt about the rightness of my view of the text is at once an act of unbelief."[18] And so the same expository impulse that promotes individuals taking notes in the pew to take home and appropriate as each one sees fit devalues the communal engagement over unclear meanings in Scripture out of humility one toward another.

Indeed, expository exegesis operates in ways that foreclose interpretive community. For in the act of expository exegesis, the text is turned into an object for examination, dissecting, and packaging for rhetorical delivery to an audience. The text becomes an object in the hands of the preacher as it is broken down into three points to be given out as something the listener can use. Once the sermon is given, the text becomes an object to be consumed by the parishioner, who in turn listens, analyzes, takes notes, and goes out to be a doer of the information just heard, which consequently distances the listener from the text. The parishioner in essence is separated as subject over against the text as object. In this way, expository preaching creates the inevitability of the domination of the text by either or both of these subjectivities: the (subjectivity of the) expository preacher dissecting it for an agenda and/or the (subjectivity of the) listener hearing it according to his or her own grid. In this sense, expository preaching fosters an interpretive violence always putting the text at the disposal of the listening or speaking subject's own structure and agenda. Instead of bringing parishioners together to participate in Scripture through submitting to it and submitting one to another in the work of the Spirit to interpret the Scriptures, expository preaching isolates parishioners into rational minds, each one receiving the sermon "nugget" for their own personal use either in agreement or disagreement with the other person sitting in the pew.

> Once the sermon is given, the text becomes an object to be consumed by the parishioner, who in turn listens, analyzes, takes notes, which consequently distances the listener from the text.

But as James Smith delineates in his *The Fall of Interpretation*, none of this need be so. The act of interpretation need not be Derridian violence if we resist the notion that we must be Cartesian modernist selves separated and isolated in the act of interpretation. Meaning need not be self-possession carried out in violence upon propositions over against alternative opposing meanings. Rather, if intersubjectivity and situationedness are the assumed conditions of our finitude before God, then it is a positive to come together as a body and mutually participate in reading, submitting to, preaching, and discerning the Bible as a communal interpretive act under his Spirit. When interpretation begins with submission to the Word and submission to one another as a communal act, when it is born out of humility, vigilance, and mutual testing, it is no longer an act of violence but an act of love.[19] We come together to edify one another in the next step needed to follow Christ.

Interpretation of Scripture therefore is always a communal act. No self can interpret outside communal structures. We embrace preaching as a practice of the church that leads the church further in its living under Scripture and acts as a function within the ongoing reading of the Scriptures within community. We truly see that it takes a community of Christ to faithfully interpret Scriptures. And the interpretation of Scripture as a community of the Spirit actually overcomes Derridian violence of one versus the other to become a practice that makes us one.

Is Expository Preaching a Giveaway?

Many evangelicals take comfort in the fact that their church preaches the Word because they have expository preaching. Because their preaching follows the text sentence for sentence, this somehow ensures them of a more faithful interpretation of the text. But, from what we have said above, no expository preaching can escape becoming interpretation no matter how close to the text the preacher follows. And faithful interpretation of the Word requires that interpretation be confirmed or worked out over time among a faithful community. Surely expository preaching can be an important aid in leading a congregation further and deeper into the faithful interpretation of God's Word. But the fact that the preacher follows the text word for word in and of itself does not guarantee that the church preaches the Word.

In fact, the danger exists in expository preaching that preachers, not seeing how their own social habits condition them to read a text in a certain way, dogmatize their own interpretive habits with no recourse to the community. Verse for verse, sentence by sentence, preachers read their own agenda into the text unaware that they even have an agenda, or worse, believing their personal agenda is directly from God. Confident of their expository method, preachers are delinquent in preaching with the necessary humility in submission to the testing of their words before the congregation. And so in the name of preaching the Word, the expository preacher inserts unawares habits of interpretation learned from other places. Expository preaching thereby hides the giveaway of the preaching of the Word.

Likewise, the same danger exists when the expository preacher is confronted with a new issue of interpretation in the church around which a consensus does not already exist. Here again, relying on the expository method, the preacher does not preach in submission to the work of the Spirit in the community to lead that community to a further interpretation. Instead, living under the modernist assumption that the author's intended meaning is there for all to see, expository preachers interpret selected texts to underwrite their own agenda, believing that this one meaning of the text should be plain for all to see. When disagreement occurs, the expository preacher digs in to defend the one meaning, doing harm or causing divisiveness in the congregation. And the congregation, living under the same modernist assumption, knows only how to accept that all they hear from the preacher is truly God's Word or else it is heresy, and they must surely leave the church. Both preacher and congregation miss how preaching the Scriptures is necessarily the outworking of a politics that is always answering the question, How are we going to live? And so the church that is so confident that "our church preaches the Word" may completely miss its own unfaithfulness because of its premature confidence in the modernist method of expository preaching.

Ultimately then, apart from a faithful community of Christ carrying on the practices of prayer, listening, and forgiveness sufficient to engage in the hearing, testing, and living out of the Word of God, the evangelical church cannot deliver on its promise that "my church preaches the Word!" Without such communal practices, expository preaching subtly yet painfully may turn out to be the ultimate irony and become the means to "give away" the "preaching of the Word" to the domination of foreign cultural agendas that preachers themselves unwittingly bring into the church, all because we do not see that it takes a testing, living community to truly interpret Scripture. As Stanley Hauerwas has shown, when we try to defend a depoliticized view of Scripture separated from the outworking of real life in community, we end up "giving away" faithful interpretations of Scripture within Christian community to the manipulations of the unspoken politics and agendas of American life.[20]

Many churches based upon expository preaching promise that "people will grow at our church" because they get "the meat of the Word" every Sunday through expository preaching. After all, we carefully learn the Scriptures sentence by sentence hearing an application or two every Sunday that we can then use in the management of our spiritual transformation. But herein lies a "giveaway." For as we have just outlined, the parishioner as Cartesian mind remains firmly in charge of his or her own transformation as one sitting in the pew, listening to the expository sermon. Expository preaching leaves the hearer firmly in charge of both what one hears and what one is to do with it. Each sermon focuses upon the thinking parishioner's mind as the rational agent capable of taking the ever climactic "point of application" home and doing something with it. And as the sermon applications pile up, and the parishioner loses ground week to week, ever hurrying to catch up with last Sunday's application point, frustration is the result. The expository sermon becomes the wellspring of yet another works-righteousness theology that depends upon the listener taking home the Sunday application and doing it. Expository preaching therefore alters the hearing of the Word from being a gift we respond to and obey to being another lecture from which we seek some

> As the sermon applications pile up and the parishioner loses ground week to week . . . the expository sermon becomes the wellspring of yet another works-righteousness theology.

"take-home points" or a motivational speech from which we seek some inspiration. It "gives away" Scripture's transforming power to be replaced as another form of self-help.

From Expository Preaching to Preaching as Reimagination: Narrative-Based Preaching

Evangelicals then must do more on Sundays with our preaching. We must do more than seek to control information about God from Scripture for our own personal uses. We need practices of reading, preaching, and hearing that embody our repentance from trying to make Scripture the servant of our own self-controlled lives. We need practices that bid us come as subordinates to Scripture, which gives us new selves that grow into the character of God.

In North America, we gather before the Word with our imaginations and character formed out of the omnipresent culture of a post-Christian narcissism and consumerism. And so we sit in the pews needing to be reshaped by the Word before we need reminding about the things we should be doing. We come needing to see the world as Scripture sees it before we receive another inspiring rhetorical climax that lasts but a moment. If we would be faithful then, we must go beyond old methods of expository preaching. If wearing scrolls on our foreheads is a metaphor for individuals seeking to control the Word of God for their own uses either in self-pride or for personal security, we must do more than wear scrolls on our foreheads.

Let us call this preaching "narrative-based" preaching. In contrast to the presentation of information to be consumed, such preaching seeks to renarrate for us the world as it is according to Scripture and call us into that reality. It is preaching that approaches Scripture first and foremost as a narrative. Its task is description and the shaping of a new imagination for all of us who have had our imaginations held captive by the foreign forces of North American, post-Christian life.

Let us then move beyond seeing Scripture as a collection of truth propositions that need to be scientifically dissected, inductively sliced, and distributed to Cartesian, rational selves sitting in the pews. Instead, let us come to Scripture as the grand narrative of God in Jesus Christ where God has revealed himself down through the ages from Abraham to Moses, the nation of Israel to the ultimate person and work of Jesus Christ. It is real history, but let us not make it into scientific history where we know it only as distanced selves dissecting an object. Rather it is the narrative of God into which we have been invited to participate. It is alive and it discloses the world where Jesus is Lord, and God is at work through Jesus Christ to save the world. Preaching must invite us into this narrative. Amidst the carnival of narratives that society has become, let us come to worship under his grand story to be engulfed by it so as to live it out in contrast to the world's stories. For this to happen, we need to preach so as to "counter-imagine" the way the world really is under Jesus as Lord over against the dark world of consumerist materialism we live in outside the church.[21] We do not need scientific artifacts but the real, true, and all-engulfing story of God.

So let us put historical-critical exegetical methods in their place as limited tools grounded in history that must be submitted to the traditions and history of God's work in the church. These methods still have service, but they must serve the explication of Scripture's narrative, not the narrative of any scientific presuppositions we bring to the text.[22] We must see that Scripture, far from being an object to be dissected, is rather a glorious narrative from which all else is seen and put into order. As quoted famously by theologian Hans Frei, literary theorist Eric Auerbach once described Scripture as follows:

> Far from seeking, like Homer, merely to make us forget our own reality for a few hours, [the Bible] seeks to overcome our reality: we are to fit our own life into its world, feel ourselves to be elements in its structure of universal history. . . . Everything else that happens in the world can only be conceived as an element in this sequence; into it everything that is known about the world . . . must be fitted as an ingredient of the divine plan.[23]

Once we see Scripture in this way, we cannot come to Scripture with the purpose of putting it at our own disposal. We move from historical-critical dissecting to always respecting the narrative structure of the text. Even the epistles of Paul have a narrative that lies behind them. There's a world in there to be disclosed and unfurled so we can invite the congregation into it. Preaching is the means to call us out of the world that lives as though God does not exist and into the world that knows his lordship. It invites us in to find our selves in that reality in submission to Christ.

Let us then see the first task of preaching as description. Let us move from the first goal of preaching as the production of a set of application points to the goal of unfurling a reality we could not see apart from being engulfed in the story of God from creation to redemption. This first task

> Let us then move beyond seeing Scripture as a collection of truth propositions that need to be scientifically dissected, inductively sliced, and distributed to Cartesian, rational selves sitting in the pews.

of preaching then is not to dissect the Scripture into "nuggets" that the isolated self can put to use at its own disposal. Rather it is to preach the reality of the world as it is under the good news of the gospel, which renders all things new. It is from such preaching that we can receive a self. As hermeneutician Paul Ricouer puts it:

> Ultimately, what I appropriate is a proposed world. The latter is not behind the text, as a hidden intention would be, but in front of it, as that which the work unfolds, discovers, reveals. Henceforth, to understand is to understand oneself in front of the text. It is not a question of imposing upon the text our finite capacity of understanding, but of exposing ourselves to the text and receiving from it an enlarged self, which would be the proposed existence corresponding in the most suitable way to the world proposed.[24]

Such preaching then will always call the person into a new self, not put Scripture at the behest of the already existing selves sitting in the pews. As such, the first task of preaching must be description.

As with Old Testament theologian Walter Brueggemann, let our preachers purpose to "fund counterimagination" for our congregations so they might live faithfully amidst the false worlds of the post-Christian world.[25] Let our preaching establish an imagination that contrasts with the one we are constantly being formed in, outside the church. Let the evangelical preacher compellingly describe the new Easter reality as it is in Christ so as to counter the alternative worlds that are engulfing us in North American society. And then, once the world of his lordship has been renarrated, we can invite the congregation into it by the Holy Spirit so as to truly live.

Some evangelicals may complain that to make preaching purely a matter of "Christian self-description"[26] is to make Scripture less morally directive. But this again misses the point. For to say that Scripture is primarily narrative, as Hans Frei claimed over against the Enlightenment,[27] means that Scripture will form our experience and give us an orientation for our Christian lives. Out of this orientation will come moral directives for how we should live and how we will want to live our lives. With narrative preaching, however, the preacher's first job will not be to hand out more "to do" lists. Rather it is to unfurl the reality of who God is past, present, and future so that all men and women who would submit to live in that world would then be able to understand themselves, who they are, where they are going, and what they are to do in terms of Jesus Christ and his story.

Likewise, some evangelicals may complain that our approach to preaching makes Scripture less objectively true. But saying Scripture is primarily narrative in no way minimizes the referential nature of

Scripture or its historicity.[28] Rather, what we must acknowledge is that we must first truly engage and live into the world of Jesus Christ as Lord, as expounded in the Scriptures, in order to know truly to what these theological descriptions refer. By "living into" I mean learning to walk, see, converse in the language, and participate in the reality that Jesus has died, risen, and sits as Lord over all things. As opposed to using Scripture as knowledge to achieve my own end, this "living into" requires discipleship, takes faithfulness over time, and provides a basis for truly knowing what it means to say "Jesus is Lord." We cannot truly know the truth of Scripture apart from becoming a participant in it through the preaching of his Word and the outgrowth of that in our lives as the work of the Holy Spirit.

Such an all-engulfing view of Scripture will shift the way we preach. For example, modern preaching (whether expository or other) has often taken the best wisdom from culture and found comfort in harmonizing it with Scripture.[29] As a result, what often happens is Scripture becomes interpreted by culture instead of the reverse. Narrative-based preaching, however, resists the goal of being relevant to modern or postmodern culture. Instead, narrative-based preaching will paint the worlds we are invited into through Jesus Christ as a contrast to the disorientation and chaos of the world out there. Instead of relying on psychology and the human sciences to explicate what Scripture is saying, we explicate the truths of Scripture and the derivative experiences therein and point to divergences and comparisons that make compelling the world of Jesus as Lord. We may use, for example, existing emotions of current society as a starting point for a sermon. But we do not appeal to such emotions in the congregation as truth, but instead contrast such emotions with the world of emotions waiting to be born out of our life in Scripture. Faithful preaching can then invite parishioners out of pagan emotions into new emotions born out of the world of Jesus as Lord. Postmodernity and its varied hermeneutics surely tell us now that emotions are formed in narratives, and so in Christ, through faithful preaching, we can be invited to be made new.[30] In this way, narrative-based preaching resists syncretism with other worlds without first describing the reality that is true under the lordship of Christ.

Narrative-based preaching does not eliminate all need for applications. What it does mean, however, is that prescriptions will only make sense after descriptions. Narrative-based preaching follows the writing model employed by the apostle Paul, who often initiated the teaching part of his letters with a description (what biblical theologians have called "the indicative") and only after followed with the prescriptive part of the message (what biblical theologians have called "the imperative").[31] The power of the gospel is to change the way we see and to enable us to enter a world where Jesus is already Lord ahead of the rest of the world, a reality that the rest of the world will see one day when "every knee shall bow." The preacher, however, sounds the reality of that kingdom's existence in the here and now for those who have ears to hear and eyes to see. He calls us to see our world in light of the lordship of Christ, to see our marriages, our work, our communities, our celebration, our various other tasks in light of that lordship. He describes what it means to live in a world under that lordship where God is sovereign and working for our salvation.

These descriptions lead to imperatives, but these imperatives are inevitable, because after hearing about the way the world is under Christ, having embraced these beliefs as our own perception of the world, it only makes sense that we act, think, and feel in certain ways. Applications, "things we need to do," therefore come only as the outworking of a prior description of the narrative world of Christ. These applications often come in the form of invitations into seeing things a certain way, confessing sin, and obeying God faithfully for the day that lies ahead.

The expository preacher tends to view the preaching task as the distribution of truth to the mind wherein the mind is asked to directly subdue the body. The modernist evangelical model of sanctification is the control of the body directly by the mind's cognitive assent. The narrative preacher instead presents the narrative of the story of God. The listener is invited to submit and see the world as presented before him out of the Scripture. Here the person, by the Holy Spirit, through submission and obedience, sees things differently and embraces them into the soul so that these descriptions and reasons for doing things become part of the way the person sees things through "the eyes of the heart." This is most often in Scripture associated with the unveiling of the eyes or ears by virtue of the work of the Holy Spirit. The move is never one from the mind straight to the body or vice versa, it is the transformation that comes from a new way of seeing. Such preaching does not appeal to an already existing self but rather invites one to receive a new self in orientation to the God of Israel and Jesus Christ.

Paul often uses visionary metaphors to describe such Christian transformation. "I pray that you will grow in depth perception and understanding" (Phil. 1:9, 10, my translation). "Having the eyes of your hearts enlightened, that you may know what is the hope toward which you are called, what are the riches of his glorious inheritance, what is the immeasurable greatness of his power" (Eph. 1:18–19, my translation). Jesus often talks about having eyes to see, ears to hear, or having your eyes opened. "Your eye is the lamp of your whole body; when your eye is sound, your whole body is full of light; but when it is not sound, your body is full of darkness. Therefore, be careful lest the light in you be darkness" (Luke 11:34–35, my translation). The role of descriptive preaching is to unfold before the eyes of our hearts what is true of the world we are called to live in under the lordship of Christ. When we become open to, attracted to, and taken over by these stories of God through the preaching of Christ in the Holy Spirit, our vision is formed by the reality of Scripture, and we embrace these realities as our own: our emotions, desires, and reasons for behavior are formed. Our character is formed in our response to the Spirit.

Narrative-based preaching therefore resists legalism. Scripture is seen as a narrative describing the world in which we live. Only after we have been captured by the vision of the world formed under the lordship of Christ, by the work of the Holy Spirit, is it possible to demand that we live in integrity with our beliefs. We see and understand our lives in terms of the language of sin and we are then able to repent. We see Christian vision for our sexual lives in terms of the created order God has given, and we commit to marital purity. We come to see and understand that God is taking care of our needs because he is our Father, and he is the giver of all good gifts, and we are stewards of his resources in the "in-between times" (Matthew 25). As a result we can no longer be miserly with our money and instead become stewards and givers toward the goals of the kingdom. Character is formed through submission to the Word, and obedience follows. Description precedes prescription and thereby resists legalism.

> **The role of descriptive preaching is to unfold before the eyes of our hearts what is true of the world we are called to live in under the lordship of Christ.**

The narrative-based sermon then often concludes not with more applications and "to do" lists but rather by invoking postures of response: submission, obedience, confession, or silence before the Lord.[32] It will not so much be another application we take home to do in our lives. It will be a submission to a way of seeing, it will be the acknowledgment of my own blindness, it will be the submission in trust to a course of obedience, it will be just sitting in this world that is real because Jesus has died and risen to the right hand of the Father. Slowly over the Sundays, I am brought into the light from the darkness, from seeing things as if God did not exist to seeing that he is Lord over his people and the world. From Sunday morning worship the preaching of the Word is carried into our small confessional groups where we read it again and ask ourselves the questions again, and through confession of our sins and prayer we participate in Scripture. From Sunday morning worship, the Scripture is invoked in our house gatherings, prayer meetings, men's and women's meetings, and business meetings of the church.

And when there is a disagreement over which way we are to go, we can come together to discern in the Spirit what is the way we are to follow because we are formed in humility to the Scriptures. The exposed myths behind expository preaching reveal that it takes a community to preach the Word, to discern, and to live Scripture.

Practices for Returning to the Faithful Hearing of the Word

What practices can evangelicals engage in to sustain the faithful preaching of the Word in our churches? What practices can we restore to train our minds differently so people like John and Sue from this chapter's opening paragraph can identify the preaching of the Word in ways that mean the faithful preaching, interpreting, and living into the Word of God? What practices can lead to narrative-based preaching in our congregations? I suggest the following.

Return to the Lectionary

Let us evangelicals return to the practice of the lectionary. Let us learn the practice of reading three or four readings for each Sunday, one from the Pentateuch, one from the Psalms or the Prophets, one reading from the Epistles, and of course one reading from the Gospels. In this way we can resist the de-narratizing of the text à la expository preaching. Instead, by reading a lectionary each Sunday, we will be forced to view the primary text for the sermon in its context of the whole narrative of God in Christ. Such a lectionary forces the preacher to refer to the other texts or at least interpret the one text in light of the other texts. And likewise when the congregation hears all the readings performed, they rightfully receive that we as his people are being invited into the whole narrative of God down through history.

At our church, we often follow the actual Anglican *Book of Common Prayer* lectionary texts from Advent to Pentecost. However, during the Ordinary Time part of the calendar, we often do series based in certain lectionary texts or even diverge from the lectionary. Yet even when we diverge from the lectionary proper, our church continues to read three or four texts in lectionary fashion, providing readings that can give a total narrative context for the preaching of the day.

Practice Performative Reading

Let evangelicals practice performative reading of the Scripture texts on Sunday mornings. By performed readings, I mean let us perform

Scripture as if it were being told as a story, or in the case of an epistle, let it be read as if it were a letter just delivered and read from the apostle himself. At our church we have had a Scripture Performance Reading Team that practices and studies how to read and perform Scripture. Such a practice elevates the narrative authority of Scripture among the church. After we have completed the reading of the Gospel in our church, with the congregation standing, the reader raises up his or her Bible and declares, "The Word of the Lord!" and the congregation responds, "Thanks be to God!" This traditional liturgical response followed by Christians throughout the ages fosters submission to the authority of the Scriptures as delivered through the prophets and the apostles and practiced among a people. It removes Scripture from the modernist tendency to put its veracity in the mind of each individual. Instead, we gather on Sundays to submit to the ongoing work of God in Christ through history and to carry on the narrative of God canonized in Scripture.

Tailor the Conclusion of the Sermon for Response

I have argued that the expository sermon's propensity to end with a set of application points defeats the believer's growth and ability to live into the Word. Instead, the Word of God is preached, the congregation hears, and then responds. In other words, the sermon should lead to responses of submission, repentance, obedience, and praise. What should the congregation confess? How should the congregation see the situation at hand? What issue of surrender, submission, and obedience lies ahead? How can we submit to that? And then, after the sermon, as often in the history of the church, the service should simply be silent maybe for five or ten minutes. The point here is that taking notes to sermons is not sufficient to shape and form a people into a full submission to and participation in the Word of God.

> **The sermon should lead to responses of submission, repentance, obedience, and praise.**

Of course, no preaching of the gospel is complete without the Lord's Supper. In some way, the only proper response to the hearing of the Word is the participation in the story through the celebration of the Lord's Table. The rehearsal of the Table in fact narrates the story from which all our other stories can make sense for the Christian. The Table of our Lord therefore provides the context that the preaching of the Word flows out from and returns to. Without it, the narrative integrity of the preaching of the Word is lost. Evangelicals must therefore reinvigorate the Eucharist as both the response to the Word and the context out of which it can even make sense in the life of the believer.

Employ Narrative-Based Preaching

Let evangelicals practice narrative-based preaching.[33] By narrative-based preaching, I mean first, that the narrative structure of the text or what forms the context for the text is always respected. I mean second, that the modus operandi of each sermon is to describe the world that is being envisioned by Scripture and then invite the congregation into it. Obviously, storytelling is one important means of doing this. This is often more than retelling a Scripture story. When I preach, I often use stories to unfold experiences such as are common in the world; to these stories I then juxtapose the story that a given Scripture is depicting and the experiences native to its world so they become known to us. Third, by narrative-based preaching, I mean that we do not examine the grammar of each verse, word for word, sentence for sentence. Nonetheless, when I preach, I often choose one, at most two, crucial exegetical points and use them to illumine the world of the text we might have missed otherwise. I may proceed orderly through the text, but I feel no need to go sentence by sentence, verse by verse. Instead, I am looking to have our vision of who God is clarified, the reality of how he works in history remembered to us, the reality of how the world is ordered under his lordship described for us. I am seeking to paint the reality as it is under the lordship of Christ. With each sermon, I try to invite the hearer of Scripture into another way of seeing the world out of Scripture and to ask what kind of faith, confession, obedience, or submission this requires of us. I ask questions such as:

How am I to respond to this God?

In light of who God is, in light of what he has done, in light of what he has said, what step in my life should I be taking in obedience?

How should I be seeing a current situation in my life?

What sin should I confess?

What attitude should I repent of?

How should I see myself before God?

What am I not acknowledging about God?

How should I celebrate this in my own life?

How am I to respond in worship?

Promote Communal Discourse

If we can agree with the thesis of this chapter, that we as evangelical Christians must resist the isolating, individualizing tendencies of expository preaching, churches would do well to promote spaces for living communal discourse over texts and their application to our lives. At our church we seek to promote spaces for discussion with the pastor about the texts: Sunday school morning classes, Sunday night coffee times, after-church luncheons, and midweek fellowships devoted to more diligently searching and discussing the Sunday worship texts. Another example of this is Solomon's Porch in Minneapolis, Minnesota, where Tuesday nights are devoted to discussion of the upcoming Sunday's texts. According to the pastor, Doug Paggit, his sermons are birthed out of these discussions.[34]

The interpretation of Scripture must be tested (1 Thess. 5:20–21; 1 John 4:1; 1 Cor. 14:16). At our church we have the reading of Sunday's texts with a formation question in the bulletin to be used at our confessional groups during the week where we can respond then in confession and searching out what this means for our lives. The overriding goal is the fostering of humility and vigilance in the hearers and teachers for the interpreting of the Scriptures in the church and into our lives. In Sunday morning worship, our service sets the stage for all of this when the pastor gets up to preach. The pastor says the liturgical words, "The Lord be with you," and the congregation responds, "And also with you," thereby acknowledging and praying for mutual dependence upon the Holy Spirit both to preach and hear the Word faithfully. At our church, these words signify that the time of the sermon is not a time spent sitting in a lecture hall but an arena of the Holy Spirit where God begins and continues his work among us to faithfully live into the Word.

Persevere in Times of Conflict

The true test of our humility and vigilance as readers of Scripture comes when there is conflict among us. Here we must learn that the faithful interpretation of Scripture takes more than one man's or woman's exegetical skills; it requires prayer, humility and patience, and diligence. And so it is at our church, whenever conflict arrives, we try to treat it as an opportunity to learn humility and vigilance. Whether it is a disagreement over women's roles in the church or the use of Christmas trees in the sanctuary, we will come together to consider Scripture as well as the historical teaching we have lived under, and we will not leave until we have reached a consensus in the Spirit. In my church experiences, when conflict arrives we certainly recognize those ordained with the responsibility to teach, we recognize those in denominational leadership, and also those from the congregation. And those who have questions must be heard, and those who have a position to advocate must be patient. We have at times sat, prayed, discussed, waited in silence often into the night until we too could say, "It seemed good to us having become of one mind" and "it seemed good to the Holy Spirit and to us" (Acts 15:25, 28). Always out of this, sometimes with great pain, we learn what it means to live into Scripture faithfully. We are attempting to learn what it means to do more than wear scrolls on our foreheads.

6

Justice (Our Understanding Of)

Practicing Redeemed Economics:
Christian Community *in* but Not *of* Capitalism

For anyone united to Christ, there is a new creation: the old order has gone; a new order has already begun.

2 Corinthians 5:17 REB

We were a small gathering of about forty-five people meeting in an old church on Sunday nights in Chicago. This night, a person stood up during congregational prayers and announced to everyone that she had cancer. She told us that she needed an operation and had no health insurance and did not know how she was going to pay for it. No one knew how to react, so we just prayed for her. To my knowledge, no one did anything else significant that night to help this woman. Prayer is good but empty if we separate it from social justice. Several months later this woman with cancer cautiously asked someone in the church to second mortgage his house and help her pay for her operation. That person responded with the question, "I don't own my house free and clear, besides have you second mortgaged your house?" This perhaps was a legitimate question but no one, including the woman with cancer, would dare get involved in discerning the answer to this question. It seemed too big of a threat, not only to the homeowner but also to the woman with cancer. As a result, this woman with cancer was basically left alone with her economic problems despite being part of a close community. This same community, however, could get enthusiastic about volunteering aid to the local soup kitchen, offering financial help to the homeless, or walking miles to raise funds for pro-life and anti-poverty campaigns. But we did not know what to do when someone in our own community stood up and announced such a great need. Eighty thousand dollars (the cost of the operation) would surely have bankrupted us all. It seemed that this woman threatened everyone else's financial survival. She put all of our own individual securities at risk and we were paralyzed. We didn't have a way to "be the church" in the moment of her need. We didn't know how to discern justice or mercy, what we should do, or what she needed to do.

I contend this episode is a metaphor for what happens in various and sundry ways in the majority of North American evangelical churches. Larger congregations may have benevolent funds to help out such a woman, but rarely do we take communal financial responsibility for one another. Larger evangelical churches may have committees to meet needs of hurting people in times of emergency, but rarely do we engage in what it means to restore justice and righteousness among us as a body of Christ in terms of economic disorder, conflict, and other issues of injustice. Yet when it comes to ministering social justice outside of the church, evangelicals are more active today than they have ever been before.[1]

I contend this disparity is dangerous because it leaves our churches prone to compromising the justice of Jesus Christ in society at large. If we do not practice justice among ourselves as Christians under Christ's lordship, we will not have the skills to discern it out in society either. Inevitably, we will be influenced by a formula for justice that comes from some place other than the body of Christ. In the case of evangelicals, this place often proves to be America's own liberal democracy and capitalism. The social politics of democratic capitalism ends up determining the way we do justice more than the politics of Christ. This then renders our justice unrecognizable as Christian justice in the world.[2] Truly, without the local church as a visible reference point, any justice we practice in society in Christ's name inevitably will blend in with other forms of contested justice active in the postmodern societal marketplace. And if we do separate our justice from society's, our justice becomes just another disingenuous argument without a living visible representation of what justice looks like among a people of God. In either case, we end up "giving away" the justice of Christ to forces external to the church.

This chapter argues that the work of social justice in Christ begins with the woman with cancer standing in the middle of the congregation. Only from such a concrete outworking of justice under his lordship can we then locate and do justice in the world. The following seeks to uncover how and why evangelicals do justice and why it fails as a work of Christ's justice in a society at the end of modernity. It asks how we can return the work of justice to the concrete body of Christ. It then suggests the reinvigoration of an old church practice through which we can receive back Christ's justice as his church *in* but not *of* capitalism and then offer it to the world.

Evangelicals and Our Detached Social Justice

The predominant majority of evangelicals today support social justice as integral to the work of the church of Jesus Christ. Admittedly, in the past, evangelicals shunned the redemption of society's social structures. They viewed the present world through famously pessimistic and apocalyptic eyes.[3] But since evangelical theologian Carl F. Henry published *The Uneasy Conscience of Modern Fundamentalism* in 1947,[4] mainline evangelicals have moved beyond these pessimistic, hyper-otherworldly views of salvation to embrace social justice as the work of the church. Today, we embrace more than pro-life and pro-family social agendas. We now also embrace ministries for societal justice and mercy such as Habitat for Humanity and World Vision as well as legislative reform for public education funding and improved low-income housing.

Amidst these advances, however, evangelical churches still have trouble practicing social and economic justice right inside the local congregation. We seek to minister to the poor or the disadvantaged by going out to them. But rarely do we actually minister to the poor or disadvantaged among us. We have programs to reach out to the homeless, destitute, or broken peoples, but rarely do we minister to them by making them part of our congregation. Our local congregations therefore look strangely homogeneous in terms of racial and economic composition.[5] And within the local church, evangelicals largely act as private individuals in regard to money with little sense of common liability one toward another in the congregation. We preach regularly about tithing

> We seek to minister to the poor or the disadvantaged by going out to them. But rarely do we actually minister to the poor or disadvantaged among us.

but rarely preach about our financial responsibility toward each other. For evangelicals, the work of economic and social justice is much easier done outside the church than inside.

We embrace that Christ's salvation includes both the deliverance of this world's social structures from sin and injustice as well as the redemption of individual souls. This is what evangelical ethicist Ron Sider labels "holistic" salvation.[6] Sin is not only attributable to persons as individuals but also to nonpersonal social structures as well. A half century after Carl F. Henry, Sider therefore can speak for most evangelicals when he espouses a "full-blown biblical theology that affirms both personal and social sin, both personal conversion and structural change, both evangelism and social action, both personal and social salvation, both Jesus as moral example and Jesus as vicarious substitute, both orthodox theology and ethical obedience."[7]

Throughout this new articulation of social justice, however, evangelicals still keep personal salvation separate from social justice. For most evangelical congregations, salvation happens to individuals through personal conversion who then take their place in the church while the work of social justice takes place in relation to social structures outside the church. Salvation in Christ is over personal sin and guilt while social justice is the engagement of sinful social structures outside the church.[8] In relation to social justice, the local church acts as the equipping training site from which to send individual Christians out to engage the sinful structures and powers of the world for Christ. The local church can provide the background to give integrity to what Christians advocate socially in the world. The idea, however, that the local church itself can be a social politics of justice doesn't exist for evangelicals. We do not see the community of Christ itself as a politics that can engage the world. For evangelicals therefore social action is primarily saved individuals acting as Christians out in the world against powerful sinful social forces.[9] And we confine the work of social justice largely to the arena outside the church.

This theology influences the strategies evangelicals choose to do justice ministry in their local congregations. The common denominator among these strategies is that evangelicals carry out social justice as individuals detached from the internal politics of the body of Christ. For instance, when evangelical congregations seek to do justice ministry, often the first thing they do is seek a target outside the church to offer relief from some social deprivation. And so evangelicals sponsor numerous "soup kitchens," "clothes hampers," and efforts to build improved housing. But rarely is there the means to invite these victims into the life of the church that is doing these activities. All of these social engagements are exemplary acts of mercy in Jesus Christ, but the people that are affected are mostly separated from the regular worship or fellowship of the congregation doing them. We should of course encourage these isolated acts of generosity because they are valid acts of mercy in the name of Jesus Christ. But is this a justice that is truly social and accomplished under the reign of Jesus Christ?

Another common evangelical strategy is to engage in activism aimed at changing a governmental or civic policy. This is done through protests or active lobbying of governmental bodies in the legislative processes. This activity again is worthy but is still located external to the local congregation. A third common strategy is the use of parachurch organizations to do the actual work of social ministry in the targeted places of need. These ministries often target the so-called "inner-city areas" of poverty and blight. This targeting reveals the suburban nature of evangelicalism as well as the propensity of evangelicals to dispatch justice ministry unto locales that are separate from our own place of living. It also reveals the propensity of evangelicals to opt for expertise and efficiency when it comes to getting ministry done. These parachurch experts are not part of the local congregation from which they raise money.[10] They are hired guns to do the work of justice for the churches who can pay their way. All of these strategies are noble acts of God's mercy, but they illustrate how justice ministry for evangelicals is largely separated from the local church. We practice justice detached from the inner workings of congregational life.

The Modernism That Shapes Evangelical Assumptions about Justice

Evangelicals can detach justice ministries in this way from the local congregation due to our individualizing habits inherited from modernity. We view the church as a voluntarist institution composed of and in service to individuals.[11] Evangelicals view salvation as an issue of individual conversion as opposed to individuals being invited into God's cosmic work of salvation in Jesus Christ. In this way the individual is kept distinct from the social.[12] None of this changed when evangelicals moved toward a more holistic view of salvation.

In the move toward holistic salvation, evangelicals by and large kept personal salvation primary and simply added on the Protestant liberal concern for social justice. We did not change our emphasis upon God saving individuals. We simply changed our view of individuals to include both the spiritual and bodily aspects of persons and therefore agreed that salvation should address both. We recognized we could not preach the good news of personal salvation if we did not also address the physical and social structural needs of the person.[13] Yet in all of this, the individual remained primary. The connecting link between personal salvation and the work of social justice remains the individual.[14] The social space of the church stays irrelevant to social justice except as a place to raise up individuals for the work of salvation in the world. The church gets individuals saved. Once they are saved, they are transformed toward genuine Christian concern for suffering in the world and the work of reordering unjust social structures.[15] The individual remains the unit of salvation. It is no problem then for evangelicals to detach the work of social justice from the inner workings of the church because in the end salvation is all about individuals.

This is part of the way the theological shift to social justice happened for evangelicals. When evangelicals of the 1970s embraced the Protestant liberal concern for social salvation, they did not critique its modernist tendency to marginalize the church's societal role in social justice. On the contrary, evangelicals unwittingly absorbed the liberal Protestant approach to the church that divorced God's work in the world from the social politics of the church. Liberal Protestantism did this when it replaced the church with "the kingdom of God" working in the world.[16] When evangelicals finally joined hands with the liberal Protestant work for God's justice in society, they also more subtly concurred with the Protestant liberal assessment that the church is invisible, temporal, and not to be the arena for social reformation.[17] Evangelicalism's individualism made this easy. Evangelicals, because we were already prone to seeing salvation as solely personal and individual, unwittingly acquiesced to the liberal Protestant understanding that the church can at best be marginal in a society that has displaced God to the realm of one's individual private beliefs and feelings. As a result, the gospel of Jesus Christ is not capable of a meaningful social manifestation among a specific people.[18] We are left to seek justice in the temporal social structures of the world as individual Christians relieving individual suffering wherever we find it until Jesus comes. The church as a political entity is again irrelevant for evangelicalism.

Evangelicals further marginalize the church from the work of social justice with our approach to Scripture. Evangelicals typically assume that Scripture aided by some good exegesis can give a good working definition of justice to any individual Christian, who can then carry it out into the world irrespective of context. With modernist confidence,

> Evangelicals unwittingly acquiesced to the liberal Protestant understanding that the church can at best be marginal in society.

scriptural exegesis is a matter of objective science for evangelicals. We believe there is no communal cultural hermeneutic needed to interpret Scripture.[19] We are unaware of how interpretations of Scripture are prone to being shaped by the culture we are working out of. We think therefore that all justice is God's justice and should be obvious to all Christians anywhere if we just think it through hard enough according to the Scriptures. We do not readily see how faithful interpretation of Scripture requires the culture of his body to test it and authenticate it under the auspices of the Holy Spirit.[20] We do not understand that faithful interpretation requires discerning the justice of Christ one situation at a time in the body. Only then will our working understanding of justice be determined by Scripture as authentically engaged by the Spirit-driven community of Christ. So most evangelicals operate out of modernity, assuming that individual reasoning can rise above culture's corrupting powers. This assumption is what enables us to practice justice as individuals detached from the inner workings of the body. For most evangelicals, there is no need for the outworking of Christ's justice concretely in the church in order then to discern it outside. The work of Christ's justice can be detached from his body.

The evolution of evangelical social justice therefore reveals how indebted to modernity we evangelicals really are. Despite a commitment to social justice, we remain individualists. And like most Enlightenment modernity, we believe justice to be self-evident to all individuals, Christian and non-Christian, if we will all just think rationally about it. Justice is justice and surely God is behind all justice. Christians should therefore just dive in to work for it wherever it may be found.[21] Who can argue that a soup kitchen is not a good thing? In classic Protestant liberal fashion, we assent that the church is at best the voluntary association of individuals getting saved to help humanity. We accept that liberal democracy (especially for liberal Protestants) and capitalism (especially for evangelicals) are good compromises for a just society because they supposedly allow individuals freedom to make their own decisions to follow Christ and to associate freely with other Christians.[22]

But in the process, this approach to justice marginalizes the church itself as a politics for justice. Evangelicals may be the capitalists and liberal Protestants may be the advocates of liberal democracy, but in the end they are two sides of the same coin: a modern worldview that sees Christ as a personal and private belief on the one side, and justice as something God is doing irrespective of the church's politics and knowable to all people on the other. And our commitment to scriptural authority cannot guide our work for justice because we do not see the necessity of the church to interpret and embody scriptural truth. All in all, the church's role is to produce individuals to work for a more just society. For evangelicals, the social politics of the church is temporal and secondary to what God is doing in the world, and the work of Christ's justice can be done separate from the body of Christ.

Why There Can Be No Social Justice Detached from the Local Church

But modernity is passing and its modernist confidence in one justice for all reasonable individuals is eroding. Postmodern thinkers now record the triumph of the pragmatic and the uncovering of power interests and interpretive communities behind all acts of justice.[23] Suddenly what is justice for one is the manipulation of power for another. From the O. J. Simpson trial to the United Nations Iraq weapons inspections, justice has become either "one side versus another" or another form of performance in the vein of "reality TV." There is no more one justice, justice qua justice. Even democratic liberal versions of justice are not safe. After years of public debates on issues from homosexual rites to pedophiliac rights to children of divorced parents' rights, so-called "self-evident" human rights have been reduced to what is useful, pragmatic, or most fascinating. Equal rights and poverty levels are the ideologies of power struggles and fragmented social agendas. And so democratic liberal justice itself has become fragmented within North American society. And justice carried out by individuals takes on the interpretation into which it is thrown.

All of this reveals how the detached justice of evangelical churches is prone to being compromised. Evangelicals, with no actual community of reference, cannot clarify or demonstrate what the justice of our Lord looks like in a society of multiple justices. Evangelicals assume that justice should simply be obvious to reasonable people. But amidst the end of modernity, one person's justice is another's imperialism. Justice is fragmented. Our efforts therefore become enveloped by whatever justice dominates the cultural context of our work. The defining characteristics of Christ's justice get lost amidst the world's economic and social redefinition of what we are doing.[24] Whenever justice does not first take shape in the local church body, the giveaway of Christ's justice is inevitable. For when we go outside the church to do his justice before defining it via its practice inside, the righteousness of Christ gets subsumed by a justice already defined outside the church. With no prior practice of justice in place in the church, we just tend to hop on board with things already recognized as justice in the world. And in the process, we end up unwittingly "giving away" our justice to the forces of external culture.

In this vein, evangelicals predictably appeal to democratic liberal ideals in their work for justice. Because we do not practice justice inside our congregations first, we look to democratic ideals to articulate what justice is when we seek to practice it outside the church. We most often find ourselves defending our justice ministries in democratic terms like "individual rights," "equal opportunity," or "minimum standards of living." I will give examples of this in the following section, but the fact that we use these categories should not surprise us. Evangelicalism originated in the womb of democratic individualism and the American frontier. Therefore evangelicals naturally feel comfortable with the forms of justice canonized within democracy and American capitalism. Unaware of the postmodern fragmentation of democratic justice, evangelicals persist in describing the work of justice in these terms. Our churches seek to minister to conditions we find exterior to the church and framed in these terms. This is how we do justice ministry. And so evangelical forms of justice often look strangely akin to liberal democratic forms of justice with proof texts from Scripture. And the victims rarely find their way into our congregations or our homes. Doing isolated acts of generosity to the poor is always easier than inviting them into our house to be wholly redeemed. What most often makes it possible for evangelicals to separate the work of social justice from a justice defined internally among the body of Christ are the theories and language of democratic justice.

At the end of modernity, however, the justice of democracy and capitalism is "up for grabs." The justice language of human freedom, individual rights, equal opportunity, and minimum standards of living is not as self-evident as it once seemed.[25] Even worse, these democratic liberal forms of justice may not even be compatible with living the Christian life. Alasdair MacIntyre explains how this could be so.

In his book *Whose Justice? Which Rationality?* MacIntyre shows how liberal democracy has become a tradition all its own with a power agenda that produces its own kind of people. According to MacIntyre, the "project of founding a social order in which individuals could emancipate themselves from contingency and particularity of tradition by appealing to genuine universal, tradition-independent norms [in other words the democratic liberal agenda] . . . has itself been transformed into a tradition."[26] In so doing, democratic liberalism, though "initially rejecting the claims of any overriding theory of the good" in an effort to emancipate the individual to pursue his or her own preferences, became a tradition itself embodying a form of justice and rationality all unto its own.[27] Democracy therefore extols specific goods like egalitarianism and freedom to express and to become what each individual chooses. This is justice for democracy. Democracy, in other words, requires a commitment to values and goods as strong as any religious commitment. And yet these goods may or may not be compatible with being a Christian. As MacIntyre delineates, this liberalism does not provide a neutral tradition-independent ground from which Christians and anyone else may determine our own claims for justice individually.[28] It is a tradition in and of itself that forms us into certain kinds of people acting for certain kinds of reasons and certain kinds of justice. The question now is, Are these kinds of reasons, kinds of justice, and kinds of people we are being given in democratic liberalism worthy of the justice of Christ?

Stanley Hauerwas answers this question famously by stating that liberal society and its justice forms us into people that work against us being followers of Christ. "[Democratic] liberalism," he says, "becomes a self-fulfilling prophecy; a social order that is designed to work on the presumption that people are self-interested tends to produce that kind of people."[29] He states, "As Christians we will speak more truthfully to our society and be of greater service by refusing to continue the illusion that the larger social order knows what it is talking about when it calls for justice."[30] Hauerwas questions the idea that freedom, equal rights, and a justice qua justice in a liberal society are good things to be upheld and worked for by the church. He illustrates how working for liberal forms of justice like equality and freedom, the separation of politics from economics, may in fact "reinforce those practices that are implicated in the creation of poverty in our society" in the first place.[31] He sees the liberal accounts of justice as training and reinforcing people to be the kind of self-interested, cutthroat competitive people that such a society needs to survive. The solution then for Christians should not be to join hands with the accounts of justice in democracy as evangelicals have done. Rather the solution is to engage in the diligent practice of God's justice under the lordship of Christ in his body. As Hauerwas is famous for saying, "The first task of the church is not to make the world more just, but to make the world the world."[32] The church must begin by being the church and working out what Christ's justice is in the church before we can offer it to the world or call into account the forms of justice in the world. At the end of modernity there can be no justice of Christ detached from the church.

John Milbank carries the stance of MacIntyre and Hauerwas further by describing how democracy and capitalism are built upon an ontological foundation of violence. For Milbank therefore, democracy's as well as capitalism's very foundations are so disparate from the Christian vision for humanity that Christians cannot participate in it in any way that makes sense. According to Milbank, capitalism and democracy assume that people are individuals with discrete wills pitted against one another. For democratic capitalism, the natural state of humanity is as individuals each born for unlimited freedom who must somehow now live together. According to Milbank, this is a politics built upon an "ontology of violence," one person against the other.[33] But Christians assume something totally different. We assume that the world and all therein were originally created as a unity together participating in the ever-flowing work of God into the world.[34] There was no individual versus individual or individual versus group because these conditions were the effects of sin.[35] The work of Christ was to restore this peace. Christians therefore cannot participate in capitalism and democracy because to do so rejects the underlying assumption that God's work in Christ redeems us to an original order of participation and unity in God. If we agree with Milbank then, any justice articulated in the terms of democratic capitalism assumes the separation of individual versus individual. If we articulate justice in the terms of individual equality or equal opportunity, we are in essence maintaining the violent terms of democratic capitalism. It is a politics born from assumptions of conflict as opposed to the Christian assumptions of reconciliation and peace in Christ.

> **Democratic capitalism, according to Milbank, is a politics built upon an "ontology of violence," one person against the other. But Christians assume something totally different.**

Democracy and capitalism therefore fundamentally play on a politics that does not restore humanity to a mutual participation in God but replaces such participation with a politics based on the discrete wills of all individuals getting along without killing each other.[36] The justice based in democracy and capitalism does the same. And once we see democracy and capitalism in these terms, evangelical participation in such a justice is heresy.[37] The only politics we can truly participate in is the church as the restoration of God's relationship with humanity in creation. The only justice that makes sense is that worked out in relation to God through Jesus Christ in the church. Only from this standpoint can we then enter society with Christ's justice.

Evangelicals as Christians therefore must recover a Christian language and set of practices that do not "give away" our justice to the categories of ontological violence inherent in capitalism and liberal democracy. We must locate our justice in the work of Jesus Christ among a people called out to be his church. Only by returning to the practice of justice in the local church can we find our way to a justice that is born out of Christ, which we can then give to the world. Thus, MacIntyre, Hauerwas, and Milbank reveal the task for evangelicalism in America if we are to practice the justice of Christ. We must throw off our careless modernism and our alliance with democracy and begin practicing the justice of Christ in our churches so that we might then manifest it in the world. For the Christian, there can be no social justice detached from the church.

Evangelicals and Our "Liberal" Ways of Justice

Unfortunately, evangelicals remain mired in the language of justice as defined by liberal democracy and capitalism. We consistently push a justice based in individual equality, equal individual opportunity, and personal rights. We do not see how this is not Christ's justice and how in fact this may be working against Christ's justice. I offer the following examples.

First, Ron Sider of Evangelicals for Social Action begins his book *Just Generosity* by defining poverty and explaining how to recognize it through liberal democratic ways of defining inequitable structures in the U.S. economy. For Sider, living below the U.S. poverty rate of $16,530 a year is unjust when the mean family income is $56,902.[38] Sider argues that this is poverty because "it means stretching every penny and having no budget for many things such as furniture, vacations, recreation, private health insurance, and so on that most of us take for granted."[39] Basically Sider delineates why this is unjust in terms of equal opportunity and living standards as drawn from democratic and American capitalist terms. Sider goes on to detail how the United States has the greatest income inequality of all developed nations.[40] In Sider's classic 1977 book *Rich Christians in an Age of Hunger*, he makes the oft since repeated comparisons between the rich countries and the poor, stating, for example, that the "rich 34 percent claims 87 percent of the world's total GNP [gross national product] each year. The poor two-thirds is left with 13 percent."[41]

What Sider did not consider is that these ways of quantifying justice might perpetuate the ills of capitalism and democracy upon the poor. Certainly Sider is to be commended for his massive work in drawing attention to the Christian's obligation to the poor. But Sider missed the way he allowed the capitalist machine to determine what poverty is. And what goes unnoticed is that part of rectifying that injustice in this way assumes the sucking of all the poor into the full rigors of the agonistic system of capitalism. Perhaps those who make $56,902 have a nice house but live a nonstop, stress-filled lifestyle in which they never see or spend time at the local church or with their children. Maybe the two-income family has to shove their children into a day care facility three days a week in order to participate in $56,902 a year. Maybe addictions like unhealthy eating at McDonald's just to have time to eat are a necessary part of the two-income, capitalistic-driven character of life in society. Even worse, maybe these capitalistic ways would spatialize the poor into relationships of contract and exchange incapable of communing one with another as a unity in Christ. Maybe this is a life of capitalistic justice Christians should wish on no one.

Back in 1977, Sider compared the wealth of United States to the wealth of underdeveloped countries, using the GNP statistics in currency at the time. This means of comparison is still used regularly by evangelicals today to talk about economic injustice. I certainly agree heartily with Sider that North Americans are guilty of ignoring their obligation toward the world's poor some twenty-seven years later. But should we be using a capitalistically driven GDP (gross domestic product) statistic to define the terms of poverty? (GDP is now the term that has replaced GNP in government statistics since Sider's book in 1977.) Does not GDP itself assume the defining myths of wealth creation in capitalism? Could it be that GDP really represents for the Christian the production of a lot of nonessential things and the arousal of non-healthy desires to consume them, which amounts to a lot of nothing in the lives of these people or the economy of God? Should not Christians examine whether all this proposed wealth creation is really about the production of many things and the arousing of many desires we could all do without? Capitalism may quantify this as wealth creation or GDP, but the Christian may see this as a lot of misdirected energy that indeed inflames desires away from the purposes of God.

It is therefore not morally neutral to use the measure of GDP to compare a country's wealth and determine means of redistribution. Inherent in any diagnosis and solution that uses the capitalist measure of GDP is the propagation of a consumeristic, production-oriented, stress-filled existence upon people who may indeed be better without it. These are the agonisms of capitalism. Surely we should at least consider whether Chileans may be better off living more simply and less consumerist lives than their American counterparts. None of this means we should not spend more effort in works of mercy and relief to all those in poverty. The point is this justice should look a lot different than we are describing it. But we will never see it this way because evangelicals are prone to see justice in democratic and capitalistic terms. When we do not practice righteousness first in the community of Jesus Christ, we do not have the means to discriminate what God is really after in restoring righteousness to those who are suffering injustice.

A second example of this same evangelical blind spot is illustrated by the following episode I have seen repeated in many evangelical churches. A pastor of a large suburban evangelical megachurch presents the need for Christians to get more involved with social justice. He describes the hurting plight of people in the urban setting. Then the pastor tells how he decided to personally seek out a man he noticed was in need of help. So the pastor invested his own sweat labor and personally helped the man fix up a building, which allowed the man to start a business. The pastor described the triumph when this man started working for himself. The man was given back his dignity by actually owning his own business. The climax of the story was when the pastor asked the man how much he had in his bank account. The man replied, "Seven hundred dollars." The pastor asked, "When was the last time you had seven hundred dollars in the bank?" and he said, "Never." Though there may have been other overtures to this man's personal salvation, the act of justice that was highlighted was this man's acquiring an independent bank account with seven hundred dollars in it.

Few would doubt that much good was accomplished in this work of mercy. But what defines this particular act as a work of Christian justice? Does a "seven-hundred-dollar" bank account owned for the first time qualify as a work of justice? Does restoring a poor person to financial independence constitute Christian justice in and of itself? Does helping a man accomplish a seven-hundred-dollar bank account count as a work of justice if it also unwittingly trains the man into centering his life on wealth accumulation? Highlighting a "seven-hundred-dollar bank account" as an achievement might be susceptible to such an interpretation. In fact, the goal of acquiring a bank account in and of itself could easily turn into the pursuit of greed and wealth accumulation as well as plain old independence from God, all of which are forms of unrighteousness. As theologian Stephen Long reminds us, "A just ordering of economic life assumes the order of charity."[42] For the Christian, an act of justice cannot be discerned as justice apart from it being the outgrowth of charity in the life of Christ. And this "charity is not natural to us."[43] It comes only as an infused virtue (Aquinas) born out of the life of the Spirit. This means that a "seven hundred dollar bank account" can only be known as justice as it is related to the life of stewardship, obedience, charity, and forgiveness.

For instance, a key Christian virtue in the business owner and his seven-hundred-dollar bank account would be the understanding that all our money is from God and to be owned in stewardship of his ownership. A key evidence of justice would be the life of charity offered to the world through this man via the grace given to him with the new "seven-hundred-dollar bank account." Otherwise we simply perpetuate the same sins of greed and avarice that caused the injustice in the first place. And we train this man out of poverty into isolation and a life seen in terms of private wealth and exchange. But these virtues are impossible to learn apart from being a part of a living community and body of Christ that practices these skills of stewardship one with another. Apart from such a community, this act of mercy could be training this man into another form of worship, the worship of the gods of greed, wealth accumulation, and consumerism. The community of Christ is therefore essential for Christian justice.[44] In this second example, the particular act of mercy was done many miles from the actual church community this pastor was regularly a part of (his own congregation). If we hypothetically assume that the man he helped did not become part of the pastor's church (he very well could have), we would have to seriously question whether this could be a case of Christian justice.

A third example of evangelicals defining justice in terms of democratic capitalism is the way evangelicals attempt to influence public policy. When it comes to public policy, evangelicals have gone beyond advocating legislation and court appointments that will further family and personal morality agendas. They also now advocate political agendas that will promote better welfare systems, equal access to health care, and fairer distribution of resources among public school systems.[45] While doing this, evangelicals rarely consider how being complicit in the capitalist and democratic systems damages the possibility for achieving Christian justice. It is true that evangelicals have criticized welfare for the way it trains dependents into commodifying tendencies. For instance, evangelicals and many others have examined the ways (what used to be called) Aid to Families with Dependent Children (AFDC) encouraged more out-of-wedlock births for the mother's purpose of earning more money. But rarely do evangelicals question whether these systems should be abandoned entirely unless a central role exists for the church because of the way they perpetuate capitalist problems.

We will now champion, for instance, funding equality among all public schools and decry the inequality that exists between school districts and opportunities for education between the poor and the middle classes in the United States. What we will not ask is whether public schools themselves train our children for the democratic capitalistic virtues of self-interest, being a good consumer, and earning money enough to support the practice of consuming and paying for it. Therefore we swiftly support U.S. policy changes to level the playing field of public education and ignore the changes needed in our local churches to make the church central to, or at least a part of, the public education of our children. I do not suggest we should ignore the former for the latter. We should do both. But because we rarely discern concretely in our local churches the problems of sending our own children to public schools, we miss the immediate Christian concern. We can only then respond through broader policy initiatives as determined by democratic terms. We miss asking what the role of the local church should be in educating her children in relation to public schools. We therefore "give away" justice to the determining factors of democracy and capitalism. We do not see what real education is or for that matter what other policy problems like health care can really mean because we do not engage in these concrete discernments in the local church.

So evangelicals have increased their work for social justice over the past thirty years. Yet it is a social justice that is not based in the justice of Christ as worked out in our local congregations. It is most often a justice defined by democratic and capitalist concerns and the languages that define them. We do not have a language of Christ's justice. We therefore tend to "give away" our justice in Christ to the cultural sources we have become accustomed to.

Recovering the Language of God's Righteousness

New Testament theologian James Dunn, in his co-authored book *The Justice of God*, teaches us how to speak about justice in the scriptural language of "righteousness." Drawing on the Hebrew Scriptures, Dunn expounds a justice that is faithful to God's work in Israel and Jesus Christ. He says, "In Hebrew thought righteousness is a concept of relation. In Hebrew thought righteousness is something one has precisely in one's relationships as a social being. That is to say, righteousness is not something which an individual has on his or her own, independent of anyone else—as could be the case with the Greco-Roman concept."[46] Dunn draws on the prophets (Ezek. 18:5–9; Isa. 58:3–7; Amos 5:21–24; Micah 3) to describe how being in a right relationship with God vertically was inseparable from being in right relationship with one another in the Hebrew Old Testament context.[47] God's righteousness is prior to any human righteousness because human righteousness is a response to God's righteous actions toward human beings. More basic than any form of justice based in the metaphor of the law court is the justice founded in one's covenantal relationship and the ongoing sustaining of that relationship through difficult circumstances, through forgiveness and healing. In other words, for the Christian, God's righteousness is something worked out among a people of God, and it is first and foremost a response to his righteousness.

Dunn argues against the over-Lutheranizing of the doctrine of justification where justification became individualized and defined as the isolated individual's legal status before God. Evangelicals are particularly prone to this. Dunn, however, describes how our justification in Christ is not of the individual standing before a law court so much as it is being invited into the work of God's righteousness through Jesus Christ in a continuation of the covenant relationship with Israel. Justification is not an individual possession as much as it is the offer from God to participate in his work of salvation and righteousness. It is therefore a righteousness of both a restored relationship with God and the concomitant response to that relationship with the righteousness established in the covenant people of God. Dunn explains that "God's righteousness is his acting out of that obligation which he took upon himself in creating the world and choosing Israel to be his people. And it consists primarily in drawing human persons into the appropriate relationship with himself and in sustaining them in that relationship."[48] The conclusion then is, as Dunn states, "The biblical understanding of justification/justice/righteousness is all of one piece. In particular, it involves two important aspects: righteousness as essentially involving relationships; and righteousness, as both horizontal and vertical, as involving responsibility to one's neighbor as part and parcel of one's responsibility towards God."[49] Unless these two are held together, justification and justice can get distorted.

> **Justification is not an individual possession as much as it is the offer from God to participate in his work of salvation and righteousness.**

For Dunn then, it is a mistake to individualize justification in a way that separates that justification from the work of God's righteousness in a people. Evangelicals err when they separate personal salvation from its outworking as righteousness among a people of God. The doctrine of justification by faith alone is part and parcel of an entire cosmological work of God to work righteousness in a people and through this people to the world.[50] Therefore evangelicals err scripturally when they over-individualize salvation to the extent it becomes a possession and a commodity. Instead, we should maintain salvation as God's work in establishing a righteous relationship between himself and his people and then manifesting that righteousness horizontally as the inextricable extension of that new relationship.

James Dunn helps us see then what justice looks like as it has been revealed to the people of Israel and culminated in the person and work of Jesus Christ. He uncovers that there is righteousness in Christ that fulfills the justice of God in Israel and surpasses any justice that democracy or capitalism can give us. He helps us see that the all-engulfing righteousness of God should be the only real justice we Christians are interested in. Dunn shows that there is a justice in Christ that is thicker, less individuated, and more compelling that the church should not relinquish as we engage society. Dunn challenges us to reacquire such a language for justice in the church. Using this language, we will not be able to claim that we are participating in Christ's justice by merely providing financial, physical relief to people external to the church. We will not be able to claim as justice some sort of structural change that offers equal opportunity in a democratic society unless it reflects the already existing change in the society of Christ. Likewise, the work of this justice will not be done until the relationships one with another and with God have been restored in the way God himself calls us to be with himself. Justice then is never just about money; it is also about stewardship. It is never just about equal opportunity; it is about restored whole political relationships. It is never just about aid to dependent mothers; it is about a healing and restoration of the broken down and a restoration to their place in a renewed people. It is about the work of God for a new humanity and the restoration of that humanity into relationships not governed out of the ontology of violence upon which democracy is built but gifted out of our mutual participation in the body of Christ. It is about a restored and redeemed economics.

> **There is a justice in Christ that is thicker, less individuated, and more compelling that the church should not relinquish as we engage society.**

This kind of justice can only begin in the church of Christ. This kind of justice supersedes all other kinds of procedural justice in America and cannot be done in complicity with the terms laid down for us by the powers of democracy and capitalism. It must be done first as the work of God in his church through Jesus Christ from which we then display it to the world, engage the foreign injustices with it, and ultimately invite the victims and the victimizers out of the agonistic society to sit as one with us at the Table of the kingdom of God.

Community *in* but Not *of* Capitalism

The work of James Dunn challenges our evangelical churches to manifest a justice among ourselves that displays the kind of righteousness that can only be God's. This has never been more important as society fragments into its multiple justices and communities. But this has also rarely been more difficult as late capitalism extends its dominion over all manifestations of North American life. Capitalism intrudes upon every living space. North American society imposes enormous capitalist pressures on its inhabitants that impede this kind of community. So our congregations must work incessantly, paying off larger credit card bills and mortgages on bigger homes. Capitalist competitiveness and consumerism as well as liberal individualism shape us into being wealth accumulators, consumers, and parents who must take every possible produced advantage for our child's growth and development. There is little time for our people to be the body, and so the local church often is reduced to being the distributor of religious goods and services. When we do come together, we come shaped as we are out of capitalism as individuals protecting our interests. We do not come determined first by our citizenship in Christ.

As a result, instead of being communities of God's redeemed economics, many evangelical churches take on the communal characteristics of capitalism in strange ways. In the way evangelical churches organize, we curiously choose elders who are more successful as businessmen and accumulators of wealth than they are capable of giving wisdom and Christ-centered shepherding to the local congregation. We project budgets based upon how many people are actually "giving units" in the church. Our people walk and look like capitalists. When anyone is in need or going through rough economic times, we do not talk about it because we are ashamed. It is a shame to be poor or unsuccessful in capitalism. We do not look upon each other with "unlimited liability" one toward another.[51] We surprisingly get our identities more from our jobs than our life in a Christian community pursuing God's kingdom on earth. And we treat our money as our own. We live in fear that to give up our possessions will leave us alone and destitute when our time of need comes. The last thing our people will talk about in church is how much money we make or our investments at the bank. Our imbedded individualism hurts us as we hoard our money, keep private our personal finances, and die a slow death of the soul as we never learn how to truly live, rejoicing with those who rejoice, weeping with those who weep (Rom. 12:15). All of this makes practicing the justice of Christ in the local church more difficult.

> **We surprisingly get our identities more from our jobs than our life in a Christian community pursuing God's kingdom on earth.**

Evangelical churches therefore face a significant challenge in being the church without withdrawing in toto from capitalism. How can we be a community of Christ in which the righteousness and justice of God are worked out among us without being determined by forces of democracy and capitalism? How do we eat, live, and have jobs in capitalism and yet not become driven by the emotions and desires of "consumeritis," career success, and the protection of our financial security? How do we see justice as more than leveling the economic playing field or providing the basics necessary to give someone an opportunity to be successful in democratic capitalistic society? Community in capitalism is so difficult because consumerism is always making us ask, Are we meeting your needs? But we do not need another pseudo community that gathers to support its members in each other's striving for self-fulfillment and career advancement.[52] For we will again blend in to the all-pervasive forces that make justice about getting more of what I want out of capitalism and democracy. Instead, God calls us in Christ to a righteousness of another kind. How do we live as community *in* but not *of* capitalism (John 17:14–18)? How do we practice the redeemed economics born out of his righteousness? How do we practice justice as righteousness as a people *in* but not *of* capitalism?

The answer to this question for many has been to withdraw from capitalism entirely and become an intentional community. Intentional community, with no private ownership of property, is certainly an option. Yet is there another way we can still live in capitalism but not be of it? Can we live together in a manner in which we retain private ownership yet view that ownership so differently that it actually binds us together as members of a body as opposed to separating us by the fears of securing our own interests?

Ron Sider has expounded how private property was not so much the issue in the New Testament church. Rather the issue in the New Testament church was how each member was to see that all his or her property and money was a gift from God to be held in such a way that there was an unlimited call on that property to meet the needs and mission of the community.[53] The determining factor on wealth was the *koinōnia* in Christ, the common lordship of Christ over all things (including wealth) for the common living out of his righteousness. Roman Catholic traditions have also not excluded the right to own property but at the same time placed limits upon that ownership. According to some Roman traditions, to hold on to capital surplus in the presence of another's need was a violent act. In some canon law, to steal from another's surplus in time of mortal need was not a sin.[54] Property was always held for the common good. According to Sider, an expression of that *koinōnia* was financial responsibility one toward another as evident in Paul's agreements with the Jerusalem church and the sharing of the Gentile church in their need (Gal. 2:9–10).[55] As John Yoder has advocated and Ron Sider affirmed, the early church lived under the shadow of the Jubilee tradition that practiced the holding of property only for a limited period as a steward or manager of that property for the benefit of God and his people. At the end of every fifty years the ownership of land and property would be returned and equalized among the people (Lev. 25:10–24). The property was not to be owned in perpetuity; it was to be owned as a steward would manage the property for his master. God and God alone owned the land (Lev. 25:23). In many respects, the community described in Acts chapters 2 and 4 is a reflection of these principles.[56] It was this attitude toward private ownership that governed the church.

It is disputable whether or not the Year of Jubilee was literally carried out either in the nation of Israel or for that matter in the early church. But the principle provides a backdrop for how we are to live as the eschatological people of God called into living out his righteousness and justice one with another *in* but not *of* capitalism. Intentional community of one purse is not the only option to make this happen. As many such communities have discovered, becoming a community of one purse does not totally insulate the community from the influences and pervasive corrupting forces of capitalism.[57] What does, however, make possible the living together *in* but not *of* capitalism is the fundamental disposition wherewith we hold our privately held property together, in "unlimited liability" one toward another and to God, recognizing that the property is not ours in the first place, just placed into our stewardship for a short time for the blessing of God's people. It is a disposition toward ownership that rejects capitalism's contention that it is something I have done that merits the ownership of my property and wealth.[58] Instead, I hold property in the service of the King.

Whether intentional community of a common purse or whether we come together maintaining separate bank accounts, I contend that the development of this crucial disposition of stewardship and practices to live in that disposition are what shall enable us as evangelicals to carry out justice as a community *in* but not *of* capitalism. Similar to the early church, which lived with slavery as an economic reality hardly capable of displacement, so too we might have to live with capitalism as an economic reality not soon to be displaced. Nevertheless, as theologian Oliver O'Donovan has described, the early church carried the conviction that the church itself was a society without master or slave within it.[59] And so likewise, the evangelical church must carry the conviction that the church itself is a society where no one holds goods and resources in private ownership, but as gifts from God for his faithful stewardship one to another for the pursuit of justice and righteousness in our midst and then to the world. It might then be necessary for us evangelical church members to maintain private ownership and bank accounts in order to live in capitalism, but as his church we shall not live as if there are any owners among us, only stewards of God's gifts for the benevolence of all under his lordship.

This kind of disposition toward wealth can only be formed inside the church community through the concrete practice of justice one situation at a time. Indeed, Christian justice begins with that woman who stands in the middle of the congregation and says, "I have cancer, I have no health insurance." At this point we can neither argue about governmental health insurance policies nor write an easy check that will not hurt our bank accounts. Evangelicals may be prone to seeing this woman as derelict in her duty to work and be responsible for herself and his family. This is the justice of capitalism. But it cannot be this easy when the woman stands up and speaks amidst the congregation. This woman must be heard and talked with. We must discover why she has no health insurance. We must examine her own life and ours as to why we allowed this to happen in the first place to someone who has been in our midst for three years. We must pray for her medical care and see that her family has sufficient support to make it through. We must serve this woman in such a way that not only is she taken care of medically but the overall status of this woman's relationship to God, her secular community, and her church community is restored. We must also ensure that the church somehow does not contribute to her dereliction in not having health insurance if there was in fact dereliction. We must in fact deal with everything that has to do with this woman being in righteous relationship to us her community and to God and to the world. The regular practice of such restoration forms the disposition of justice in the community.

Only after we have walked through this process can we see similar situations in the world and make comparable discernments as to what it means to restore such situations to righteousness in God outside the church. Only after we have been formed into the disposition of Christ's justice in community do we have the disposition necessary to carry out his justice in the world. Only after we have walked through this process with someone can we go to the government and propose broad solutions that can model the community of Christ in caring for the one left destitute without health insurance. When a woman comes forward in the middle of the congregation, we are tempted to give her money so that she will go away, or we are tempted to slough off her request as someone whose irresponsibility should not be rewarded. But because she is in the middle of us, we cannot treat this woman as the detached stranger who panhandles for change in the street. She is in the congregation of Christ and we must come into relationship with her. This practice of engaging her in our midst forges the new justice that is ours in Jesus Christ. It is the New Order coming into being in our midst. And it forms the basis for the justice of Christ to be worked out in the world.

Reinvigorating the Practice of the Benevolence Fund

Evangelicals therefore require a practice that counteracts the determining forces of capitalism upon the way we see justice and money in the local church body. We need a practice that spatializes the world for us in terms of the reconciliation we have in Jesus Christ's death and resurrection. In theologian William Cavanaugh's terms, we need a practice "that organizes the very spaces into which we walk."[60] Out of such a practice, the local community should not only be formed into a disposition toward Christ's justice but be able to resist the alternative forces of capitalism that seek to form our imaginations in contrary ways.

I propose that the "benevolent fund" be such a practice that can form this kind of community *in* but not *of* capitalism.[61] Simply put, at the time of the celebration of our oneness in Christ, around the reception of the gift of God in Christ, in the Lord's Supper, we must reinvigorate the practice of benevolence as the outgrowth of that time around the Lord's Table. Of course this may imply that most evangelicals recover the true depths of the Lord's Supper first before going on to benevolence. But here I wish to propose as well that the eucharistic practice be reinvigorated and extended to include the age-old practice of benevolence. By this I do not mean that we simply collect a benevolence offering after celebrating the Lord's Supper. Rather, let us make the benevolent fund an intentional practice among us. Let us make visible verbally and ritualistically that we receive everything we are and have from the work of God in Christ and we return it to him as well. That as we are all one in Christ's body, we are mutually financially liable to one another. That as we have so bountifully received, we in return give with the same unlimited bounty. We do this in such a way that it is not a shame but an expectation that those who are in need will come forward to be ministered to. Once those in need have come forward, this committee of benevolence sits with them around a meal and discerns their needs as well as issues of sin and then invites them into reconciliation, restoration, and righteousness through financial assistance and community restoration. This should be reported to and supported by the local body. In this way, we should discern one's financial problems one person at a time with a deep sense of mutual accountability.[62] In the process, this practice of benevolence orders the participants together into a new relation financially one with another, a new foretaste of a redeemed economy, in essence the body of Christ.

We must find ways to embody these things through rituals in front of the whole congregation. Each member, for instance, can write on a piece of paper what each one's total assets and annual income are and put it in the plate to be placed on the altar as a sign that all our assets are God's and are "on call" at the behest of the benevolence ministry and the body of Christ. And all this will be done as a direct outgrowth of our times around the Table where we are truly made one. We do these things here at the altar where Paul once chastised the Corinthian financial inequalities that were allowed around the Table of our Lord (1 Cor. 11:17–22).

Such a benevolence practice will require that we locate those among us who are gifted in discerning matters of financial justice and righteousness. Such a benevolence committee discerns both the needs of the member, his or her sins and victimization, what needs to be set right, and the communal claims on each member's property to meet the needs if the benevolence fund cannot. Such a committee signifies both the communal claim on each member's assets as well as the illegitimacy of any one individual's unilateral claim over another member's assets. We must admit that such unilateral non-communal claims destroy community just as much as individuals privately hoarding wealth. Because when a Christian says to another Christian in the body, God has called me to pursue this goal and therefore you should support me, or I need a cancer operation and you should mortgage your house for my hospital bill, he or she makes a claim that can only be discerned within a community. Otherwise, anyone with a personal dream for ego aggrandizement can avoid work and baptize their personal dream in the name of the Lord's calling and make a unilateral claim on God's assets. Likewise, anyone with a medical bill can ignore what they must do out of obedience to Christ for their whole restoration. Unilateral behavior destroys community and sets the members up for abuse all in the name of the Lord. Without a local body to discern, members can abuse the body of Christ, leaving the community devastated. Therefore the benevolent fund committee that acts on behalf of the body to "discern the body" (1 Cor. 11:29) is an inextricable part of being a body of Christ *in* but not *of* capitalism.

Such discernments of the body often entail options other than distributing money to a person in need. Certainly, there are many times when distributing money is the only option that can meet a person's need in a given situation. But there may also be times when the gift of money alone may perpetrate injustice by encouraging the disadvantaged to be even more enmeshed in the consumerist ways of modern capitalism. Christian justice may require other more creative solutions involving the community. For example, if a member needs a car due to financial hardship, the congregation may organize to offer their cars on a rotating basis to the one in need. Instead of providing money for a car or worse yet, the means to acquire "car payments," the community provides an in-between arrangement that can forestall burdensome indebtedness, maintenance, and insurance costs. Such a solution would provide immediate transportation, create a communal basis for fellowship and restoration, and resist the potential for an unnecessary slavery to car ownership and loan indebtedness. Such a practice may be the means to resist captivity to the consumer capitalist forces that seek to further imprison the poor and make spiritual paupers of us all. A new communal simplicity can challenge every one of us. The benevolent fund committee therefore should be ready to engage in these types of discernments that resist the forces of consumer capitalism in order to yield a true justice of Christ that is in but not of capitalism.

Perhaps proposing an intensified practice of the benevolent fund seems ridiculous as the solution to the world's injustice. But *perhaps* this is the point. Our God in Christ has chosen in ridiculous fashion to come into the world at one location at one time and to start there for the redemption of the whole world. And so from God's work of justice in that one local body in that one person who is restored to righteousness, the church can then meet that one person outside the congregation who has succumbed to the same unrighteousness. We can then engage this one person on the same terms. One situation at a time, God's people mete out his justice. The hurting are engaged on all the levels of victimization, restoration, and personal obedience in relation to one's relationships and obligations as given by God and his people. This person will not be left outside the community to figure everything out on his or her own. He or she becomes one of us, invited into the new righteousness that is of Jesus Christ. The reclamation of one such person into God's righteousness here on earth is a glimpse of where we are all headed for eternity. The witness is powerful. From here we can go to government and make proposals that are undeniable in credibility because we are witnesses to what God can do among his people.[63]

In the end, such simple and concrete workings out of God's righteousness make the church visible. Such a physical engaging of justice one person at a time through the practice of benevolence avoids making justice a private possession to be gotten on our own by secretly writing a check. Instead, it forms the beachhead from which more and more justice can flow into the world from the church.[64] As we learn from William Cavanaugh's powerful depiction of the church in Pinochet's Chile, "if the church is to resist society's masquerades of justice, then it must be publicly visible as a body of Christ in the present time, not secreted away in the souls of believers or relegated to the distant historical past or future."[65]

> **When we minister love, restitution, redemption, restoration, and reconciliation to even one person, a truly revolutionary justice has taken place under the banner of Christ's justice.**

So therefore, what starts with a woman standing in the midst of the congregation at the Table of our Lord, telling everyone, "I have cancer, I have no health insurance, I have three thousand dollars in bills this first week, and I need an operation," leads to those with the means to help, sitting in a room, asking her, "What do you need to make it to the next day, week, and month?" After the immediate relief, this committee asks more questions about her family and work history. There is no sloughing off this woman's life with an easy check. They may ask her why she hasn't had a job in ten years. They may inquire about her family history and why her finances are mismanaged. They may see the unfortunate cycle of victimization she has been caught up in well enough to thwart its repeat. They may discern what sin, if any, needs to be dealt with as well as in what way this woman needs forgiveness, restitution, and restoration. They will ask not only how to get her through her immediate financial need, but what needs to be done to restore her obligations to former bosses, her community, those she has gone into debt with, and her children and family. Together as a community we are mutually liable, together we see how she was left most vulnerable at the hardest time. When we minister love, restitution, redemption, restoration, and reconciliation to even one person, a truly revolutionary justice has taken place under the banner of Christ's justice.

So then comes the encounter outside with the homeless person and the same story is carried out except this person at the end is invited into the fellowship of Christ's righteousness in his body. We then think about self-insuring the whole church for medical costs and including those who need to be insured in our group. We then extend this new social justice to the poor all around us.[66] We discern in the Spirit as a body what goes wrong and what goes right. We then go to the government with a proposal to make such medical insurance co-ops available to all just as has been done in the body of Christ. But the power of such a visible justice as this lies in the fact that we cannot be relegated to the status of just another competing lobbyist or special interest group. We have rejected the commodifying tendencies of capitalistic medical practices by living out an alternative righteousness under the lordship of Christ.

What therefore begins as a tiny concrete engagement for justice becomes a regular practice, extended from the Lord's Table, flowing into everyday life. Each local church becomes a subversive community undermining the injustices of capitalism, extending its reach into its daily contacts with the world. Its tiny presence undercuts the foundation of any false justices the world may seek to mete out. The one tiny victory in the restoration of a woman destroyed by hospital bills stands as a witness to that justice that is coming in the name of the Lord. And just as the regular Roman Catholic Church practice of the Eucharist bred a politic that slowly undermined the politics of torture and of a brutal dictatorship, as William Cavanaugh depicted for Chile,[67] so also the extended practice of benevolence can perhaps breed a politic among evangelical churches that undermines the total determination of capitalism upon all our relations in North America.[68]

The practice of benevolence, of giving and submitting to one another financially, can de-spatialize us out of relationships determined by capitalism and order us into a new way of being in relation to one another economically. Through such a regular practice, churches can in fact participate in a redeemed economics that is already the ongoing work of God through Christ. We can imitate an economics that, through its physical practice, becomes the way we see all other economic transactions. The righteousness of God becomes visible through the regular practice of the benevolence fund, and thereby fundamentally threatens the way capitalism carries out justice. It is tiny in its beginning. It requires the real functioning of the body of Christ. But perhaps if North American evangelicals make the real practice of "the benevolence fund" central to being the body, perhaps if we make it an inseparable outgrowth of his Table, then his justice will be spread. It will undermine the imposters of justice in society, spread Christ's justice to the poor, and extend Christ's reign to the victimized until he returns.

7

Spiritual Formation

The Need for More Preaching (and Penance)
in the Psychologist's Office, or Why Therapy Never
Should Have Left the Church in the First Place

Confess your sins one to another, and pray for one another, so that you
may be healed. The prayer of the righteous is powerful and effective.

James 5:16 NRSV

One morning, a man named Jim came to my office for a counseling session, acting quite disturbed. Jim was a regular in our community, and I knew he was struggling. I asked him what we needed to talk about, and he started to tell me about his heightened struggle with sadness, depression, and indeed, thoughts of suicide. As most pastors know, this is a serious matter. Pastors are often told that this kind of issue is one for the professionals. Nonetheless, I continued to probe Jim by asking him to describe his emotions. He described his hopelessness and despair. I asked him to describe any events that might have triggered his immense sense of hopelessness. After talking for two hours, Jim clarified some things for himself and me. Jim stated he was angry because he had no meaningful sustainable relationship with a woman. He articulated that his situation was determined by the way he had been raised by his parents. And most of all, Jim clarified that he was angry at God for not giving him the life he saw everyone else have.

After these two hours of conversation, it seemed appropriate for me to ask Jim questions like the following: Do you believe God can overcome the victimizations and personal sins of your past? Do you believe God through Jesus Christ and his Holy Spirit can be working even now in these sufferings to lead you to his greatest purposes for your life? Do you see any sin you need to confess and repent of in your most recent relationship? Can you seek restitution for sins you have committed against the one you once loved? By considering suicide, is it possible you are telling God he was wrong in creating you in the first place? Can you repent of that sin and seek reconciliation with God? I offered Scripture as the means to focus on these questions. Curiously, most of these questions came as a shock to Jim. He resisted answering the questions. He considered them guilt-inducing and judgmental.

Why were these questions inappropriate? None of these questions would have been unusual if we were in a medieval confessional and I was a priest. And in revivalist times, these signs of depression and sadness in a person might have been welcomed by the church as a sign that a conversion experience was near and that these questions needed to be asked. Perhaps even a modern therapist could ask questions similar to these yet using other language. But as two evangelicals sitting in the office of an evangelical pastor, these questions were somehow intrusive, naïve, or dangerous in light of modern psychotherapy. These questions about confession, repentance, discerning one another through Scripture, and prayer had somehow become inappropriate at the most crucial moment of spiritual formation.

I contend that this episode reveals much about who we evangelicals give authority to for interpreting our spiritual lives. I also contend, that though this session was an extreme case, it actually is quite typical of spiritual formation among many evangelical churches; for it reveals the surprising authority that Jim and many suffering evangelical parishioners give to modern therapy in their lives. Jim gave enormous authority to the therapeutic interpretations he had been given in other counseling. He believed that his life and personality were determined by the first three to eight years of life. He accepted that his personal emotional structure was innate and needed to be managed toward productive life. He believed that his interpersonal relationships and the navigation of his life's decisions needed to be managed for the acquiring of self-fulfillment in accordance with the ways "God had gifted him." These were nonnegotiable beliefs he had learned through his therapy, and any questions that contradicted those beliefs were not acceptable. Jim then could hardly allow himself to consider questions that pondered the Christian merits of his suffering, the discernment of sin and confession, the claim of God's kingdom upon him in vocation and marriage. In the same way, I contend, many evangelicals give enormous authority to modern therapeutic practice in their lives. We see it as science and good medicine. Consequently, at the most crucial times for the formation of our souls toward Christ, we evangelicals look to modern therapy, and the opportunity for spiritual formation is lost.

This state of affairs is the result of psychology's newfound place of approval in North American evangelicalism. Whereas forty years ago, evangelical parishioners would look askance at the prospect of a fellow church member visiting the local therapist, today's evangelical boomers and their children go regularly to therapy for personal emotional struggles or marital problems. Evangelical churches join hands with psychological service providers regularly. They dedicate offices on-site for therapists or develop referral services with "Christian" psychologists. Many evangelical preachers are now as comfortable with psychology as they are with Scripture as an authority for their preaching. Christian men's and women's therapy movements have spun off from their secular counterparts: Robert Bly, Sam Keen, and the Warrior Weekend. For most evangelicals, all of this is a positive development. Christian counseling is finally accepted in the church.

> **At the most crucial times for the formation of our souls toward Christ, we evangelicals look to modern therapy, and the opportunity for spiritual formation is lost.**

Ironically, this all takes place amidst devastating postmodern critiques upon modern psychotherapy. Amidst the evangelical and American acceptance of psychology's legitimacy, postmodern thinkers question its authority,[1] challenge the kind of character it produces,[2] chastise its alignment with individualist, self-centered culture,[3] uncover the nonscientific interpretive nature of its enterprise,[4] and assail it for its complicity with certain power interests of society.[5] In short, the purveyors of postmodern hermeneutics shake the foundations of psychology as practiced in the modern world. And they reveal just how much we evangelicals are married to modernity in the way we collaborate with therapy as an extension of the church.

Even more illuminating, however, these postmodern critiques awaken us to the possibility that the church may be "giving away" the spiritual formation of her people to the modern therapists. Postmodern critics argue that therapy forms "selves." They warn that therapy cannot help but form a particular kind of character in its patients. Therapists train the patient to look constantly inward and to center oneself on one's emotions. Therapists ask constantly, "What does that say about you?" As a result, modern therapy cannot help but shape a certain kind of person. If all goes well, the patient may emerge as more efficient, independent, emotionally in control, and capable of functioning in democratic capitalist society. But is this the character we want as Christians? Yet rarely is the question asked, "Is this the character of Christ?" Postmodernity uncovers the reality that evangelicals may be "giving away" spiritual formation in the ways we make use of modern therapy in our churches.

The following chapter describes the postmodern critique of psychology. It will illustrate how psychology can produce character in individuals that works against living the Christian life. It also shows how evangelicals "give away" spiritual formation when they sponsor therapy as the means to emotional health as defined by modernity. The chapter will finally illumine the need for evangelicals to recapture spiritual formation for the church of Jesus Christ and point to some practices for the church that can recapture "therapy" for the kingdom of God and his lordship.

The Therapist Revealed

Evangelicals give surprising authority to modern psychology and its therapy. We regularly go to outside therapists for guidance. We allow the therapist to function autonomously as an avenue for emotional and spiritual healing. This is largely because evangelicals accept psychology as a scientific medical enterprise. That, for evangelicals, lends psychology an inherent authority. We may see the need for psychology to be informed by Scripture.[6] But for evangelicals, this most often takes the form of harmonizing the truths of Scripture with the truths of psychology. We see psychology and Scripture as two different approaches to the same knowledge that lead to the same truth, the same core experiences, and the same realities. Psychology is based upon science and scriptural accounts are based upon God's revelation. And so the two should naturally harmonize. Evangelicals see no problem with this.

But the writers of postmodern hermeneutics reveal how psychology is not the so-called objective science it claims to be.[7] They uncover that all sciences, hard or soft, are not neutral producers of objective truth to be harmonized in one great "university."[8] And this is especially true of psychology. For postmodern hermeneutics, psychology is an interpretive enterprise that shapes the very way we make sense out of our lives and see the world. For sure, there are so-called facts upon which these various therapeutic theories are based, but they are no less an interpretation of a person's life than a religious narrative.[9] Each psychologist interprets a patient's problems according to preconceptualized language and a list of dysfunctions. A therapist will interpret your disorder differently according to a Freudian model versus a Jungian or a Rogerian or a Behaviorist model. Psychology is not objective, scientific truth in the modernist sense. It is a structure for the interpretation and understanding of self-identity.[10] In the world of postmodern thought, schools of psychology have as much interpretation in them as any religious history or other system of knowledge.

> **Psychology is an interpretive enterprise that shapes the very way we make sense out of our lives.**

As a result, postmodern writers reveal how the therapist occupies the power position over the patient. Not only is psychology an interpretive structure to help me understand and interpret my life. As German philosopher Jürgen Habermas has detailed, the therapist sits in a position of power over me imposing this prestructured story line upon how I am recounting my life.[11] The patient is virtually submitting his or her life to be analyzed and renarrated according to a particular brand of psychology. As postmodern thinker Michel Foucault enumerated, the psychologist is one of modernity's pervasive means of structuring the self, what Foucault labels as the "technology of the self." He labels the psychiatrist as "the master of truth" for the patient.[12] Therapists might say things such as, "This is your work," or "Only you can decide that," but the questions belie the formation going on. I am learning the language of self-control with the understandings the therapist gives me to understand what that means. This process is never questioned because the therapist operates under the cloak of authority provided by modernity (and medical science). So not only does therapy mold the character and emotions of the patient, it operates from the power position to do so.

> **Therapy is spiritual formation of a suspicious kind. It is the formative religion of democratic capitalism.**

And so, as with Foucault, it would be naïve for us to think that there are not power interests at work in therapy. We should be asking whether the goal of most therapy is to better acclimate the patient to a manageable life in democracy and capitalism. We should examine whether or not the stresses we seek to deal with better or the depressions we seek to manage are not themselves the product of the demands of an excessive capitalist culture or the thin purposes offered to us by a democratic culture of self-fulfillment. Is the psychologist's office in fact a place for the shaping of our characters to become better suited to live in our sick society? Therapy therefore is spiritual formation of a suspicious kind. It is the formative religion of democratic capitalism.[13]

Giving Away Christian Formation in the Name of Therapy

Once we see psychology in these terms, we see that therapy is not necessarily always aligned with the Christian's spiritual formation. Before postmodernity, we could have believed that counseling at worst was a benign enterprise causing no harm. If it did no good, at least it did no harm. But postmodernity dispels this myth. As we now see, psychology shapes the very way I make sense out of my life and see the world. It is an interpretive scheme into which I give my life to be understood, narrated, and formed.

Psychotherapy therefore is a powerful form of spiritual formation. It does all the things Christianity is supposed to do in terms of one's spiritual formation. When we walk into the psychologist's office, we submit ourselves to the therapist's interpretations. As in a confessional of old, we recall our pasts and then together with the therapist we interpret them. In the therapist's office, we interpret our pasts via the language of dysfunction, codependence, inner child, and other languages of therapy. In the Christian confession we interpret our pasts through the language of sin, redemption, and the story of forgiveness through Christ's sacrifice on the cross. Our identities are shaped through these understandings. Each is a narrative out of which I interpret my life. Christianity enables me to see my life in certain terms, make sense out of my life and my experience and myself in certain ways. Psychology does the same. In the light of postmodern hermeneutics, both practices powerfully shape spiritual formation.

Psychology and Christianity, however, may differ in important ways. In contrast to most evangelical assumptions, psychology may provide me with interpretations of myself and ways of seeing the world that diverge dramatically from the ways of the gospel of Jesus Christ. There is a difference, for instance, between construing something as a dysfunction and as something labeled as sin. These are two different languages, two different meanings, two different shapings of experiences. There may be stark differences in the ways each one deals with anger. For instance, some Jungian psychologists recommend getting in touch with my anger, retrieving from my past a destructive voice from a negative parental figure and acting out the killing of that voice in a psychodrama. A Christian pastor on the other hand might recommend recognizing injustice and sin done against me in my past, being righteously angry, and dealing with those sins through a forgiveness born out of a relationship with Jesus Christ.

The two approaches differ in the way reality is construed, the way each one sees the world, and the quality and shape of the experience produced. The Jungian-formed person experiences the resolution of anger through separating from and eliminating the cause of injustice in the past. The Christian-formed person recognizes the injustice through anger, seeks healing from the damage, and resolves the anger relationally by extending mercy and forgiveness to the cause, doing so out of a relationship of forgiveness in Christ. Jungians and Christians may both forgive, but Christians forgive out of recognizing and experiencing their own forgiveness in the cross of Christ. The cross of Christ produces a forgiveness that is different in texture and depth to the forgiveness formed by Jungian psychodrama. It reunites the victim and the victimizer in the way psychology cannot. And each forgiveness produces a different kind of character peculiar to its own narration of the world.

It turns out then that Christianity and psychology do not necessarily lead to the same truth and experience. Instead, they are two different ways of interpreting our reality, producing two different ways of experiencing and living in the world. Indeed, it is possible that psychology and Christianity may diametrically oppose one another. As sociologist Phillip Rieff has argued, there is nothing at stake in a therapeutic understanding of the world beyond "a manipulatable sense of well-being."[14] Psychology focuses the patient on "self-actualization" while Christianity teaches the patient to "deny oneself and pick up one's cross and follow Christ." Psychology aims for satisfaction in one's self while Christianity aims for a satisfaction in Christ. Psychology looks inward for goals and well-being; Christianity looks outward toward God and his purposes.[15] Psychology and Christ therefore form two different kinds of people. We can no longer naïvely say psychology is true because it is science and "all truth is God's truth." Now the all-important question for the Christian entering therapy becomes, Out of what story will I allow my life to be formed, Jung (or some other theorist) or Christ?

Despite this incompatibility, under modernist assumptions about psychology most secular and Christian psychologists operate as if secular psychological insights and principles are in effect religion-neutral and can be applied equally to all religions. They believe that by ensuring that the therapy is client centered, therapy will not intrude upon an individual's beliefs. "Christian psychologists" consider therapy to be Christian when it is framed with questions like "What role does God play in this?" or "How can you draw on your relationship with Christ to get strength to pursue this?" Perhaps a proof text or two will be used by a therapist to reinforce a therapeutic insight. Nevertheless, the discernments and interpretations remain Jungian, Freudian, or Rogerian. The goal remains self-centered not Christ-centered. The "rights and wrongs" are framed out of the structure of modern therapy. The answers are determined by the structure of modern therapy. Yet evangelicals so widely accept the modern myth of psychology's harmony with Christianity that we overlook the kind of character being produced in the psychologist's office. We baptize the formative powers of therapy with Christianity even though it produces character that adapts to the purposes of living better in capitalism, consumerism, career-ism, and not necessarily the kingdom of God.

In essence then, to give such elevated authority to the psychologist is to make a religious decision as profound as opening oneself up in faith to the Christian preaching of the cross. Therapy isolated from the church and in the power position over the use of Scripture threatens the Christian's spiritual formation. This is what postmodern hermeneutics illumines. In essence this results in the "giveaway" of the Christian's spiritual formation to therapeutic places outside of the lordship of Christ.

> To give such elevated authority to the psychologist is to make a religious decision as profound as opening oneself up in faith to the cross.

The Example of Jungian Psychology

To expand further on this "giveaway" to modern therapy, let us look closer at the example of Jungian psychology and its relation to Christianity.[16] We could choose another school for illustration purposes. But Jungian psychology is especially popular among Christians and provides a case study of how Christians try to Christianize therapy.

Robert Moore and other Jungian thinkers have popularized the thera-pies of Jung among men's movements in the last twenty years. Many Christians have used its powerful tools in their own healing and the start-ing of various therapeutic programs themselves.[17] One possible reason for this popularity of Jungian therapy among Christians is that Jung's approach (such as his push for the integration of the self, the recognition of emotional energy, and its proper "canalization" and overall integra-tion within the self's structures) pushes several buttons for children of Christian fundamentalism. It undoes the muting or repressing of the emotions and desires that is necessary under a fundamentalist system of salvation where you get "justified by faith" and then proceed to a military mechanical approach of living in order to live under the demands of that salvation. At the same time, sin is recognized through "the shadow" and "shadow work" in Jung, and the integrity that is demanded in Jungian therapy coincides with the Christian value of honesty and confession. Indeed, the Jungian retrieval of emotions and the unwinding of past negative associations in personal histories can act as a necessary structure for repentance and restitution, something that evangelicals don't get to do very often in church.

But some of the differences between Jungian therapy and Christianity are striking when it comes to spiritual formation. For instance, let us look at how one interprets one's actions in terms of sin/shadow. For Christians, we come to see our pride and self-deception as "sin," which at their root are efforts to overreach our boundaries as creatures of the Creator. We have stepped out of God's design and purposes for our lives. We have attempted to secure our own existence over against our dependence upon our Lord and Savior.[18] We repent and move toward the pursuit of God's purposes through knowing the world under his sovereign will.

For Jungians, however, we come to understand disorder in our lives in terms of our "shadow." Jungians seek to bring up these "animal spirits" from inside themselves and productively channel them. For Jungians, repressing them leads to disorder and perverse manifestation of these energies elsewhere. These energies must be brought to the surface and individuated. Through accessing an archetype like Warrior, these energies can then be transformed into life-enhancing forms of self-expression. There is a difference therefore between the Christian disciple locating one's sin and forming character around Christian visions for one's life and the Jungian patient bringing up emotions, integrating them through the "proper channeling" of the Jungian patient's "shadow." The Christian experience of disorder is shaped in relation to submission to our Creator and his designs for our lives found in our history in the Scriptures. The Jungian patient's experience is shaped by a reordering of energies toward an archetypal symbol, found in the myths of the human subconscious. The Christian experience is centered outside itself, the Jungian looks within. The two experiences are different and will shape two different kinds of persons.

Let us look again (as mentioned above) at Jungian psychodrama as another striking example of the differences between Christian and Jungian spiritual formation. For the Jungian, when there is dissonance within a person between a parental figure telling him "you are no good" and another voice, a healed parental figure telling him "you are worthy," the patient often is invited to act out through psychodrama the murdering of the bad parent and the keeping of the good parent. This imagery, perhaps useful in some contexts outside of Christ, goes against the Christian approach to conflict born out of the forgiveness available in a relationship with God through Jesus Christ. The Christ-follower certainly will be angry and it will be a righteous examined anger (Eph. 4:26; cf. Ps. 4:4), but the next step is to engage this person in forgiveness, and we do it out of a perception that we too have been forgiven by the grace of God (Matt. 6:12–14; 18:27). We do it out of a character formed (maybe in that moment) in the perception that the God of Jesus Christ is sovereign and working for the redemption of all people, and despite the evil, he is at work in all things (Eph. 3:20; Prov. 16:4–5). In this perception of the world, should the patient embrace it, we have our anger formed by a forgiving God's actions toward us. Christian interpretation therefore shapes our emotions differently from the Jungian forms of interpretation.

This illustrates something fundamental to postmodern understandings of how the self is constructed: emotions, desires, and experience are all socially constructed. There are no uninterpreted emotions. They are not merely primal emotions given through evolution. Emotions are social constructions, and different interpretations or constructions will form different emotions.[19] In therapy therefore we not only retrieve primal energies or past emotions, but we are actually forming them according to the way we interpret them.

Experimental psychology has substantiated this. Many emotion theorists now tell us that human emotions are formed as the result of a prior cognitive appraisal. There may be primitive emotions, visceral responses biologically received to perform certain bodily functions within us, but humans form much more complex emotions that are based upon our appraisals of reality.[20] For instance, how we perceive the value and place of work in our lives will affect what kind of frustration, anger, and happiness we experience in our work. I may be afraid of losing my job because of a recent corporate merger and an anticipated round of layoffs. I feel insecure, irritable, and frustrated. On the other hand, I may see the world in which I live as governed by the lordship of Christ where God is actively working in and around my life. As a result, I may have confidence in God's ability to lead, direct, and provide during this time if I will but engage, follow, and respond to my situation. My fear is shaped by a trust in what God is doing and I can enter the world differently with a more confident disposition. My emotions are shaped by an appraisal of reality informed by the way I see the world. My emotions are shaped by the value I put on things, the commitments I make, the social world out of which I construct my appraisals. Understood like this, therapy at its core is character formation.

And so it is at the point in therapy when emotions have been retrieved, the past renarrated, and we sit raw with our emotions, that the Christian requires descriptions and understandings of the reality as it is under the lordship of Christ in order for these emotions to be shaped into Christ.

It is at this point that the Christian seeks to form his or her emotions, desires, and character around the understanding of the world as it is in light of the life, death, and resurrection of Jesus Christ. This is spiritual formation of the purest kind. Here we Christians can face our sin out of our forgiveness in Christ. We can repent because we know we are already forgiven. Here we can share forgiveness toward others out of the knowledge of our own forgiveness. And it is at this point that Christians will form a distinct set of emotions and dispositions based upon the way they understand the world in Jesus Christ while followers of Jung will likewise form a set of emotions and character based upon the understanding of the world they are given. Our emotions are formed out of the interpretations we give to things and the world. And Christians cannot afford to give up these interpretations to the psychological languages of the therapists.

> **Our emotions are formed out of the interpretations we give to things and the world. And Christians cannot afford to give up these interpretations to the psychological languages of the therapists.**

Christians need therefore Christian understandings of their lives in order to have a therapy that forms them into Christians. Christians need exposition and application of the world according to Scripture in order to have their emotions formed out of that. In essence, Christians need some preaching and penance in the psychologist's office. They need the scriptural wisdom of the gifted priest in the confessional. These understandings provide the prescriptive descriptions of the way things are, into which we submit and form our emotions. Even if we could rely on the psychologist to lead us to a correct interpretation and reconstruction of our past histories, we still require understandings of our lives and the world in order to be shaped and formed toward the future. We need to understand where to go with our fear, anger, and sadness. We require a knowledge of who God is and how to move in trust in relation to him. We require the application of his forgiveness and the emotion-forming nourishment that comes at the Lord's Supper. We require an understanding of a good marriage, of a proper relationship to our work, of a meaning and a purpose for our life found in the kingdom of God. And for this, the Christian requires the church.

When it comes to such prescriptive understandings that form emotions, Jungian therapy offers the primal archetypes such as the King, Warrior, Magician, Lover archetypes offered by Robert Moore.[21] Beyond the vision of the integration of our beings with the shadow side of our existence, the followers of Jung call for the patient to get in touch with, access, and align himself with the "energy" of the archetypal images. According to Jungians, these are primal imprints available to us all. There is no need to mention a particular god behind these images, as these primal archetypes are seen across the wide visage of world religions and mythologies. This hero has "a thousand faces."[22] It is "in-born" in our "natural history."[23] And so Robert Moore, Joseph Campbell, and other Jungian thinkers will offer numerous examples throughout mythology as well as Christianity of the archetypes. Influenced strongly by the "history of religions" approach to theology, Moore and his colleagues homogenize all religions into one primal experience and kindly allow the patient to plug in his or her particular god.

But is this really a primal experience or is it a very specific interpretation of religious experience forced upon other religions and mythologies in an imperialistic manner? Is it Campbell and Moore forcing other religions into their favorite "Jungianized" version of Western democratic liberal manhood? Though these archetypes are offered as primal experiences within us, they offer particular powerful interpretations for our lives in the forming of who we are to be. They prescribe a certain kind of marriage and a certain view of work and a certain approach to community and celebration. And as we compare, we discover that there is a difference between a husband of the archetypal "Warrior King energies" and Ephesians 5 where the husband gives himself up for his wife as Christ did for the church.[24] There is no escaping it. The archetypes are a substantive vision for our lives as strong as any other particular religion, and they are different from the Christian vision found in Scriptures and heard in its faithful preaching.

This is sometimes missed because most Jungian psychologists again understand their therapy to be "patient-centered." "This is your work," the therapist tells the patient. What particular faith the patient chooses is up to the individual and does not diminish the effectiveness of the therapy. The therapy will only bring the patient in touch with his or her own emotions. The patient will be brought to his or her own resolution and management of these emotions through the integrity of the process and the patient's own participation. There is no enforcement of a right or wrong upon the patient. There is supposedly no one doctrine enforced upon the patient as morally true. All of this is supposed to come from the patient. The archetypes are universally true and lie within. If the patient is a Christian, the patient may simply choose to use his or her chosen faith in the process. The patient can fill in the blank with "Jesus" for these statements: my higher power is _____, or my god is _____. The therapeutic approach is most at home in America where individualism and tolerance are the most prized values. But this approach still is not Christianity because Jesus becomes interpreted via Jungian therapy and practices. Jesus is domesticated on Jungian terms. Jesus becomes a "higher power" subservient to the religious imperialism of the archetypal interpretation of all religions. The patient becomes a Jungian user of Jesus, not a follower of Christ.

And again, these interpretations cannot help but form a certain kind of person. This Jungianized self-actualization will form a highly autonomous, individualized person who views and interprets work, marriage, and the other aspects of his life in the terms of individualized, self-expressivist goals. In Jungian language, these are the goals of Jungian wholeness of the psyche where the various energies and drives are brought into individuation and integration. Even though I may have "plugged in" Jesus, I am becoming a person quite different from the one envisioned who "must deny himself, and take up his cross and follow" Christ (Matt. 16:24).

The therapeutic approach is most at home in America where individualism and tolerance are the most prized values.

As a result, marriage for the Jungian will often become a negotiation of the fulfillment of needs and desires. For the follower of Christ on the other hand, marriage models Christ's relationship to the church (Ephesians 5). It is a place of commitment to the other in vulnerability for the purposes of mutual growth, the raising of children, and the fulfillment of God's purposes for their lives for the glory of his kingdom. For the Jungian, work becomes an expression of a passion, something "I want to do." For the Christian, work can be a vocational space, an offering unto God, to be inhabited for the glory of God in all excellence, integrity, and gratitude. It is here that we discover that the Jungian interpretation and goals for the self may not be the same as the Christian gospel's. And it is here that we discover just how different the kinds of people are that Jungian therapy forms versus the life of Christ.

We see then that psychotherapy is a work of spiritual formation as profound as any religious conversion. It offers a vision of how we should live. For Jung it is the goal of the integration of the self, a depth equilibrium where the various opposing pieces of the self as evidenced through energy sources become integrated, managed productively, and unified in a way that is harmonious with certain primal archetypal visions. For Christians it is the vision of a life redeemed from sin through the forgiveness of the cross of Christ to live out the full purposes of God in creation as described over the pages of the story of Scripture. As with all psychologies, Jungians must have a vision of what is healthy and what is unhealthy as well as what is appropriate and what is inappropriate

Psychotherapy is a work of spiritual formation as profound as any religious conversion.

behavior, in order to conduct therapy. Christians have the same. In any therapy there are good and bad reasons for guilt. It tells us what is right and what is wrong. Christians have the same. By its very nature Jungian therapy, as in all psychology, is a confessional that forms our lives in the deepest and most religious of ways. Christianity is the same. So for the Christian to be a Christian in all of this, one must subsume one's therapy to the faithful preaching of the story of Jesus's death and resurrection. For the Christian, not only can Jungian psychology not stand alone, it must be subservient to the preaching of the cross.

On Making Therapy Christian: Why There Is No Therapy Apart from the Church

The above does not mean that Christians have nothing to learn from psychology. Indeed, we should not ignore therapy's profound effects upon people's lives both in and outside the church. The intense communities of AA (Alcoholics Anonymous) and other addiction recovery groups serve as models for what we have lost in evangelical churches. These powerful therapies serve to call evangelical churches to the practices of confession, repentance, and learning to speak truth in love in the context of community. Evangelicals have lost practices like these. Today, the practice of confession rarely happens among evangelicals except possibly at heightened so-called revivals. We have much to learn from Jungian and other traditions of therapy.

We can learn from the therapists how necessary it is for Christians to unwind personal past history (James 5:16), speak truth in love (Eph. 4:15, 25), be accountable, and "be a mirror" one to another (Eph. 5:11–14). We can learn the necessity of owning our sin and restitution. Since Protestantism rejected the practice of penance, we have lost these sacred practices of spiritual formation and we need to retrieve them. We can also recognize the ways depression changes the balance of chemical relationships in the body and seek medical practices to address such changes in ways that are faithful to Christ. All of these therapeutic practices make sense for the Christian. But all this will be for naught for the Christian, if he or she is not shaped out of these places into the character and will of Christ.

This is why therapy requires Christian preaching, teaching, and wisdom. Preaching provides the language of sin, which in turn makes possible the retrieval and interpretation of our pasts specifically as Christians. The church community provides the context of acceptance and forgiveness by God through the cross of Christ, which makes possible the confession of our sin and the removal of repression and denial in the Christian life. Scripture provides powerful visions of life under his lordship, which makes possible the forming of our emotions and desires for marriage, for our work responsibilities, for our responsibilities to justice, and every area of our life as it is within the kingdom of God. And above all, preaching provides the call to faith and openness to the power of the resurrected Lord in the person of the Holy Spirit, which makes possible a redemption and a healing that is beyond what is possible in other human terms. These are all skills of the body of Christ (1 Corinthians 12). Christian therapy therefore needs the body of Christ.

But we cannot do therapy like this sitting in the pew. Because evangelicals are so sermon-centric, we are tempted to think good therapy happens by taking good notes in the pew. But ironically, the more we concentrate on good biblical instruction as central to the Christian life, the less we talk to each other about our lives and especially about sin. Most of our "small group" processes are either inductive Bible studies or involve more intense, scholarly study of the Bible that never deals with the emotional and character issues that are destroying our lives. It is a testament to how unsafe the church has become for sinners that we rarely discuss with each other our sin and failures and seek the healing of the Holy Spirit. Rarely do we have confession and repentance in our "small groups." We need to find safe places where we can share our lives, confess our sins, receive scriptural wisdom, and be prayed for. To do this, we cannot just get together and simply share our sins and quote Bible verses at each other. We must retrieve from therapy the needed skills to practice biblical confession and bring it under the lordship of Christ. This is of utmost importance to the future of spiritual formation in the evangelical church.

The postmodernist Michel Foucault argued that the confessional of the medieval church was the means of structuring "the self" in the European Middle Ages. For Foucault, the confessional formed the very identities of medieval persons within the language of sin, and the practices of repentance and restitution. He skillfully showed how the church's sacrament of penance was then recodified into psychology and its practices through modern science.[25] The ways of Christianity, the "denying of our selves," were replaced by the secular discourses of the psychiatric institutions and modern science.[26] Foucault wrote of the power interests of psychiatric care that lurk within a society, which depends upon consumption and the myth of self-determination. Psychiatry was forming different "selves" for different purposes (power interests) than the church. His analysis compels all Christians to consider the many ways in which evangelical churches "give away" the formation of our selves to secular forces of therapy under the legitimating discourse of modern science. It is the "giveaway" of the formation of our "selves" into Christ.

We should take back the confessional from modern psychology and return it to the church.

I contend that the evangelical church should respond to the Foucaultian transformation by undoing it. We should take back the confessional from modern psychology and return it to the church. The church should engage the practices of psychology and take up the ones that make sense under Jesus's lordship and form confessional communities. By so doing, the church can bring therapy back to its rightful home for Christians, the body of Christ. Therapy outside the church will form persons into ways of seeing, values, purposes, and the language of the world, most likely using some utilitarian school of therapy such as Freud, Jung, Rogers, or Adler. Christian therapy will form persons into ways of seeing, values, purposes, and the language of the world where Jesus is Lord. For the Christian therefore there can be no real therapy outside the church. We should bring therapy back into the church.

Practices for Returning to Confession

Recapture the Confessional

Evangelicals, like all Christians, need therapy. We need a therapy as defined by the epistle of James: "Confess your sins one to another, and pray for one another so that you may be healed" (James 5:16). We need therapy to unwind our pasts, uncover our sins, receive forgiveness, and then forgive. We need therapy to physically receive absolution and engage restitution under the cross of Jesus Christ, a place akin to the Roman "confessional." We need therapy that intervenes by speaking truth in love into our lives when we are blinded from seeing our own sinful patterns, interventions akin to the old Christian Anabaptist practices of "binding and loosing" where two or three gather to confront on truth (Matt. 18:15–20).[27] We need therapy for direction and wisdom when we don't know how to make a decision, akin to the old Wesleyan "class meeting." We need a therapy born of the Spirit and the discursive powers of Holy Scripture set loose in the Christian community. We require such practices that bring us together to work out our salvation in "fear and trembling" (Phil. 2:12).

To do this kind of "therapy" we need safe and confidential places in our churches to confess, discern, receive scriptural admonition and wisdom, and support and edify one another. One such place Christian therapy could be practiced is within the ever popular "small group" so common in evangelical churches. Yet we need to go beyond mere inductive Bible study and the intellectual study of Scripture. We need a small group where we can confess sin, locate sin, and deal with sin in a restituting manner. We need a small group where we can hear truth spoken into each other's lives. We need a small group where we can discern what lies immediately ahead for obedience as a confessional community empowered by the Spirit and guided by prayer. We need a small group where we can do all this guided in Scripture under Christ's lordship. These groups will need to be as confidential as the "Roman confessional." These groups will need to be as reconciling as an Anabaptist community. These groups must be as intrusive and accountable as the old Wesleyan "class meeting."

> **One such place Christian therapy could be practiced is within the ever popular "small group." Yet we need to go beyond mere intellectual study of Scripture.**

In our church, these groups are most often formed in threes. They are small enough to be both intimate and yet safe and confidential. We call them "triads." We carry on three simple practices: (a) checking in with what has happened in our lives since we last met, (b) confession of sin and restitution (James 5:16), and (c) "putting things out into the light" and "speaking truth in love" into each other's lives (Eph. 4:14–15; 5:11–13). After each confession of sin, we hear the words "We have heard your confession, and in Christ Jesus you are already forgiven and loved." When we speak truth into each other's lives we read Scripture as the basis of our comments. In these groups, people often recount their past, become transparent and honest about it, and retrieve it. The group often facilitates a conversation to explore the location of sin. Pastoral direction is available when needed. In these groups, people often take in Christ's forgiveness anew and in time forgive others. In these groups, we often choose paths of restitution and new life. Many times we confess new commitments for the first time before a community of memory. Often powerful emotions are dealt with as if we are in a therapist's office. Every time we meet, we baptize our discernments with prayer, putting all under the lordship of Christ.

These practices of confession and penance are a therapy as profound as any found in the therapist's office. Such spiritual formation practices form desires, emotions, experiences, and a character that is different from those formed by Jungian or any other kind of therapy. It trains people like Jim, at the beginning of this chapter, to see suffering and depression in the ways of Christ, to develop new emotions for the sufferings we must go through, and to overthrow patterns of thought that are foreign to the gospel. Such triads for our church are powerful places of formation where the body comes together in the gifts of the Holy Spirit to be formed into Christ.

These triads resemble the confessional in the Roman Catholic Church. They also resemble the old original Wesleyan "class meetings."[28] The loss of the Wesleyan class meeting in North America testifies to the church's capitulation to modernity.[29] But if we would recover the mission of the church from the giveaway of spiritual formation in our times, these "meetings" may be precisely the practices that could lead the way.

Practice Therapist Agreements within the Church

The church I believe still needs her therapists. Yet a therapist detached from the church can foster the "giveaway" of our spiritual formation. The therapist hears only one side of the story for an hour a week. Therapy can therefore become a dividing discourse over against a spouse who is left out of the therapy, or a church or friends or a co-worker. In addition, Scripture can become the tool of therapy and thus subordinate to therapy when such therapy is separated from the worship of the church. So even if the therapist uses Scripture, if he or she is not worshiping God with the patient, the therapist inevitably must resort to interpreting Scripture for whatever lies expedient ahead, not the outworking of Scripture in a body of people.

These problems can be avoided through the regular practice of therapist agreements within the church. Here the therapist, through some form of an agreement, becomes a co-laborer alongside the small group, the pastor, the elder, and the patient. Through some form of agreement, the therapist, patient, church elder, and small group all become partners for the healing and edification of the patient. They all become available to the therapist to check out truth claims, hold each other in accountability, and oversee the whole process under the lordship of Christ and governance of Scripture. This defies current rules of professional conduct. And admittedly our church has been unable to accomplish a therapist relationship like this. It is likely that such a church-therapist working relationship agreement is impossible for all but the biggest of churches that can hire in-house therapists. Nonetheless, evangelicals need to explore this kind of internal communal relationship for its churches. And evangelical schools of psychology must seek new ways to train practitioners for the future Christian confessionals that evangelical churches sorely lack.

Therefore the role of therapy for the Christian needs to be returned to the church where faithful preaching exists and scriptural wisdom resides to form faithful lives. Return the therapists to the church. They can do everything they do out there in here but with the explicit commitment to the gospel out of which we understand and illumine our lives in terms of the person and work of Christ. Confession, the articulation of past mistakes and past sins done to us, should be going on in the church where the forgiveness of Christ can shape our guilt and shame and can form our anger toward those who have harmed us. Repentance and the disavowal of past mistakes and wrong patterns should be conducted in the church where faith in the sovereign God acting in Christ can help lead us into the formation of new experiences our bodies and minds do not yet know because we have been held addicted to the chains of sinful patterns for so long. To escape these, we need faith and openness to the work of God to accomplish things we cannot think or imagine (Eph. 3:20). And the work of describing what it is we want in our marriages, our work, our communities, our worship, our celebrations, and the total ordering of our lives should take place in the church where the vision of what God's glorious kingdom in redeeming all creation calls us to, and can be made clear and powerfully attractive out of the story of Scripture. In short, the church needs to return to being a community of confessional practices, and I am sure the therapists, under an allegiance to the cross of Christ, can help us in that.

8

Moral Education

Evangelicals and the Training of Our Children
to Be Good Americans: The Example of Character
Education in the Public Schools

Train up a child in the way he should go:
and when he is old, he will not depart from it.

Proverbs 22:6 KJV

And you shall teach these ways diligently to your children and shall talk
of them when you sit in your house and when you walk by the road, and
when you lie down and when you get up.

Deuteronomy 6:7, my paraphrase

Every pastor knows the difficulty of getting church started on time. Some
say it is a cultural thing and of course that is true. Yet if we took a survey,
the average evangelical parishioner who cannot make it to Sunday worship on time would rarely report late for work, for the start of a movie,
or for a sporting event. I have equally noticed the same problems with
Christian parents (of many different evangelical churches) in getting
their children to Sunday morning catechesis on time and regularly. Yet

here too these same parents probably rarely allow their children to be late for public school and they probably get their children to the soccer, music, and art activities on time come hell or high water. These patterns of behavior, I contend, reveal an understanding about moral education that is prevalent among North American evangelicalism in general.

Many evangelicals treat Christian education (and church for that matter) as though it is one more educational activity alongside many others. It is important and no child should be without it. But at the end of a busy week (although Sunday really is the beginning of the week) with all kinds of activities we can only do our best. And maybe since we are not paying directly for it, or being graded, or since maybe it will not harm my child's economic future or my child's ability to compete in sports, music, or art, I can be a little less frantic about getting my child to his or her Christian education class. After all, what is most important is that my child learns how to think, compete, develop his or her whole personality, and make independent decisions. Evangelicals certainly expect their churches to teach the basic foundational knowledge of the Bible to their children. But after all is said and done, moral education and Christian education are still the job of the family. And so "yes," the church is important, but the family ultimately can make up for any lacks the child might experience from missing church.

If the above in any way accurately describes a portion of evangelical churches, then we evangelicals are facing a significant challenge in the moral education of our children. Because as critics of modernity contend, education is not so much about information as it is about formation. And our children are being less and less formed by Christian ways as they spend more and more time being shaped by the educational forces of our post-Christian culture. And so our modern notions of education may be failing us. The statistics suggest that more of our children are deserting the church at the time they leave for college.[1] We must then ask, In the post-Christian culture of North America, are the ways we prepare and initiate children for the life of following Christ adequate for the day?

The following chapter pursues this question by looking closely at the ways Christians think about public education and the notion of character education in the public schools. It reveals the ways public education teaches our children in ways we never contemplated. And so when we get our children to public school on time and to their various sporting events, we must ask, In what ways is their character being trained? Could it be that we are "giving away" the moral education of our children to the forces of American society and leaving their Christian education behind as an afterthought? A close look at our assumptions about public schooling reveals the ways our children's character is being formed away from Christ and how we must reclaim catechesis for our children in a living body of Christ if we have any hope of raising our children to be followers of Christ in a post-Christian North America.

Evangelicals, Church, and Public Schools: The Current State of Evangelical Moral Education

Most evangelicals are comfortable with modern notions of education. In other words, we subscribe to teaching our children to think critically, to develop the child's creative personality, and to learn basic technical skills and foundational knowledge necessary for living in the modern world. Going back to John Dewey, we agree that education must flourish the individual by teaching him or her how to function as a thinking contributor within democracy and to develop one's full actualization as a person.[2] These modern ideas translate into our Christian education, when we emphasize the individual development of the child's "personal relationship" with God and the delivery of basic information each child needs to read his or her own Bible and know right from wrong. These emphases are still important. Yet in the process, evangelicals can overlook the need for a living community of Christ to habituate our children into Christ and form their character. As a result, we separate our children into classes away from the parents and teach them foundational knowledge. In worship and in fellowship, evangelicals tend to isolate the youth into their own "youth groups" away from the adults. By so doing, we separate the youth from the social world of adults who can model the life we are teaching. Unintentionally then, evangelicals quarantine the development of the individual child from the community at large. In these ways, evangelicals follow the modernist individualist developmental approach to education.

Evangelicals further reveal their modern prejudices toward education when we resist formal initiation processes in our educational programs. Most evangelicals are foreign to the notions of a first communion, a confirmation ritual, or a baptism that has significant initiatory processes around it. In modernist fashion, evangelicals view Christianity as a set of beliefs not a way of life that one must be initiated into.[3] We lack the sense that Christian education initiates our children into the world of following Christ and in the process must equip them for engaging the cultural forces of the secular world.[4] So we educate for individualist developmental goals, skills for personal Christian development. We don't do catechesis, the initiating of the child into the language and ways of Christian life and practice. We treat Christian education as another educational piece alongside several others in a whole developmental program for our young. As a result, sixteen years into our children's lives, evangelical parents often find their children oriented to another world, entirely different from the Christian world the adults know and assumed their children were learning. We are surprised when we discover that our teenagers are governed more by the secular cultures of media, sports, and capitalism than the ways of Christ.

In modernist fashion, evangelicals view Christianity as a set of beliefs not a way of life that one must be initiated into.

This evangelical understanding of education is reflected in how we engage public schools. When we send our children to public schools, we engage the issues of information that offend Christian sensibilities such as sex education or the teaching of evolution. We ignore, however, the character-forming effects of the public school's culture upon our children. Evangelicals do not readily see that the public school is a community inducting students into a way of life, the ways of democracy and capitalism. We push for "good grades" from our children while we ignore how the school's culture promotes certain goals, visions, and character traits that may impede living life as a Christian. We argue for the right to pray in public schools but ignore how learning to pray to the pluralist god(s) doesn't teach our children how to pray at all if we are Christians. We don't see that our children are being initiated into a way of life foreign to the gospel through secular media and public schooling. Meanwhile we often lack a compelling alternative way of life in the church that we attend hurriedly one hour a week on Sunday. Capitalist society fragments our lives so much that the church can at most be just another fragmented moment in the child's life in order to get some needed religious information to the child. In the meantime, the thirty or so hours spent at public schools every week are powerfully initiating our young into America's way of life, and by default our children receive it.

This issue is not easily solved by other options to public schooling. Many evangelical parents opt for homeschooling when they recognize the problems with public schools. But without the compelling way of life (in the church) discussed above, the child is still left without a community and culture to be initiated into. Homeschooling may protect children and teach technical skills and information well, but apart from the church, homeschooling still lacks when it comes to an initiation into a way of life that is bigger than one's own family. In regard to the option of parochial schooling as part of the local church, evangelicals have traditionally lagged behind their Roman Catholic and mainline European Protestant church counterparts. And when we do erect parochial schools we often model them after the public schools except for some curriculum omissions and an occasional chapel. Evangelicals seem oblivious to the reality that our children's moral education must be about initiating our young into a way of life. Sadly, evangelical ways of educating children remain impotent in the face of the secular post-Christian cultural forces forming our children.

I contend then that in many instances, evangelicals unintentionally "give away" the training of their children's moral character to the public schools and the other cultural forces of our day. Because of our modernist understandings of education (described above), our children's education cannot help but be irresistibly centered elsewhere than in the church of Jesus Christ. Because we teach Christian life through the passing of information in a small time frame on Sunday morning, our efforts are dwarfed by the hours spent in public school, television, and children's soccer, art, and music programs. Because what we say and pass on is not backed by a powerful cultural community of life into which the children are initiated, the secular culture overwhelms our children by the time they are sixteen. Through our modernist methods therefore I contend we "give away" our children's moral education to the secular post-Christian forces. As a result, our children fall victim to these forces. And they are left bereft of the skills needed to live the Christian life in a world that no longer knows God exists. And when the time comes to send our children off to college or into the workplace, our children are better trained to be good Americans than followers of Jesus Christ. The virtues of their character are more aligned with American aspirations than those of the people of God. In the face of current postmodern cultural challenges, evangelical churches therefore need to become communities of faith that initiate and nurture children into the ways of Christian life. We need to find practices of community and catechesis that train our young *out* of the world and *into* Christ.

There is no better illustration of this "giveaway" than the Christian collaboration with public schools in the teaching of character. Evangelicals among other Christians support character education in public schools as a positive development for their children.[5] Yet I contend that such character education cannot help but initiate our young into Americanism in ways unbeknownst to evangelical parents. Evangelicals therefore cheerfully "give away" our children's character formation to non-Christian processes. In what follows, using former U.S. Secretary of Education William J. Bennett's proposals for teaching character as a test case, I will describe how virtues taught by public schools become powerfully imbued with the values of liberal democracy and market capitalism and therefore train our children into a morality that is much more American than Christian. Evangelicals and other Christians may believe that good character is good for all people. But thinkers like Alasdair MacIntyre and Stanley Hauerwas reveal how there can be no universal set of virtues. Sending our children to public schools' character education classes turns out to be a "giveaway" of our Christian moral education to the ways of secular society. Evangelicals therefore should take the teaching of virtue more seriously.

Evangelicals are not alone among Christians in their general support for character education in public schools. Yet they are peculiar among churches for their resistance to formal catechesis as a rite of the church. From this analysis of teaching character in public schools, I will then suggest that evangelical churches require a new focus upon initiation and catechesis to meet the challenge of a post-Christian culture for our children. We need to reinvigorate the church as the center of our children's moral education.

The Virtues Craze

American culture had a "virtues" revival in the 1990s, and by and large evangelicals joined in. William J. Bennett's *Book of Virtues* made the *New York Times* "Best Sellers List" in 1993, followed shortly thereafter by a sequel.[6] Numerous educators pushed for teaching character and virtues in the public schools.[7] Various institutes arose to develop character curriculum for public schools (Josephson Institute, etc.). As a result, public schools all over North America now espouse that "character counts" and they teach character in public schools.[8] Evangelicals, for the most part, are their cheerleaders.[9] Opposition to "character in the public schools" comes mostly from those who see it as a breach of the separation of church and state.[10] Little or no noticeable opposition appears from evangelical concerns. Evangelicals and their publishing concerns embraced William Bennett and his *Book of Virtues*. One could assume then that evangelicals, by and large, feel more comfortable sending their children to public schools after the character education initiatives than they did before.

But do Christians share virtues in common with these public producers of virtue? Should evangelical Christians participate in public schools' character or virtues education? And if so, in what way? It certainly is a relief that schools are teaching something besides the hedonism and violence that dominate the key media of popular American culture. But is the honesty taught in the public schools the same as Christian honesty or honesty in other religious traditions? Could it be that Christian virtues like honesty, patience, and courage look a lot different when they are taught within the confines of the public schools? Could it be that these public school virtues actually obstruct the formation of Christian character in our children?

William Bennett and the Postmodern Culture

William Bennett answers these questions by asserting that there are virtues common to all Americans. Therefore Christians, evangelical Christians, and even non-Christians should all participate equally in supporting these common virtues. According to Bennett, Christians share many virtues with all Americans because we all belong to the common culture of America out of which we can form character in our children across all ethnic, cultural, and religious boundaries. For Bennett, "the vast majority of Americans share a respect for fundamental traits of character—honesty, compassion, courage and perseverance."[11] "[T]he first mistake is to say that we cannot agree on the basic traits of character we want our children to have and that we want our schools to develop."[12] There is a common culture, a common "civil religion," and a common language that unites us all that transcends cultural-religious lines.[13] All Americans, evangelical or not, should therefore feel comfortable in teaching their children common virtues based in the history and literature of the West through the public schools.[14]

> According to Bennett, Christians share many virtues with all Americans because we all belong to the common culture of America.

Evangelicals generally warm to this kind of talk. Bennett's strategy resonates with many of the popular evangelical arguments for universal moral absolutes. But recent multiculturalist and postmodern positions undercut Bennett and his defense of a "common culture." The academic fight of the 1990s for the university canon has uncovered the power associated with specific interpretations of history. It reveals a lack of consensus for which version of history we will follow in Bennett's America. Bennett's "common Western heritage" therefore is not as common as Bennett wants to assume. It is a very specific tradition that must align with specific power groups. Postmoderns approach this so-called common heritage and see specific value agendas that are capable of impinging on someone's religious values no matter how "pluralist" its appeal. America has multiple cultures with thick and living traditions. And so when we view Bennett's "common heritage" with this postmodern lens, each tradition is a powerful ideology carrying deep allegiances sometimes centuries old. Consequently, there is no common culture in Bennett's sense. Bennett's common culture and even "pluralism" itself must take its place alongside all other competing ideologies and cultural traditions and ways of life in the melting pot of American life.

Character education cannot be separated from this fragmented post-modern reality. If there are different cultures, there will be different virtues. Virtues like courage and honesty are attached to communities, ethnicities, histories and traditions, ways of life, and their corresponding purposes, agendas, and values. Following Alasdair MacIntyre, a virtue is a different thing depending upon where it comes from. It changes depending upon whether you are working out of Homer, Aristotle, or the New Testament.[15] Virtues only make sense within the moral world that created them. They are only useful and worth having when aligned with purposes and ways of life in which they make sense. They are driven by powerful ways of seeing the world, and they take shape in a person as they make sense within certain achievements and practices that are the essence of living a good life.[16] Their formation and their content are therefore dependent upon the specific cultural context that births them. And if a social context has sufficient of these resources to teach virtues, it will not only define the virtue but also support the way of life behind it. MacIntyre, postmodernism, and multiculturalism therefore uncover the painful truth: if we are really teaching virtue to our children, we are giving them a way of life. And the Christian way of life differs from other people groups in the public school. It is therefore inevitable that disagreements will appear as you must get more substantive about the cultural and religious details of the virtues you are teaching.

> If we are really teaching virtue to our children, we are giving them a way of life.

Why There Are No Universal Virtues

There still remains the allure that there are virtues that everyone can agree on. Are there not some virtues that transcend postmodern suspicions or multicultural fragmentation? Who could disagree with the virtues of honesty, courage, or courtesy? Is not Christian persever-ance the same as perseverance for a Muslim, an atheist, or an agnostic? Surely there are some virtues that are universal to all beliefs, creeds, and cultures.

A closer look at specific virtues, however, reveals how virtues become very differentiated once we define them, once we describe what they mean and show how they make sense in a social and moral world. Muslims have a certain way of seeing the world and it forms their character in specific ways. The character of a Christian is shaped by the way he or she understands the world under the lordship of Christ, the story of the cross and the resurrection, and how this defines what it means to live unto the glory of God. As Hauerwas explains, "To have Christian character is to have one's attention directed by the description of the world that claims it has been redeemed by the work of Christ."[17] It is from within the depths of these social contexts that the differences between these virtues appear.

Let us illustrate this process by using two "character words for the month" at Chicago public schools—"courtesy" and "courage."[18] At first blush, the Chicago school board is merely trying to teach our kids some civic decency and perhaps the courage to "say no to drugs." Hopefully, our children become so courteous and courageous that metal detectors, "drug free zones," and zero-tolerance policies become unnecessary. But a closer look reveals how problematic either one of these virtues can become.

"Courtesy," for instance, could require respect or ignoring someone because courtesy implies a way of seeing and respecting other human beings. It infers a basis upon which I should respect my fellow human beings. There are reasons that inform who I would respect and why I would respect that person. In some cultures "courtesy" may mean respecting all human life for its inherent dignity as rational, purposive, and valuable in God's sight. However, in places such as Chicago gang life, courtesy may mean respecting those who are like you, who wear their hat the same way, or who are in the same gang. Courtesy could even mean injuring an adversary who has injured a fellow gang member because that is how you show respect in that world. To reiterate MacIntyre's point in *After Virtue*, a concept of virtue "always requires for its application the acceptance of some prior account of certain features of social and moral life in terms of which it has to be defined and explained."[19] "Courtesy," in other words, may not mean the same thing in some cultures as it does in yours. And, as some Chicagoans know, it may not even mean the same thing in the next neighborhood.

Likewise, the virtue "courage" inevitably begs the question, Courage to do what? The nature of the virtue "courage" varies sharply between social contexts out of which we shape our values of what is courageous. I suspect that many gang members may find someone to be a coward who does not avenge a gang brother's death at the hand of the enemy gang member; others may label that courage. We may describe a bank robber who "braves" the Texas Rangers in an attempt to rob money from a small town bank in a Western movie as foolhardy; others may call it courage.[20] On the other hand, we may describe the soldier who risks his life to retrieve an already dead comrade's body on the battlefield as courageous ("We leave no one behind!"); others may call that foolhardy. In each case we distinguish courage from foolhardiness or cowardliness based upon what purposes one deems worthy of courage. Courage to say no to sexual advances or courage to make them is entirely dependent upon what one thinks are the proper ends of human sexuality. The meaning of courage then is based upon the social and religious context out of which one can learn the purposes and values behind the virtue of courage. Training a child in courage and courtesy therefore requires the defining of what each virtue looks like according to certain goods and purposes. It requires getting specific, and this inevitably exposes differences that arise out of the religious and cultural sources of these virtues.

In this way there are no universal virtues. Christian courage and courtesy should look different than other forms of courage and courtesy. If a child is going to be courageous in a Christian way, he or she will be so for different reasons. Children of Christians will be courageous out of a Christian way of seeing the world. They can be courageous because God is in control, Jesus is Lord, and "I can trust him to carry me through." In the same way, courtesy will be born out of a vision that every person in one sense or another is someone for whom Christ died. Ultimately, God is after each person to bring him or her to his full purposes, and "I may be an instrument of that redemption." Such a way of understanding reality changes the way we treat people. And so Christian courtesy is different from other forms of courtesy based outside of the social context of the history of Jesus Christ. There are no universal virtues for the Christian. And we would not be surprised that people from other religious traditions would have virtues that are not universal as well.

In the end then, teaching virtue requires an embodied tradition substantive enough to fill out what the virtues look like and why anyone would want to acquire them. This inevitably undermines any attempt to universalize a set of virtues. To teach honesty to children requires a tradition that can describe honesty, give stories that are illustrations of honesty, and give purposes and a way of life in which honesty will make sense. Without such definition, the virtues will be merely the presentation of interesting "take it or leave it" behavioral choices. They will not become indelible parts of our children's character. They will be as disposable as any other consumer product. The very mechanics of teaching character therefore work toward defining specifically a culture's religious moral purposes and values. And these very same mechanics of teaching character work against universalizing a set of virtues upon which everyone in America can agree.

The Public School's Brand of Virtues

When we understand virtues in these terms, we see that the public school itself must assume the status of a tradition in order to teach virtue successfully. In other words, the public school must give stories that are illustrations of virtues, give purposes behind the virtues, and offer a way of life in which the virtues make sense. Otherwise, the virtues will just be more information that is easily discarded when proved not useful. The virtues will not be compelling enough to make them worth learning. Yet any tradition this substantive will transgress at least some of the parents' religious or ethnic beliefs (assuming the school is pluralistic). William Bennett therefore cannot have it both ways: a tradition substantive enough to teach virtue yet a tradition weak enough to be inoffensive across religious and ethic lines. Even a set of "lowest common denominator virtues" will either teach purposes and a way of life or fail to teach character altogether. The question then for evangelicals is, Can the public schools teach our children virtues that do not impinge upon what Christians seek for their children in the Christian way of life?

To answer this question, let us look at the social context out of which the public school must define its virtues. The culture of the public schools is necessarily constructed to be a moral context upon which we can all agree. Via the U.S. court system, religious traditions are excluded from public schools by definition. The public school therefore is based upon that part of America's moral foundations that remains after taking everything out that we disagree on. It is by default a social world committed to the ethos of capitalism and self-interest because Americans can at least all agree that we must train our children to survive in the economy where it is up to each individual to compete for a job. Likewise, such a space in the public schools is committed to the ethos of democracy because Americans can at least all agree that we must train our children to get along with others that are different than us without violence. Americans can also agree that each individual "must learn to think for himself" if one is to maintain dignity in one's participation in the democratic process. In this way, capitalism, democracy, and liberalism make sense as the basis for American virtue, and any teachers teaching virtue will find it necessary to articulate virtues in line with this context.

Public school teachers therefore will not teach just any version of honesty, respect, and courage but a version that makes sense in this agreed-upon context of capitalism, democracy, and liberalism. In regard to the virtue of courtesy, therefore, the public schools will teach their children to tolerate people (with courtesy) who are different from them so that we can all get along (goals of democracy). Regarding perseverance, the public schools will teach the children to work hard and study so they can get a good paying job (capitalist pursuits). In the public schools, persistence pays off in self-reward because it leads to a job that pays money and security because these are the ultimate public goals of our society (capitalist goals). Likewise, in the public schools, temperance means practicing so-called safe sex so that you will not catch a life-threatening disease or bear children too early in life and harm your economic future. And every child will learn courage because without risk you will not achieve the rewards of your personal dreams (liberal happiness and capitalist goals). The public schools, in other words, will train our children in virtues that promote self-interest, self-flourishing, and the honoring of each person to do the same. These are the purposes of the American way of life. In this way, the public schools cannot help but socialize children to be good Americans.

Training our children to be courteous and tolerant because we all deserve the right to pursue individual freedom is different from training our children to see that each individual is a child of God born for redemption with created purposes.

Oddly, many evangelicals assume that such American virtues as courtesy and tolerance are universal or even Christian. This assumption, however, is mistaken. Training our children to be courteous and tolerant because we all deserve the right to pursue individual freedom is different from training our children to see that each individual is a child of God born for redemption with created purposes. I am sure these two virtues are related, and some may argue the liberal version is parasitic upon the Christian version, but they are not the same. Likewise, training our children in temperance because focus is necessary to be joined to God's greatest created purposes for sexuality is different from training children to be temperate for economic or physical health.

It is clear that virtues such as courtesy, temperance, and courage are different for a Christian, whose primary allegiance is to follow Christ, versus the American, whose allegiance is to individual freedom, capitalism, and success in business. These and other virtues are different for Christians who carry deeper goals and purposes for our lives than participation in a competitive economy and a liberal democracy. At the very least, a common pluralist tradition like Bennett's cannot place the cross of Christ in the same position in public schools that it has for Christians in the formation of our virtues and character. These more particular purposes, as extolled in the history of Israel and Jesus Christ, change the very substance of our virtues and the nature of our character. For the evangelical then as well as for all Christians, the virtues of a good American are not sufficient. Bennett is wrong to assert these virtues are common to us all. In fact, in some cases these virtues run counter to who we want ourselves and our children to be as followers of Christ.

The Illusion of the Tradition-Neutral Public School

This understanding of virtues shatters any illusion that the public school is a tradition-neutral place that is benign to our children's moral formation. For what we see now is that the public school, by teaching virtues, cannot help but be the purveyor of a way of life as powerful as any religion. In order to teach virtue, the public school must be a cultural world possessing a set of virtues, purposes, and ways of life all its own. Indeed, as the postmodern hermeneutic makes clear, any claim to "tradition-neutrality" is a disguised moral claim of its own. And so the public school becomes the social context to train children into the moral character of that world.

Postmodernity reminds us how individuals are formed in communities and their cultures, never as isolated persons. Hence, the public school's non-neutrality threatens our children's upbringing as Christians all the more. As MacIntyre and Hauerwas have shown, we can no longer assume that our children are formed morally as individuals by the development of individual rational powers à la Immanuel Kant and his follower Lawrence Kohlberg. They develop morally into their social contexts.[21] As developmental theorist Jerome Bruner has explained, the narrative faculties of children are fundamental in their moral development. The child develops moral capacity through his or her initiation into a "canonical" narrative world of meaning.[22] In other words, children learn moral meanings not through information or reasoning skills, but they incorporate the moral meanings of the stories and the modeled lives of their social context. This kind of learning starts even before the onset of formal reasoning skills.[23] In this view then, the tradition-neutral, pluralist social world of the public school becomes itself a culture into

The social space of the public school is itself a religion that powerfully shapes the character of our young.

which the child is initiated and forms the child's moral consciousness. In such a world, the ultimate values of tolerance for each other in a democratic society become moral purposes. The freedom to allow individuals to make up their own mind becomes a moral mantra unto itself. Individual freedom, self-expression, and personal self-fulfillment become goals in themselves that form the character of the child. It cannot be escaped. The social space of the public school cannot maintain its "value-neutral" status as the public educators would have it. Instead, it is itself a religion that powerfully shapes the character of our young.

The so-called "tradition-neutral" social space of the public schools therefore initiates children into significant moral character that is neither universal nor benignly neutral. Indeed, such a neutral space may actively inculcate values that are toxic from the Christian viewpoint. Teaching democratic tolerance, for instance, may communicate powerfully to children that what is moral and good is a matter of their own personal choice rather than something authoritative and created into the universe. When we teach children to make up their own minds and to respect individual freedom, the socially unintended message may be that there is no moral world worthy of their allegiance more so than any other is. It could also be that the powerful social world of democratic liberalism, that is, of the public school, socializes children into believing that anything is permissible provided it does not hurt any other individual. For the Christian, these moral purposes are not sufficient to train our children into anything more than a restrained, democratically acceptable self-indulgence.[24] The so-called tradition-neutral public schools train our children in ways that work contrary to the character produced in following Christ. Evangelicals then have good reason to pause and ask, Are we "giving away" the moral education of our children to the public schools in ways we never imagined?

Evangelicals and the Future of Christian Education: The Predicament We Are In

The above analysis of the public schools and virtues education reveals the larger predicament Christian educators find themselves in a post-Christian culture. We see that all moral education requires a culture and its community to train our children into a moral life. And yet it seems we do not possess such a communal culture in our local churches. Sadly, evangelicals often lack such a community because we act as busy, indebted, and fragmented as the rest of our capitalist culture. Meanwhile, moral education is happening now with our children, simply by living passively in the current culture.

The public school's virtue education vividly illustrates this last statement. The above analysis reveals democracy and capitalism promote not only virtues but also moral purposes that often oppose the lordship of Christ. Yet we lack the cultural resources to critically engage democracy and capitalism as cultures encroaching upon the gospel because we have no alternative communal culture at church sufficient to sustain our children's moral nurturance into Christ. The above analysis of virtues education and the public schools shows how moral education cannot be accomplished by teaching content alone. It requires a way of life, a community that lives that way of life, and a culture that embodies that way of life. Yet it seems our evangelical churches lack precisely this kind of community.

And so we who are responsible for the moral education of our children are left in a predicament. We are tempted to respond either by engaging the culture's institutions that encroach upon our children's moral training or by withdrawing entirely from participating in them. But either option will leave the problem untouched if we do not have a cultural community of Christ to initiate our children into. Without a communal way of life in Christ and the means to initiate (catechesis), engagement or withdrawal accomplishes little in the face of the dominant cultural forces. The ways evangelicals respond to public schools and moral education illustrate this.

The Evangelical Response to the Educational Dilemma

Typically, evangelicals respond to moral issues in the public school by (a) engaging the public school on moral content (the public schooling activism option), (b) withdrawing their children entirely from the public school (the homeschooling option), or (c) starting up a parochial school as an extension of the local church body (the parochial schooling option). Any of these options, however, accomplishes little for evangelicals when we lack a moral community as a way of life to initiate our children into.

The Public Schooling Activism Option

In regard to the public schooling activism option, evangelicals typically engage the public schools on one moral position at a time such as sex education, the teaching of evolution, or the censoring of immoral literature. In this approach, evangelicals assume that the public schools can teach math, science, and reading just fine, but we must watch the public schools when they are teaching issues of personal morality or biblical doctrines. In this way, evangelicals operate under modernist assumptions about education. This accommodation between public schools and the churches is uniquely modern because modernity assumes that religion is separate from science, personal moral decisions are separate from public policy, and moral knowledge is inherently different than the public forms of knowledge like science, math, and history.[25] This accommodation has been common since World War II, and it makes sense to anyone born in modernity.

Evangelicals participated in this modernist accommodation dating back to its roots in the Sunday school movement of the nineteenth century when the Sunday schools acceded the role of teaching the math and sciences to the public schools in North America. At this time, the Protestant denominations negotiated a new role for the Sunday schools: the teaching of religious and moral formation.[26] As a result, evangelicals have long been comfortable with the modernist arrangement that portioned off the teaching of math and sciences to the public schools and the teaching of religion and morality to the family's local preferred church.[27] Whenever a moral position is espoused, however, by the public schools that crosses this line, evangelicals actively engage the issue one position at a time at either the local public school level or the larger legislature level.

In light of our analysis of virtues education in public schools, engaging the public schools one moral position at a time is an inadequate engagement of the issues at stake in the effect public schools have upon moral education of Christian children. Getting sex education right or evolution removed in the public school accomplishes little because in effect it is a drop in the bucket next to the overriding powers of the public school culture itself. Amidst all these one-issue engagements, evangelicals still miss how the public school itself is a moral and social context habituating our children into a defined character for competing and living in a capitalist democracy that, according to theologian Craig Gay, "lives as if God doesn't exist."[28] The culture therefore rules over all things and dwarfs any single position or change in curriculum.

This goes for subjects like math, science, and reading as well. For math, science, and reading cannot be separated from their cosmological understandings and the reasons given for why you would want to learn them in the first place. Getting victories over public attempts to teach amoral birth control or even amoral abstinence will be only small victories unless our children are inducted into a way of life that accepts the created purposes of God for sexuality, marriage, and celibacy. And teaching math and science will undercut Christian character in our children if they learn the only reason to study is to get a job so they can get wealthy. This strategy therefore of engaging the public schools one issue at a time accomplishes little without a moral community that subverts the public school's cultural influences over our children with an alternative way of life.

The Homeschooling Option

Regarding the homeschooling option, evangelicals homeschool rightfully in order to guide their children in relation to the formative powers of the public schools. Evangelical parents homeschool to focus their children's education toward growing into the character of Christ. Their biggest challenge, however, is to find a community to initiate their children into. Homeschoolers, as they are called, know the importance of socialization. So they withdraw their children from the public school's socialization and seek to find other ways to create socialization, most often among other homeschoolers. Meanwhile their own evangelical churches often have little to offer in this regard. Homeschoolers know that a parent's teaching can only compete for so long against the cultural forces of television, the arts, sports, Internet, and the neighborhood. Yet homeschoolers often have no other place left to go than to retreat into the family. And so the problem of Christian moral education in a post-Christian culture still remains.

To reiterate the above analysis, each child must have a moral world into which he or she is initiated or the child will find one, most likely one of the prominent ones offered through public schooling, media, neighborhood, or Hollywood. The Christian family alone cannot offer such a moral world because it is too small to be a culture that can compete with the secular world. In addition, the family is prone toward the parochialization of its own sins. Apart from a commitment to community the family cannot help but be unaware of its own sins, protect itself from the exposing of its own sins, and the nurture of the dysfunction internal to its own sins. But when children are initiated into the way of life in Christ through a community of Christ, they receive formation into a way of life bigger than the biological family. They also receive a stance from which they can grow and engage the secular cultures that surround them. Homeschooling alone therefore does not solve the problem of moral education in a post-Christian culture. In the midst of these cultural forces, homeschooling by itself still leaves the children with no initiation into a world greater than their own family's. Homeschooling therefore requires a community and a culture into which the child is being initiated. This community cannot be a haphazard community brought together by homeschoolers across ethnic and religious lines. It must be a community that is centered and therefore born out of the worship of Jesus Christ as Lord in community.

> **Each child must have a moral world into which he or she is initiated or the child will find one.**

The Parochial Schooling Option

In regard to the parochial school option, evangelicals have tradi-tionally lagged behind the Roman Catholic and mainline European Protestant churches in raising up parochial schools. Nonetheless, evan-gelical churches do organize parochial schools. Often, however, evan-gelical educators seek to replicate the public school's teaching methods except that they remove certain subject matter that is offensive to the evangelical mind. Like educators of modernity, evangelicals emphasize self-flourishing, critical thinking, and acquisition of skills and forget the necessity of initiation into a way of life.[29] Modernist Christian education sees the goal of education as the flourishing and development of every individual child to become "the person God has created them to be."[30] This goal alone, however, ignores the postmodern illumination of how culture forms each person.

In addition, evangelical parochial schools in the United States some-times train their students, oddly enough, for allegiance to the nation in similar ways to the public schools. They teach and practice an allegiance to the flag and a patriotism to American values. They in essence are as much schools of the Empire of the United States as their public coun-terparts. The parochial school, however, must itself become a culture that each child is inducted into via the church. It must teach first the allegiance to Jesus as Lord over all other allegiances (Col. 1:15–17). If evangelical parochial schools only replicate their public school coun-terparts except for some curriculum deletions, and if they do not pro-vide the processes and culture to initiate children into the way of life in Christ, such schools will accomplish little in the moral education of its children in the face of the dominant cultural forces. Such schooling will only achieve its mission as it provides its children a catechesis into a way of life given through a community of Christ.

And so the analysis of virtue education and the public schools illus-trates the predicament for evangelical Christian education amidst the post-Christian cultures and it points us toward a conclusion. Simply put, without a community of Christ to center our children's moral formation into, our children are "open season" to all other dominant cultures that seek to be the moral center of their lives. We in essence "give away" the moral education of our young. Likewise, apart from such a community of Christ, all attempts at engaging secular forces or withdrawing from them will fail to save the moral education of our children into Christ. In the midst of post-Christian cultures, our children need a Christian culture to be initiated into. And our churches require a means of cat-echesis to accomplish this initiation. These statements are true beyond the problem of character education and the public schools. These statements describe the predicament for all realms of Christian education. The post-Christian culture, as represented by the public schools, incapacitates modernist approaches to Christian education that focus upon the individual. Evangelicals therefore must discard modernist understandings of education. Our churches must live as communities sharing a way of life with our children. We must reinvigorate practices of initiation and catechesis.

The Need for Catechesis and Community among Evangelicals

Unfortunately, the idea of catechesis doesn't make sense to many evangelicals. To many evangelicals, "initiatory rites" sound like primitive anthropological practices, and "catechesis" connotes Roman Catholic archaism. Evangelicals typically do not see the need for children or new converts to be initiated into something. For us, there is no initiation. Conversion happens at the moment of decision. Once "saved," the new believer immediately learns to go to church, read the Bible, and pray in largely an individualist set of spiritual practices. There is no initiation into a way of life. For evangelicals, baptism is more of a personal statement of commitment than an initiation into a way of life. There is no differentiation between the initiated and the uninitiated. For evangelicals, Christianity is about an individual relationship with God as opposed to an induction into a way of life. Evangelicals inherit all of the above from our modernist revivalist beginnings. Therefore, we do not naturally think in the terms of catechesis as an initiation into a way of life.

For most evangelicals therefore, Christian education can turn into a service to be provided to parents, not an immersion into a way of life. It is about teaching the children doctrinal information and illustrated Bible lessons. Most parents in our churches drop their children off at the children's ministry, take a number, sign the child in, and return after worship to pick up the child. The curriculum rarely matches the worship service because we do not follow a common lectionary. The family is splintered in its learning. Our churches are focused upon programs delivering religious goods and services to individuals pursuing a personal relationship with God. With this focus on programs and the achievement of modern educational outcomes, Christian education becomes a

Most parents in our churches drop their children off at the children's ministry, take a number, sign the child in, and return after worship to pick up the child.

program that cannot fit into the life of a community. Because we do not have time, or because we are too big, evangelicals bypass the processes of catechesis that require education to be a subset of a way of life.

In addition, catechesis and other rites of initiation imply sectarianism to some evangelicals. It sounds Amish to make such a big deal out of initiating children out of the pagan world and into the way of life in Christ. And evangelicals have always prided themselves on being culturally savvy and capable of "taking on" the cultural elites of society. Evangelicals therefore seek to arm their children with intellectual competency so that when the time comes they are capable of withstanding the storm and evangelizing others into the faith. They want the Sunday school program to develop basic intellectual competencies as the means to live the Christian life in the public schools. Seen in this light, catechesis might disadvantage children in engaging the world on even terms.

Evangelicals then resist the notion of catechesis. Yet in all the ways listed above, the need for catechesis speaks for itself in a post-Christian cultural context. For in a post-Christian culture, conversion cannot stand alone as the defining entry point for Christianity. Conversion is at best one moment in a believer's journey that will get lost apart from a history and a culture in which it can make sense.[31] Without an understanding of the language of Christ, the narrative of the God of Israel, and the redeemed moral world we are called to live into, a conversion will become like the seed that falls in infertile ground (Matt. 13:18–23). Without being inducted into a community to model the things Christians live for and the way we navigate our moral lives, the convert or the young child will be formed into a foreign culture that actually does model what it lives for in compelling yet evil ways.

Neither can children's educational programs be effective merely as a service provided for parents at the local church. If these programs separate the children from the adults in worship and curriculum as well as from the rest of the community, they will fail because children need to learn the language and see the ways of life modeled in community in order to grow.[32] Yet because we so segregate our children from the adults, sixteen years later we discover our children do not believe the same things that we do. The children were not initiated into a way of life. They were taught information that was disjointed from what the adults were learning and living in the worship

> **Because we so often segregate our children from the adults, sixteen years later we discover our children do not believe the same things that we do.**

service. Without catechesis that inducts children into a way of life of a living community, parents will go one way and the children another.

Likewise, far from catechesis being a sectarian retreat from a post-Christian culture, catechesis provides the basis for our children to enter and engage the non-Christian world, not be engulfed by it. Catechesis in essence provides the means for children to first learn the language and ways of Christ upon which they can then engage other ways of life. Catechesis provides the means to acquire a stance from which to see the world as a follower of Christ.[33] In a post-Christian culture, the church must initiate her young first in our own way of life because we can no longer assume a monolithic world where all assumptions about life and knowledge are built on the same foundation, the inheritance of European Christendom.

In summary then, in the face of a post-Christian culture, Christian educators are forced to define their mission via catechesis and initiation. Personal and individual development will no longer suffice as educational goals. Rather, we must depend upon the church as a moral community that lives the Christian way of life in such a way that she initiates her children into it. The church then becomes the center for the initiation of our children into Christ from which all other influences are then subordinated. The church becomes the social space where our children can learn the skills of character sufficient to live Christian lives in a fragmented world. Indeed, the church is the very social space out of which this virtue is produced, displayed, and in which it even makes sense. All other educational influences then become subordinated to the lordship of Christ, including the forces of public schooling. Catechesis is the means of initiation into this world for our young.

This is not, however, an educational retreat from the world. For the church is more than the social space out of which Christian virtue is lived. It is the culture-producing center that makes categories of discernment possible for our children out of which they can critically engage the formative powers alive in American culture.[34] As we saw earlier in this chapter, the temptation is for parents to try to engage the public schools one issue at a time, or to homeschool or start parochial schools as options to fight the foreign shapers of public school children. But none of these options will accomplish fruit apart from the community of Christ as the shaper in Christ of our children's moral vision.

In the end, the church can best engage the public schools and all of the post-Christian cultures by being a countercommunity that offers a way of life compelling enough to subvert the public schools in the formation of its own children. In this way, our children do not enter public school to get inducted into a way of life but to witness to another way of life more compelling. They enter public school not to be formed into good

Americans but to subvert the powers that seek to encroach upon the moral formation of our lives under the lordship of Jesus Christ. To accomplish this requires the church community as center for the moral formation of children and the catechetical practices to accomplish this feat.

Practices That Raise Up Our Children to Be Faithful Disciples

The evangelical church then must reinvigorate practices of communal catechesis if it is to reclaim the moral education of its children from the public schools and other forces of post-Christian culture. But what does this mean? Does this mean we should simply reinstitute the older Roman Catholic or Reformation church catechesis? Such a reinstitution may certainly be part of the process of catechesis. But catechesis is more than a given approach to curriculum. It is a way of being the church.

> Catechesis is more than a given approach to curriculum. It is a way of being the church.

Catechesis will challenge the way evangelicals think about church. A catechetical church, for instance, challenges the assumptions that large congregations and megachurches are appropriate manifestations of the body of Christ. A catechesis that truly nurtures our children into a living community of Christ will require smaller church communities that know each other. Likewise, a catechetical church challenges the way we think about gathering for church and guiding our children's entire formation. For the very idea of catechesis calls into question that any parent can categorize catechesis as just one more time slot to be worked into a schedule alongside youth soccer, art appreciation, math tutoring, or other children's programs. Catechesis cannot happen in one hour but is an initiation into a whole way of living before Christ. Catechesis requires that the family center its lives around the worship of Christ. It requires that families live intentionally in community with fellow believers.

Certainly not all evangelical churches have abandoned either community or catechesis, but the evangelical focus upon church growth of the last thirty years has created churches built more for mass distribution of religious goods and services and built less for being a community of catechesis and modeling life to our young. The degeneration of our children's moral education into large programs where parents drop their kids off, take a number, and return after worship, where few parents know other parents and their kids, is evidence of this. The megachurch threatens to turn our children's moral formation into another slotted program to be paid for and organized like any of the other myriad children's programs of our day. If this is all our children's programs are, then we face the prospect that our children's center of moral formation will be elsewhere than in the church of Christ. If this is all our children's programs will aspire to, we do in fact "give away" our children's moral education to the post-Christian forces that dominate American culture. The very idea of catechesis throws into doubt whether our children's moral formation can be accomplished in a megachurch setting. Catechesis then has as much to do about the way we live as church as the particular curriculum we choose for Sunday school.

With the above caveat in mind, I offer a few starting suggestions for ways evangelicals can reinvigorate a catechetical communal practice in our local churches.

> The megachurch threatens to turn our children's moral formation into another slotted program to be paid for and organized like any of the other myriad children's programs of our day.

Do Deliberate Catechesis

Let evangelicals practice a deliberate catechesis among our children where the children of certain ages are brought through rituals akin to confirmation and first communion at the Roman Catholic and established Protestant churches. The narratives of Israel and Jesus Christ should of course be taught. But at a certain age let the children be brought through a deliberate process akin to the early centuries of the Christian church where a deliberate rite of initiation took place that brought adults and children through a conversion rite, a covenantal rite, the baptismal rite, and an introduction into the Lord's Supper of the church.[35] Let us ensure that the children and parents are capable of knowing the basic creeds and assenting to them, knowing the practices of prayer and Lord's Supper, and knowing what the basic commitments of the new life in Christ entail at baptism. Let us change our Sunday schools into catechetical programs with rites of passage that we carefully lead, prod, and initiate our children through. Let our Sunday schools become places for powerful initiatory rites and entry into the life of the body, not only places for the accumulation of foundational biblical knowledge. Our church establishes its children's ministries toward the goals of every child to be ready for (Free Church) baptismal initiation at the age of ten. We have a specific instructional community that runs from Advent to Pentecost that takes each child through the stages and commitments necessary for baptism and life in Christ.

Use Children's Curriculum That Keeps the Church Together as a Learning Community

Let us select curriculum for our children's ministries so that the curriculum coincides with the regular worship of the church. This of course implies a lectionary-oriented approach both to curriculum as well as the worship service itself. There are several excellent such curriculum that are communal, user-friendly, and cost-effective.[36] By so doing, let us get parents and children on the same path of formation so that catechesis is a process that carries on throughout the daily lives of our families and not just on one day or one hour during the week.

Integrate Communal Worship and Children's Ministries

Let evangelicals practice children's ministries in a way where the ministry is actually part of the church community as a whole. Let us ensure from the beginning that the children are integrated into the life of the church. Let us ensure that children sit at the earliest of possible times in the worship of God alongside the adults. Let us share fellowship meals together with the children before we study and pray together. And let the whole church somehow be a regular part of the teaching ministry of the children so that parents get to know other parents, parents get to know other children, parents get to see their children interacting with other children, and children get to see their parents interacting with other parents. Parents can then share together in the nurturance of their children by sharing information, praying for each other's children, and instructing children behaviorally when the parent is not around. The church then becomes a community of the life of Christ and the adults become the guardians and mentors of the heritage we have in Christ, ever passing it down to the new generation coming along. At our church, over half of the church participates in the regular Sunday morning children's ministries through a regular rotation. We organize the sharing of cooperative babysitting practices among church parents. We organize sessions for parents to work together in discerning key issues for parenting.

Integrate Service in the Church and Teenage Youth Groups

In the same way, let us integrate our older children and teenagers into the service of the church at the earliest moments after baptism or confirmation. Evangelicals are often tempted to segregate our teenagers into youth groups isolated from the adults, with their own music, their own teaching, and their own entertainment. Teenagers certainly need social times with other teenagers, but this should be the purview of parents shared with other parents. It should not be the job of a youth professional to entertain teens because this in essence segregates the teens from the adults and creates a cliquish attitude among the teenagers toward the church and its "less than cool" ways of worship and Christian discipleship. Several years later, as the teenagers go off to college, they leave the church never having felt a part of it in the first place. They leave as jaded observers of the Christian life in the body, never having participated directly.

Instead, the evangelical church should pair adult mentors with teens so they can meet regularly to talk, dialogue, teach, model, and think through the new things each teenager must face in growing up. Here is where discipleship takes place. The church also should treat the teens as part of the church, having them read Scripture in the service, participate in leading worship, pray, minister to the poor, visit the sick, conduct missions trips, and generally be a regular part of church life. We need to expect something of them and also encourage them as they try new things and gain experience in doing them. Through such direct involvement and participation, they will learn that they belong, and in this way they become part of the living body of Christ. Of course there will be special times of gathering the teens together for a social time or a missions trip, but all this will be for naught if the teenagers are somehow segregated from the community, which is exactly where they can learn to live and breathe the ways of following Christ.

Subordinate the Public Schools

Given communal catechetical practices, our children will grow into the character of Christ sufficient to engage the post-Christian cultures when the time comes, whether we homeschool, parochial school, or even public school our children. Once our children have gone through catechesis, once armed with a stance formed in relation to the culture of Christ, our children and our parents have nothing to fear. In regard then to sending our children into the public schools and the virtues programs, they are armed and capable of critically engaging the public virtues for redemptive purposes.[37] In fact, armed with a stance, our children uncover that all such virtues programs are in effect using watered-down, lowest common denominator virtues to accommodate all within the pluralist group. Our children reveal that the public virtues are so in need of further substance that the local church body can capture it and make it a display for what it means to be a Christian. A "character education" presentation can therefore actually become a stepping off ground for presenting what it means for the Christian to be patient, courageous, trusting, loving, honest, and so forth. In this way, the church, through its children's presence, subordinates the public school into its own social field for the exercise of virtue. The public school's character education becomes the primary place for critical engagement by the children.[38] This is all made possible after the grounding of our children into the body of Christ and the life of virtue we have in Christ. Such a catechesis makes possible not only the church's recovery of the moral education of her young, but also the critical engagement of secular virtue as a witness for Christ.

Amidst the post-Christian cultures, amidst the current breakdown of the modern consensus, evangelicals require new practices for the moral education of their young. Whether it be public schooling, parochial schooling, or homeschooling, there is no returning to the medieval cultural synthesis of all things under God whereby all the sciences were the subset of the work of theology. But by being the church of Jesus Christ in the moral education of our children, by centering our children's moral development in his body, we make possible the subversion of all other forces that seek to form our children morally and make possible the captivity of those forces that are redeemable for the lordship of Christ.

Conclusion

Let Us Return to the Practices

Gerhard Lohfink, in his important book *Does God Need the Church?* says the following:

> It can only be that God begins in a small way, at one single place in the world. There must be a place, visible, tangible, where the salvation of the world can begin: that is, where the world becomes what it is supposed to be according to God's plan. Beginning at that place, the new thing can spread abroad, but not through persuasion, not through indoctrination, not through violence. Everyone must have the opportunity to come and see. All must have the chance to behold and test this new thing. Then, if they want to, they can allow themselves to be drawn into the history of salvation that God is creating. Only in that way can their freedom be preserved. What drives them to the new thing cannot be force, not even moral pressure, but only the fascination of a world that is changed.[1]

Lohfink's powerful words speak to the indispensability of the church to God's plan for redeeming the world. To many, his words convict of how far we evangelicals have fallen from God's calling to be his church in North America and yet they reveal how simple the return to that calling might be. For if Lohfink is correct, our first task must be first and foremost to come together and live as communities of faith pursuing the life of Christ together as his church. Every other task in Christian life or strategy for furthering God's kingdom only makes sense as a subset of a living body of people faithfully living the life of Christ together before the watching world.

Lohfink's words in essence magnify the seriousness of the charge of this book. For if it is true that evangelicalism has "given away" being the church in North America, the status of all of our activities before God must be called into question. Our only response can be to stop what we are doing and humbly pursue the practices of being Christ's church in North America. In the light of Lohfink, the "great giveaway" begs for us evangelicals to simply return to the basic, core practices of being the church. Admittedly, I am in no position to advocate such a pretentious sounding statement. It is questionable whether such a "simple" return is even possible. For even the most convinced of us on this position, there is no ready consensus for what practices we should pursue and what they would look like, the presentation of this book notwithstanding. Furthermore, these practices would require that our people make the church the focal practice of their lives, an allegiance we might not be ready to lead. And so there is much more work to be done to explore and attempt these practices. Returning to the practices is not so simple. Nevertheless, I do not believe that the realization as evangelicals that we have "given away" being the church calls for some new technique, new fad, or new denomination. Instead, the great giveaway calls for us as pastors, leaders, elders, and congregants to gather humbly and discern together what it might mean for us to return to the practices of being Christ's body. This book can only hope to call us to such a reinvigorated effort toward this mission.

What might such a church look like? How much different would it look from what we are doing now? I do not pretend to know. And this book has certainly failed to provide such a definitive vision. Nonetheless, as I argued in the introduction and displayed in the chapters of this book, I do believe there are basic practices that constitute the church's reality. They may take different shape from cultural context to cultural context, but the task remains the same: we need to rediscover, reclaim, and in a sense "receive back" from God the basic practices for being his church in a fragmented, postmodern North American culture. So in an effort to start the conversation, I'll take the risk! I will put out there what I imagine our churches might look like if we somehow reversed the "great giveaway" and reclaimed the practices for being the church in North America. Hopefully, others will follow with their visions. Perhaps together, out of Scripture and our life together under his lordship, God can use us to reimagine the church faithful for our times.

> **We need to rediscover, reclaim, and in a sense "receive back" from God the basic practices for being his church in a fragmented, postmodern North American culture.**

So here it goes . . .

I imagine our congregations becoming smaller, not bigger, yet teeming with the life of his body. And I hope there are more of them, so many of them in fact, that they become the alternative to the Starbucks of our day. I hope our churches become known for servanthood in the neighborhoods and warm hospitality that invites strangers into our homes. I pray that the home of every evangelical person becomes an incubator of evangelism, inviting strangers to the gospel out of their lostness and into the love and grace of life in our Lord Jesus Christ. I imagine real fellowship in our congregations, the kind that shares joys and sufferings and potluck meals. I pray our leaders take on the form of humble servants who sit, listen, and suffer with real people through many years of leading them through this life in Jesus Christ. I hope we leave behind the CEO models of leadership. I look for our worship services to become liturgical places that form our people into faithful participants in the life of God. May we renew the sense of God's mystery, beauty, and transcendence in our worship services through the rehearsal of his great work in Jesus Christ. In the process, may many postmodern wanderers be drawn into his life by his majestic wonder and the compelling story of the forgiveness and new life made possible in the life, death, and resurrection of our Lord Jesus Christ. I hope our congregations look more diverse both economically and racially. Dare I imagine that each member's bank account becomes submitted to the King and to each other through some symbolic act as we gather around the Table of our Lord. I long for the day we become model communities for a new politics that spreads God's redeeming justice to the poor and the racially divided. I hope we see small groups that renew the monastic practices of confession, repentance, reading Scripture, and prayer for our day. And most of all, may our churches become communities that nurture and care for children in the way we conduct catechesis communally, adopt the "unplanned" children, and invite all children into everyday life with God. To me this all sounds like a truly amazing way of life.

Is this a pipe dream? I certainly hope not. For I believe this is what we must be, know, and do as Christians if we are to survive the postmodern malaise overtaking us in the urban and suburban contexts of American life. We must recover the truly amazing way of life given to us as a people by God through his redemption in Jesus Christ. The only way we can resist the totalizing forces of late capitalism and its derivatives is by recovering being the church. Is this not possible? I point us all to the smattering of emergent churches that have arisen in the past ten years and the churches Robert Webber refers to in his book *The Younger Evangelicals*. And I hope this book gives hope and direction to seminarians, pastors of small churches, and all those people who have tired of evangelicalism's incessant marketing and mega-sizing. May we start gatherings of people that practice the practices of being a body of Christ. As difficult as it might be, let us join together and find our way back to the practices of being the people of God under the reign of our Lord and Savior Jesus Christ. For he truly is the hope of the world.

Notes

Introduction: The Great Giveaway

1. I allude here to those affiliated with emergentvillage.org led by Brian McLaren, *The Church on the Other Side: Doing Ministry in the Postmodern Matrix* (Grand Rapids: Zondervan, 1998), *A New Kind of Christian* (San Francisco: Jossey-Bass, 2001), as well as to Robert Webber, *The Younger Evangelicals* (Grand Rapids: Baker Books, 2002).

2. This theme of "starting where you are born" has its roots in Alasdair MacIntyre, *After Virtue*, 2nd ed. (Notre Dame, IN: University of Notre Dame Press, 1981), 221.

3. This is akin to George Hunsberger's phrase in his book edited with Craig Van Gelder, *Church between Gospel and Culture* (Grand Rapids: Eerdmans, 1996), 337.

4. Of course, this is the phrase popularized by Yoder and then Hauerwas. See John Howard Yoder, "Let the Church Be the Church," in Michael Cartwright, ed., *The Royal Priesthood* (Scottdale, PA: Herald, 1998), 168; Stanley Hauerwas, *A Community of Character* (Notre Dame, IN: University of Notre Dame Press, 1981), 85–86, 108–10.

5. This is according to the account given by John Yoder. In John Howard Yoder, "A People in the World," in Michael Cartwright, ed., *The Royal Priesthood* (Scottdale, PA: Herald, 1998), 78.

6. From "Reply to Gellius Faber," *The Complete Writings of Menno Simons*, c. 1496–1561, trans. L. Verrduin (Scottdale, PA: Herald, 1956), as quoted by John Howard Yoder, "A People in the World," in Cartwright, *The Royal Priesthood*, 77.

7. For a copy of the relevant sections of Luther's *Councils and Churches* as well as a theological engagement of all of Luther's marks, see Carl Braaten and Robert Jensen, eds., *Marks of the Body of Christ* (Grand Rapids: Eerdmans, 1999).

8. For a compendium of essays from the Regent Conference, see John G. Stackhouse Jr., ed., *Evangelical Ecclesiology: Reality or Illusion?* (Grand Rapids: Baker Academic, 2003). For a compendium of essays from the Wheaton Theology Conference, see Mark Husbands and Daniel Treier, eds., *The Community of the Word: Toward an Evangelical Ecclesiology* (Downers Grove, IL: InterVarsity, 2005).

Chapter 1: Our Definition of Success

1. The most insightful unearthing of the assumptions concerning the use of numbers and church marketing principles in theologically naïve ways is carried out by Phil Kenneson and James L. Street, *Selling Out the Church: The Dangers of Church Marketing* (Nashville: Abingdon, 1997).

2. This is strictly a characterization of a church and is not meant to be an indictment of any existing church.

3. Such a process for a large church has to go something like this: (a) The elders post new elder nominations for thirty days and allow anyone in the congregation to go to the elder nominee with complaints. (b) After thirty days, if an elder withstands such scrutiny, the congregation has no further say or affirmation. (c) The existing elders mainly direct the process from there. A church of a thousand or more almost has to have a process like this out of necessity in order to function.

4. See George Barna, *The Second Coming of the Church* (Nashville: Word, 1998), 5–8; "The Third Coming of George Barna," *Christianity Today*, August 5, 2002, 36–37. For statistics that say born-again Christians have a higher divorce rate than non–born-again Christians, see "Christians Are More Likely to Experience Divorce than Non-Christians," Barna Research Group, www.barna.org (accessed August 2000). For reports on child abuse in Christian homes versus non-Christian, see Peter Nicolai, et al., Report of the Synodical Committee on Physical, Emotional, and Sexual Abuse in the Christian Reformed Church (September 1991), and James Alsdurf and Phyllis Alsdurf, *Battered into Submission* (Downers Grove, IL: InterVarsity, 1989). These last two citations are from Rodney Clapp, *Families at the Crossroads* (Downers Grove, IL: InterVarsity, 1993), 185.

5. The most compelling example of this is the huge numbers that attend the Willow Creek Leadership Summit in Barrington, Illinois, each year through on-site or video presentation. Another example is Rick Warren's popular "Purpose-Driven Ministries" conferences. See "A Regular Purpose-Driven Guy," *Christianity Today*, November 18, 2002, 42.

6. None of these comments implies that any of these churches intend to do this. The stated goal of most churches, including evangelical megachurches, is to produce disciples. The question is whether the notion that "bigger churches are by definition more successful" promotes the building of Christ's church in a manner in which it can be his body and thereby edify and mature disciples.

7. On the roots of this evangelical-style individualism, see George Marsden, *Fundamentalism and American Culture* (Oxford: Oxford University Press, 1980), 99–101; Nathan Hatch, *The Democratization of American Christianity* (New Haven: Yale University Press, 1989), chaps. 1–2, 6–7; Mark Noll, *The Scandal of the Evangelical Mind* (Grand Rapids: Eerdmans, 1994), chap. 3.

8. On the idea of the "Spirit-filled life," a "second blessing," a second work of grace, and the whole Pentecostal holiness tradition and its determination on evangelicalism, see the work of Donald Dayton, *Theological Roots of Pentecostalism* (Grand Rapids: Zondervan, 1987).

9. This seems to be the driving force behind much church consulting. Take for instance Lyle Schaller's *The New Reformation* (Nashville: Abingdon, 1995). Schaller, in a chapter titled "Size Is Not the Issue!" writes the following: "Thus the first question should be addressed to the constituencies of the churches in the year 2005 or 2015. What institutional expression of the Christian church will be most effective in responding to the religious needs of new generations?" (60–61). Schaller goes on to say that "what sets the megachurches apart from other Protestant congregations" is their "high performance organization" (64). The baseline assumption of his work appears to be "that churches can and should be organized to operate more efficiently." On numbers, choosing a niche, and other issues of organizing, see Schaller's *Create Your Own Future* (Nashville: Abingdon, 1991).

10. On this, see particularly Alasdair MacIntyre, *After Virtue*, 74–78. On the rise of individual autonomy and its consequences, see MacIntyre's exposition in *After Virtue*, chaps. 1–9. How economic efficiency became an independent unacknowledged moral value behind modern economics and the organization of capitalism, see D. Stephen Long, *Divine Economy* (New York: Routledge, 2000).

11. The major discussion of "late capitalism" comes from Frederic Jameson, *Postmodernism, or, The Cultural Logic of Late Capitalism* (Durham, NC: Duke University Press, 1991). See also Steven Best and Douglas Kellner's discussion of Jameson in their *Postmodern Theory: Critical Interrogations* (New York: Guilford, 1991), 182–92.

12. See the classic postmodern psychology of Kenneth Gergen, *The Saturated Self* (New York: Basic Books, 1991). See also Roger Lundin, *The Culture of Interpretation* (Grand Rapids: Eerdmans, 1993), for an intentionally Christian perspective.

13. MacIntyre, *After Virtue*, 211–12.

14. Another way of saying this is the following quote from Stanley Hauerwas: "Yet a narrative that provides the skill to let us claim our actions as our own is not the sort I can simply 'make mine' through a decision. Substantive narratives that promise me a way to make my self my own require me to grow into the narrative by constantly challenging my past achievements." *Community of Character* (Notre Dame, IN: University of Notre Dame Press, 1982), 144. On the demise of modernist approaches to understanding decisions and moral reasoning as individualist, see Gergen, *The Saturated Self*, 239–45.

15. See George Barna's comments in *Boiling Point* (Ventura, CA: Regal Books, 2001), 231n5, where he states that his "research discovered that a majority of people who made a first time decision to follow Jesus Christ in response to a gospel presentation in a church service were no longer associated with that church—or any other—within eight weeks of making that decision." At my own denomination's Midwest District of Christian and Missionary Alliance 2002 annual conference, October 1, 2002, Dr. Mickey Noel, head of church multiplication for the Christian and Missionary Alliance, quoted that only one in four of the "decisions for Christ" recorded in the Christian and Missionary Alliance end up in baptism.

16. This separation has been a historical point of controversy since the Donatist controversies of the third and fourth centuries. More recent are the divisions between the Classical Protestant and Radical Reformation churches. Here Anabaptist as well as Wesleyan holiness theologians tried in various ways to mend the gap between the justification and sanctification of the believer in reaction to the cold orthodoxy of either Reformation churches on the Continent or the Church of England. The second blessing/work of grace of the holiness/Pentecostal developments in the early twentieth century can be seen as yet another attempt to mend the gap for evangelicals by providing a necessary next step between one's initial justification and one's resultant sanctification. John MacArthur's "lordship" teaching, which was controversial among more fundamentalist evangelicals, could also be categorized as another such attempt. Nevertheless, evangelicals by and large focus upon the initial decision as the largest component of one's personal salvation. And sanctification remains an individual dynamic prone to legalism once separated from the work of the body of Christ. On this subject, see Thomas Finger, *Christian Theology: An Eschatological Approach* (Scottdale, PA: Herald, 1985), 2:91–222; James McClendon, *Systematic Theology Doctrine* (Nashville: Abingdon, 1994), chap. 3. Also see Stanley Hauerwas' early attempt to propose character as a way of unifying yet making sense of the two parts within the *ordo salutis*, *Character and the Christian Life* (San Antonio: Trinity, 1985), especially chap. 5. In that text, Hauerwas states the following after quoting Calvin, "Thus justification and sanctification are but two modes of the one work of Christ for the believer. They cannot be separated, because that would result in abstracting the Christian life from its source. Yet, equally important, they cannot be mixed or confused" (186).

17. These understandings of New Testament soteriology are plentiful in evangelical scholarship. See George Ladd, *A Theology of the New Testament* (Grand Rapids: Eerdmans, 1974), chap. 5; Herman Ridderbos, *Paul: An Outline of His Theology* (Grand Rapids: Eerdmans, 1975), chap. 6, pp. 257–58. A Continental work that represents evangelical sympathies is Oscar Cullmann, *Christ and Time* (Philadelphia: Westminster, 1964), chap. 4.

18. MacIntyre, *After Virtue*, 74.

19. The most vivid and pioneering account of how "managerial effectiveness" was elevated to a moral value in and of itself in the society of Weberian modernity is given again by Alasdair MacIntyre. See his account of the "characters" of modernity, the aesthete, the manager, and therapist and take special note of his analysis of managerial effectiveness upon which this section in this chapter is highly dependent (*After Virtue*, 73–78, 25–31). On the illusions of social science as a source of knowledge independent of God and its attempts to create legitimation for a space that is in that sense "secular," see John Milbank's *Theology and Social Theory* (Oxford: Blackwell, 1990) and his critique of the assumptions of the modern sociological enterprise.

20. Yoder, "A People in the World" in *The Royal Priesthood*, 74.

21. The argument that the Pauline church order doctrine of "charisma" was foundational to the entire Gentile mission is supported by E. G. Selwyn in his commentary on *The First Epistle of St. Peter* (London: Macmillan, 1952), 416. Here Selwyn outlines what he sees as a common catechetical tradition circulating throughout the Gentile church visible in a wide group of New Testament literature. Within this study, he attempts to show such a strain in the church order and unity passages of 1 Corinthians 12–14, 1 Thessalonians 5, 1 Peter 4, Romans 12, and Ephesians 4. Through a series of charts, he is able to trace remarkable parallels between this series of letters. As Selwyn does for all the other parallel strains, he proposes that behind these parallels is a catechetical tradition which is the source for all these parallels.

22. So Yoder can state about modern Protestants that "we equate [the gifts] with commercial and industrial modes of cooperation and teamwork about which we already know. The apostle, on the other hand, says that it had not already existed or functioned before [the victory of Christ in Eph. 4:7ff]." John Howard Yoder, *Body Politics* (Scottdale, PA: Herald, 1992), 49.

23. See the illuminating editorial by Thomas Long, "Myers-Briggs and Other Modern Astrologies," *Theology Today* 49, no. 3 (October 1992), 295. I first noticed this via Phil Kenneson and James Street, *Selling Out the Church* (Nashville: Abingdon, 1997), 172.

24. Charles Taylor offers the following description of pseudo community in modernity. "The primacy of self-fulfillment, particularly in its therapeutic variants, generates the notion that the only associations one can identify with are those formed voluntarily and which foster self-fulfillment, such as the 'life-style enclaves' in which people of similar interests or situations cluster—e.g., the retirement suburbs of the South, or revocable romantic relationships. Beyond these associations lies the domain of strategic relations, where instrumental considerations are paramount. The therapeutic outlook seems to conceive community on the model of associations like Parents without Partners, a body which is highly useful for its members while they are in a given predicament, but to which there is no call to feel any allegiance once one is no longer in need." Charles Taylor, *Sources of the Self* (Cambridge, MA: Harvard University Press, 1989), 508. Sadly, this has often been an accurate description of North American evangelical churches.

25. This is nothing new to the so-called organizational sciences either. They have long understood the importance of corporate culture and the role it plays in the overall functioning of an organization.

26. George Lindbeck, *The Nature of Doctrine* (Philadelphia: Westminster, 1984), argues for a cultural linguistic way of understanding the function of doctrine. The truths,

meanings, and understandings of doctrines are only possible within a cultural world, i.e., grammar, in which they make sense.

27. Robert Webber's attempt to reinvigorate the evangelistic and initiatory practices of Hyppolytus' *The Apostolic Tradition* is a source for the implementation of such an approach to baptism for the postmodern cultural situation. Robert Webber, *Journey to Jesus* (Nashville: Abingdon, 2001).

28. Yoder, *Politics of Jesus*, 2nd ed. (Grand Rapids: Eerdmans, 1994), 154.

29. Stanley Hauerwas, *A Community of Character* (Notre Dame, IN: University of Notre Dame Press, 1981), 95.

30. At a recent megachurch leadership conference, the subject of "the empty seats principle" was discussed, which says that a church, if it is to grow, must have so many percentage of empty chairs on Sunday morning to allow new people to sit among the church. There will be discomfort for new people and the church will stop growing if a church does not make room for these people through "empty seats." Then this leader discussed the struggles of going to multiple church services, Saturday night services, video services, and of course building a bigger facility as strategies to make available empty seats. Never was the option discussed of planting churches to make way for empty seats.

31. Statistics that report two to ten times the rate of growth through conversions (see note below) in church plants versus established congregations are reported by various denominations including the Evangelical Covenant Church (www.covchurch.org) and the Advent Churches (www.geocities.com) among others. Authors such as Peter Wagner, Lyle Schaller, and Leith Anderson reporting the same phenomena are quoted regularly by denominational leaders.

32. Conversion growth refers to the growth that occurs in a church due to new conversions to faith in Jesus Christ as opposed to growth that comes from people switching churches (i.e., transfer growth). The idea that there could be these two kinds of growth is in some ways a capitulation to modernity because it assumes it is conceivable that a person can be a Christian and leave his or her church at all without being sent out by the congregation to another ministry.

33. The fact that we would start churches with two hundred to three hundred people says something about our assumptions concerning the nature of the body of Christ. It says possibly that a successful church is one thousand plus, that the goal of the church is the distribution of preaching, worship, and family education services, that the interdynamic inner workings of a small body are not the essence of what it means to be the church.

34. The current church situation is the opposite. George Gallup, in his report *The Church in the World Today* (available via his website www.gallup.org), reports that in 1900, there were 27 churches for every 10,000 Americans. In 1950, there were 17 churches for every 10,000 Americans. In 1996, there were 11 churches for every 10,000 Americans. For as Rodney Stark and Roger Fincke argue, we have no more Christians in America, just a shifting to which kind of churches these same populations belong. Roger Finck and Rodney Stark, *The Churching of America, 1776–1990: Winners and Losers in Our Religious Economy* (New Brunswick, NJ: Rutgers University Press, 1992).

Chapter 2: Evangelism

1. "The sinner's prayer" is evangelical language for a prayer designed to lead the new believer through an acknowledgment of sin and an acceptance by faith of Christ's work on the cross for the forgiveness of sin.

2. There are many studies of how American evangelical church populations are not growing, only shifting, and how our youth are leaving our churches. See, for example, Eddie Gibbs, *ChurchNext* (Downers Grove, IL: InterVarsity, 2000), chap. 1, pp. 176–79, as

well as Martin Robinson and Dwight Smith in *Invading Secular Space* (London: Monarch Books, 2003), chap. 1.

3. Academics, sociologists, and "church growth experts" have used postmodern, post-Christian, post-Christendom, postliberal as well as other labels to refer to this generation and the culture they inhabit.

4. For example, Douglas Groothius, *Truth Decay: Defending Christianity against the Challenge of Postmodernism* (Downers Grove, IL: InterVarsity, 2000); Donald Carson, *The Gagging of God: Christianity Confronts Pluralism* (Grand Rapids: Zondervan, 1996); David Wells, *No Place for Truth* (Grand Rapids: Eerdmans, 1993), 65; Millard Erickson, *The Postmodern World* (Wheaton: Crossway, 2002).

5. See, for example, Robb Redman's description of the mind-set of postmodernity, the "GenX" generation, and how worship services have responded to it. "The Sound of Enthusiasm: How Generation X Is Reshaping Contemporary Worship," *Worship Leader* 10, no. 5 (2001): 27–29.

6. Thomas Kuhn, *The Structure of Scientific Revolutions*, 2nd ed. (Chicago: University of Chicago Press, 1970). On Quine and Popper, see Nancy Murphy and James McClendon, "Distinguishing Modern and Postmodern Theologies," *Modern Theology* 5 (1989): 191–214. Lesslie Newbigin has written on this issue in *Foolishness to the Greeks* (Grand Rapids: Eerdmans, 1986). On the demise of realism in science, see Stanley Grenz, *Renewing the Center* (Grand Rapids: Baker Books, 2000), chap. 7.

7. Jean-François Lyotard, *The Postmodern Condition: A Report on Knowledge* (Minneapolis: University of Minnesota Press, 1993), 25, 29, 34. See further John Milbank, *Theology and Social Theory*, 269–77.

8. See, for instance, "Can Gays Switch Sides?" *Time*, May 21, 2001, in which the article debates the scientific data for both sides of the homosexual moral arguments.

9. Indeed, John Milbank views the demise of science as freeing theology from having "to measure up to accepted standards of scientific truth or normative rationality." John Milbank, "Post Modern Critical Augustinianism," in *The Postmodern God: A Theological Reader*, ed. Graham Ward (Oxford: Blackwell, 1997), 265.

10. Alasdair MacIntyre, *After Virtue* (Notre Dame, IN: University of Notre Dame Press, 1982).

11. Lesslie Newbigin articulates the ways in which the authority of traditions works both within the scientific community and within the Christian community. *The Gospel in a Pluralist Society* (Grand Rapids: Eerdmans, 1989), chaps. 3–4.

12. For a description of the sociological milieu of the religious wars, which gave rise to modernity, see Stephen Toulmin, *Cosmopolis: The Hidden Agenda of Modernity* (New York: The Free Press, 1990). This accepted narration of modernity is questioned in a brilliant analysis by William Cavanaugh, *Theopolitical Imagination* (London: T & T Clark, 2002).

13. For an excellent reading of influences in this direction, see Lundin, *Culture of Interpretation*.

14. Martin Heidegger's analysis of the problem of ontotheology occurred in his "The Onto-theo-logical Constitution of Metaphysics," in Joan Stambaugh, trans., *Identity and Difference* (New York: Harper & Row, 1969). For a helpful treatment of this whole movement in theology, see Thomas A. Carlson, "Postmetaphysical Theology," in Kevin J. Vanhoozer, ed., *The Cambridge Companion to Postmodern Theology* (Cambridge: Cambridge University Press, 2003).

15. Or as Derrida was famous for saying, "There is nothing outside the text." Jacques Derrida, *Of Grammatology*, trans. Gayatri C. Spivak (Baltimore, MD: Johns Hopkins University Press, 1997), 158.

16. On this subject of the way we approach truth in postmodernity and the demise of so-called objective truth, I recommend reading Phil Kenneson's "There's No Such Thing

as Objective Truth, and It's a Good Thing, Too," in *Christian Apologetics in the Postmodern World*, eds. Timothy Phillips and Dennis Okholm (Downers Grove, IL: InterVarsity, 1995), 155–70.

17. For an exposition of this entire landscape and a Christian response, see Roger Lundin, *The Culture of Interpretation* (Grand Rapids: Eerdmans, 1993).

18. Josh McDowell, *The New Evidence That Demands a Verdict* (Nashville: Thomas Nelson, 1999); Lee Strobel, *The Case for Christ: A Journalist's Personal Investigation of the Evidence for Jesus* (Grand Rapids: Zondervan, 1998).

19. It produced three different "quests" for the historical Jesus, each time producing a different Jesus that proved to have more in common with the cultural outlooks of the researchers than any of the particular changes in new data. See Ben Witherington III, *The Jesus Quest* (Downers Grove, IL: InterVarsity, 1995), 9–13; N. T. Wright, *The Challenge of Jesus* (Downers Grove, IL: InterVarsity, 1999), 28–34, for a brief retelling of the history of "quest." The question is, as the standards and conclusions shift outside of Scripture and the church itself, should we continue to pin our defense of Scripture and its concomitant authority upon these outmoded places?

20. See G. A. Pritchard's extensive discussion on these issues in *Willow Creek Seeker Services* (Grand Rapids: Baker Books, 1996). More specifically, on the professional and entertaining presentation, see chapters 5–7; on "anonymity," see pages 104–8; and on "felt needs," see pages 68–72. For another example, see Rick Warren, *The Purpose Driven Church* (Grand Rapids: Zondervan, 1995). In Warren's book, regarding "felt needs," see chapter 11, and on "anonymity," see pages 258–64.

21. See Pritchard's extensive observations in *Willow Creek Seeker Services*; see especially chapter 17 and pages 249–57 among other selections in the book.

22. The critique of consumerism in church growth and marketing is extensive (led by Kenneson and Street, *Selling Out the Church*; Os Guinness, *Dining with the Devil* (Grand Rapids: Baker Books, 1993); and Pritchard, *Willow Creek Seeker Services*. Many church postmodern theorists write about the skepticism toward truth and certainty as well as the need for image and art in communication versus pure cognitive communication. See Leonard Sweet, *Post Modern Pilgrims* (Nashville: Broadman & Holman, 2000), 85–108, 145–56; Eddie Gibbs, *Church Next* (Downers Grove, IL: InterVarsity, 2000), 120–70; Brian McClaren, *The Church on the Other Side* (Grand Rapids: Zondervan, 2000), 159–70. I would like to go one step further than these theorists and caution that our presentations and art must be authentic and historically grounded to avoid the culpability of so many consumer advertising practices that create desire for a product that does nothing of benefit for the consumer.

23. See Pritchard, *Willow Creek Seeker Services*, 138–41, 249–57; and Kenneson and Street, *Selling Out*, 71–83.

24. See Phil Kenneson's analysis on this issue, *Selling Out*, 49–62. See also Pritchard's analysis of the "Unchurched Larry Problem," *Willow Creek Seeker Services*, 268–71.

25. I believe that I first heard the term *osmosis* used by Brian McClaren on a tape recorded lecture.

26. See, for example, Thomas Oden, *Agenda for Theology: After Modernity . . . What?* (1979; repr., Grand Rapids: Zondervan, 1990), chap. 11; this book was one of the first to make this connection in relation to postmodernity (in his first edition).

27. This is what lies behind Craig Van Gelder's statement about missions to a postmodern society, "The building of living communities that practice wholeness and healing will constitute one of the greatest missiological challenges for the church in the twenty-first century," "Defining the Center—Finding the Boundaries," in *Church between Gospel and Culture*, 32. The notion that the church is to be its own apologetic is the prominent theme of Stanley Hauerwas. See Stanley Hauerwas, *Community of Character* (Notre Dame, IN:

University of Notre Dame Press, 1982). Also see Phil Kenneson, *Beyond Sectarianism* (Harrisburg, PA: Trinity Press International, 1999), and Lesslie Newbigin, *The Gospel in a Pluralist Society* (Grand Rapids: Eerdmans, 1989), chaps. 10 and 18. The fact that this theme now spans the globe, both Methodist and Reformed Protestant lines as well as European (Newbigin) and North American lines, reveals a broad sweeping coalescence around this theological position in the church.

28. The common theme of John Howard Yoder's writings in the tradition of Anabaptist thought.

29. On this idea of witness, see Stanley Hauerwas, *A Community of Character* (Notre Dame, IN: University of Notre Dame Press, 1982), 105. More recently, see Hauerwas' Gifford lectures, *With the Grain of the Universe* (Grand Rapids: Brazos, 2001), chap. 8; On "epistemological crisis," see Alasdair MacIntyre, "Epistemological Crises, Dramatic Narrative and the Philosophy of Science," *Monist* 60, no. 4 (October 1977): 453–72. It seems to me MacIntyre's notion is central to understanding evangelism in the postmodern fragmented era. A similar concept to "epistemological crisis" is developed by George Lindbeck, *The Nature of Doctrine* (Philadelphia: Westminster, 1984), 39.

30. For this critique as it applies to both missions and evangelism, see David Bosch, *Transforming Mission* (Maryknoll, NY: Orbis Books, 1991), 488; Dallas Willard, "Rethinking Evangelism: A Conversation with Dallas Willard," *Cutting Edge*, Summer, 2001.

31. Michael Green, *Evangelism in the Early Church*, 2nd ed. (Guilford, Surrey, UK: Eager Inter Publishing Service, 1995), therefore refers to the early church, how "the quality of their fellowship broke down their barriers" (219). He says, "It is very noticeable that the home provided the most natural context for gossiping the gospel" in the early church context (xx). On the centrality of the house for early church evangelism, see pages 250–70. Hospitality is also a central theme for George Hunter's account of Celtic Evangelism, *The Celtic Way of Evangelism* (Nashville: Abingdon, 2000). Numerous other strategies around this theme have appeared including the "Alpha group movement," "servant evangelism," "friendship evangelism," and "peer to peer" evangelism. See also Christine Pohl's compelling argument for recovering hospitality as a tradition for Christian life in *Making Room* (Grand Rapids: Eerdmans, 1999).

32. See chapter 6 for a full exposition of this theme.

33. Perhaps traditions deep in the practice of community and fellowship that are close to evangelicals in some doctrinal issues, like Mennonite or Brethren traditions, can lead us in recovering these ways of community that have been lost amidst the efforts to organize the church using megachurch models.

34. Thanks to Roland Kuhl for jogging my memory and stimulating my thought on this issue through his own explorations on "businesses run like churches instead of churches run like businesses."

35. "Worship Evangelism" is the phrase first popularized by Sally Morgenthaler's book with this same phrase as its title: *Worship Evangelism* (Grand Rapids: Zondervan, 1995). Although not postmodern in its emphasis, Morgenthaler leads us in the issues important for a postmodern evangelism.

36. Robert Webber, *Journey to Jesus* (Grand Rapids: Baker Books, 2000).

37. Stanley Grenz makes this point about evangelical churches in general in *Renewing the Center* (Grand Rapids: Baker Books, 2000), 289–90.

38. In other words, a convert in postmodernity is not defined by his or her isolated decision for Christ in a guilt-ridden or fear-driven moment of crisis. Instead, this first decision merely defines that person as a seeker beginning a journey toward initiation. The end goal of this beginning is the decision of the whole person to enter the death of Christ in baptism and rise again in the Spirit out of these waters to new life, i.e., existence under his lordship in the body of Christ.

39. Newbigin makes essentially the same point for different reasons in *The Gospel for a Pluralist Society* (Grand Rapids: Eerdmans, 1989), 121. He states that the goal of missions is "the presence of a new reality" in the Spirit before the world. Newbigin argues that the apostle Paul believed his mission was to plant living vibrant communities of Christ, not save all the world's individuals. He defends this thesis by pointing to the apostle's words in Romans 15:23 that he "no longer has any room for work in these regions." This implies for Newbigin that Paul believed the missionary task was completed through planting believing communities in every region because obviously every individual had not been presented with the gospel. According to Newbigin, Paul therefore can say he has "fully preached the gospel" in these regions even though there are still those who have not heard. This is part and parcel of Newbigin's collectivist understanding of the church as embodying the gospel as a witness to the world of a way of life made possible because of what Jesus has done. The idea of "missional communities" in a postmodern world is also an emphasis of the Vineyard movement, a major force for church planting in North America in the past fifteen years.

40. This is the suggestion of Robert Webber, *Ancient Future* (Grand Rapids: Baker Books, 1999), 141–63. It is developed further in his *Journey to Jesus* (Nashville: Abingdon, 2002).

Chapter 3: Leadership

1. The Harvard Business school's interest in Willow Creek organizational behavior is noted in a book by their pastor Bill Hybels, *Courageous Leadership* (Grand Rapids: Zondervan, 2003), 69–70. On Forbes's infatuation with the megachurch's leadership, Rich Karlgaard writes, "I give you the best book on entrepreneurship, business and investment I have read in some time. It's not new and it's not a business book. . . . It's titled *The Purpose Driven Church*. . . . Saddleback [Church] has spawned dozens of so-called daughter churches throughout the country. Were it a business, Saddleback would be compared with Dell, Google, or Starbucks. . . . So let's engage our imaginations, substitute the word 'business' for 'church' and see what Warren has to tell us." "Purpose Driven," *Forbes*, February 16, 2004, 39. Karlgaard then ironically lists Warren's best advice for pastors in the book and lists them as some of the best business advice any entrepreneur could have.

2. Bill Hybels, Ken Blanchard, and Phil Hodges, *Leadership by the Book: Tools to Transform Your Workplace* (New York: William Morrow, 1999), xi–xii.

3. John Maxwell, *The 21 Irrefutable Laws of Leadership* (Nashville: Nelson, 1998), xx.

4. These were the words of David Staal of the Willow Creek Association in explaining why Bill Clinton was being invited to speak at the Willow Creek Leadership Summit despite significant protests both in and outside the Willow Creek Church. *The Daily Herald* (Chicago) August 8, 2000. Bill Hybels in his response to his church's complaints said that the Leadership Summit has always prided itself in bringing in the best leaders and leadership experts, Christian or not, to learn from them about leadership.

5. Alasdair MacIntyre traces the modern rise of this confidence in *After Virtue* (Notre Dame, IN: University of Notre Dame Press, 1981), chap. 8. He also traces its demise in the same chapter (8) in the face of the breakdown of modernity or what MacIntyre calls "The Failure of the Enlightenment Project."

6. In Alasdair MacIntyre's words, the manager's claims to authority are based in part upon "the law-like generalizations and their applications to particular cases derived from the study of this domain." This is a claim "made by the natural sciences; and it is not surprising that expressions such as 'management science' should be coined." *After Virtue*, 77. For MacIntyre this is characteristic of modernity.

7. MacIntyre outlines the origins of this notion and its dominance in modernity in *After Virtue*, 74ff.

8. The characterization of all political, social, and economic relations as sources of domination is most prevalent in the writings of Michel Foucault. For an overview of Foucault's thoughts on this, see Steven Best and Douglas Kellner, *Postmodern Theory* (New York: Guilford, 1991), 54–68.

9. John Milbank details the development and discrediting of the social sciences as a neutral discipline in *Theology and Social Theory* (Oxford: Blackwell, 1990), chaps. 3–5. See also Richard Rorty, "Method, Social Science, and Social Hope," in *Consequences of Pragmatism* (Minneapolis: University of Minnesota Press, 1982), chap. 11.

10. "Getting It Done Leadership" is the title of Bill Hybels's third chapter in *Courageous Leadership*.

11. MacIntyre, *After Virtue*, 74.

12. John H. Yoder, "Christ, the Hope of the World," Cartwright, *The Royal Priesthood*, 203.

13. Richard Rorty, *Objectivity, Relativism, and Truth* (Cambridge: Cambridge University Press, 1991). Part 1 is just one voice among many that argue the nuances of this claim.

14. John Milbank, *Theology and Social Theory* (Oxford: Blackwell, 1990), 380.

15. Yoder, "Christ, the Only Hope," 202–3.

16. These phrases are all headings in Hybels's book *Courageous Leadership*. In their book *Leadership by the Book*, Bill Hybels, Ken Blanchard, and Phil Hodges say in the introduction, "We believe there is a perfect practitioner and teacher of effective leadership. That person is Jesus of Nazareth, who embodied the heart and methods of a fully committed and effective servant leader." *Leadership by the Book: Tools to Transform Your Workplace* (New York: William Morrow, 1999), xi–xii.

17. Don Soderquist, *Life@Work Journal*, Special Leadership Summit Edition 2000, 28.

18. Hybels, *Courageous Leadership*, 71.

19. Ken Blanchard, "Servant Leadership Revisited," in *Insights on Leadership*, ed. Peter Block, Ken Blanchard, Margaret Wheatley, and James Autry (New York: Wiley & Sons, 1998), 26.

20. Although not an evangelical, a book that could be accused of this same practice of using Scripture and the life of Christ in relation to leadership is Laurie Beth Jones, *Jesus CEO: Using Ancient Wisdom for Visionary Leadership* (New York: Hyperion, 1995).

21. Notable exception where the word *leader* is used in the context of the church is in Hebrews 13:17, 24.

22. Hans Küng, *The Church*, trans. Ray and Rosaleen Ockenden (London: Burns and Oats, 1967), 496–97; E. Schweizer, *Church Order in the New Testament* (Naperville, IL: Allenson, 1961), 174–76, §21c–d; E. Kasemann, "Ministry and Community in the New Testament," in *Essays on New Testament Themes* (London: S.C.M. Press, 1964), 63–64; Robert Banks and Bernice Ledbetter, "Reviewing Leadership," in *A Christian Evaluation of Current Approaches* (Grand Rapids: Baker Academic, 2004), 38.

23. For example, Romans 11:13; 16:1; 1 Corinthians 3:5; 2 Corinthians 3:6; 6:4; 11:23; Ephesians 3:7; 6:21; Colossians 1:7, 23; 4:7, 12; 1 Thessalonians 3:2; 1 Timothy 1:12; 2 Timothy 4:5, 11.

24. Küng, *The Church*, 498–502.

25. I thank Brian McLaren for reminding me of this text and its meaning in a speech he gave to an Up\Rooted meeting, March 15, 2004, at North Park University, Chicago, Illinois.

26. See Focus on the Family surveys as reported in *Dr. Dobson's Newsletter*, Focus on the Family, August 1998.

27. John LaRue Jr., "Forced Exits, A Too-Common Ministry Hazard," *Christianity Today*, March/April 1996.

28. As reported in "Forced Terminations of Pastors, Staff Leveling Off, Survey Results Show," *LifeWay News*, August 2001. The surveys showed that forced terminations had been increasing during the '90s but leveled off in 2000.

29. Stanley Hauerwas, *Character and the Christian Life* (San Antonio: Trinity University Press, 1985), 203–4.

30. For an excursus on this model, see Stephen Fowl, *Engaging Scripture* (Oxford: Blackwell, 1998), 101–19.

31. According to Bill Hybels in his book *Courageous Leadership*, in a chapter entitled "The Art of Self-Leadership," he states that "[f]ollowers will only trust leaders who exhibit the highest levels of integrity" (189). Leaders should therefore take care of their character. "Whose job is it to maintain a leader's character? It's the leader's job, of course" (190). The axioms are true that leaders require good character. What unfortunately underwrites Hybels's notions of character and leadership here is that character can be sought for the purpose of becoming a more effective leader. And leaders can see their own faults without the help of the people whom they lead.

32. This isolation of the pastor from his or her congregation, in regard to any meaningful accountability or vulnerability, has ironically been institutionalized by the evangelical organization Focus on the Family with its efforts to promote "The Shepherd's Covenant." The Shepherd's Covenant is a list of five covenants that include "genuine accountability" with colleagues who I assume are ministers either outside the congregation or on staff with Focus on the Family. Either way the accountability remains separated from the congregations. The other four covenants relate to having a good family life, having a servant-oriented heart, installing safeguards in ministry from moral failure, and maintaining a good devotional life. All of these are excellent commitments. Nonetheless they are institutionalized by the Shepherd's Covenant so as to separate the pastors from the congregation, which is in the best position to walk alongside them in their daily lives. The Shepherd's Covenant then begs the question, Why manage the clergy's moral health with a strategy that is parachurch and takes the pastor's moral life outside the church body, where it can best grow? The answer is because evangelicalism has indeed structured the clergy so as to make the pastor's growth in Christ impossible inside the inner workings of the body.

33. Robert Greenleaf, *Servant Leadership*, 3rd ed. (New York: Paulist, 2002), 29.

34. Roland Kuhl of Northern Seminary, Lombard, Illinois, has written how "the terms for leading in the New Testament help describe this servantship as a 'witness,' an 'amongness,' or an 'alongsidedness.' They are words that do not describe persons who are leading from up front or above the congregation. Rather they are persons who are with and among the people they are now serving." "Leadership in Christ's Community: A Different Direction," in an unpublished paper delivered at proceedings of an Up\Rooted meeting (February 2, 2004), 9. Roland goes on to flesh out this thesis with the way leadership would then look in the church as opposed to the various CEO models of our day.

35. The split of competency from character in this regard is a development of professionalization within modernity. It is only within modernity that one could consider one's competencies for a particular task as separate from one's character for the particular task. This in effect is the professionalization of a task where one acquires accreditation of certain competencies within a group, yet is rarely tested for character qualities. One's character, for instance, as a medical doctor used to be a prerequisite for entrance into the medical field. Today, rarely is a doctor excluded from medical practice because of malfeasance of character (until it is too late). Foucault traced this separation to modernity in the rise of the modern competent political ruler. In contrast to Christian medievaldom, the modern ruler, armed with knowledge and competency, no longer required a certain virtue to maintain his rulership (See Daniel Bell, *Liberation Theology after the End of History* (London: Routledge, 2001), 23–24, on Foucault's genealogy in this regard.) Today, the

same phenomenon is witnessed when an American president or presidential candidate claims (à la Bill Clinton) that his or her moral character has nothing to do with his or her ability to be president.

36. John Howard Yoder, *The Fullness of Christ: Paul's Vision of Universal Ministry* (Elgin, IL: Brethren, 1987), 17–18. Other writers argue for a "plural leadership" based in New Testament understandings of giftedness. R. Paul Stevens, *Liberating the Laity* (Vancouver, BC: Regent College Publishing, 1977). My own "The Charismatic Structure of the Church: The New Testament Concept of Authority and Structure in the Community of the New Age" (M.A. thesis, Northern Baptist Theological Seminary, 1981), argues for the necessity of church order in history tied to the multiple gift structure of the New Testament. In regard to leadership in the Brethren context, see Alexander Strauch, *Biblical Eldership: An Urgent Call to Restore Biblical Church Leadership*, rev. ed. (Littleton, CO: Lewis & Roth, 1997).

Chapter 4: The Production of Experience

1. Of course I am not addressing so-called Anglo-Catholic and other liturgically minded evangelicals. There are other challenges here to these worship services, but this is not the subject matter of this chapter.

2. Of course many evangelicals seek to blend the two.

3. I owe the clarifying suggestion to use the example of lecture hall and feel-good pep rally to my friend Jim Poole, for many years programming director of Park Community Church in Chicago, Illinois.

4. Zwingli believed that Christians would tend to minimize the significance of the Lord's Supper if they did it every week. It might become a dead ritual. Therefore Zwingli limited its practice to monthly and then even quarterly.

5. This was particularly true for the Radical Reformation à la Zwingli. On this theme in Zwingli, see Charles Garside, *Zwingli and the Arts* (New Haven: Yale University Press, 1966). For a retelling of the history of the development of the Protestant principle that rejects any finite manifestations of God, see Hans Urs von Baltasar, *The Glory of the Lord, Vol. 1, Seeing the Form* (San Francisco: Ignatius, 1982), 45–70. On the whole development of worship in the Reformation Free Church traditions, see Robert Webber, *Worship Old and New* (Zondervan: Grand Rapids, 1994), chap. 10.

6. Even after the evangelical battles with Protestant liberalism of the 1920s, the broad North American culture remained largely benign to Christianity as typified by 1950s television. See for instance Garry Wills' explanation of the twentieth-century American culture after the fundamentalist–liberal controversies of the 1920s in *Under God* (New York: Simon & Schuster, 1990).

7. Whatever you think of *The Andy Griffith Show*, *I Love Lucy*, and other 1950s TV shows, it is hard to imagine them as anything more than harmless wastes of time for the one who truly seeks to follow Christ.

8. This seems to be what lies behind Leonard Sweet's work on postmodern culture. Although I do not agree with Sweet's ecclesiological assumptions, he gives a helpful account of how our culture has shifted from logo-centrism to image-participatory driven approaches to knowledge. *Post Modern Pilgrims* (Nashville: Broadman & Holman, 2000). See also *SoulTsunami* (Grand Rapids: Zondervan, 1999) among his myriad of books.

9. I realize this statement is controversial. There are those who argue that entertainment and media have always been hostile to Christianity even before the 1950s. And certainly we must acknowledge that certain discriminatory and social justice practices prior to the '50s were worse culturally than what we have today in terms of media forces. What I am specifically pointing to is the mammoth growth and influence of culture industries to form hearts and minds in a way that is hostile to Christian life since the 1970s. On this see, for instance, Michael Budde, *The (Magic) Kingdom of God: Christianity and*

Global Culture Industries (Boulder, CO: Westview, 1997), or the populist book by Michael Medved, *Hollywood vs. America: Popular Culture and the War on Traditional Values* (New York: HarperCollins, 1992).

10. Of course I am aware that in other ways American culture has progressed toward certain Christian ideals. For instance, culture became less tolerant toward racism, segregation, and became a more open society for woman in the workplace and other societal institutions. These transformations in society, however, have been largely articulated not in specific substantive terms but in the proceduralist terms of democratic liberalism, that is, equal rights and egalitarianism. (On this distinction, see Ronald Dworkin, "Liberalism," in *Public and Private Morality*, ed. Stuart Hampshire [Cambridge: Cambridge University Press, 1978]). The reasons for outlawing discrimination are for a better liberal society where "selves" can flourish as selves for whatever purpose they want, not for reasons specifically related to Christian purposes or meanings. As a result, we may be more tolerant toward women having equal rights in our workplaces, yet our imaginations are still being trained by a consumeristic hedonism, which demeans and sexually abuses women. We may be more tolerant toward other races, but our imaginations continue to be trained into ethnic pride and locating our self through national identities. In the end therefore, even with the so-called societal gains of procedural liberalism, we still have a society more hostile to Christian life.

11. George Marsden, among others, has detailed the history of the American university from a shaper of character to the role of inducting citizens into democracy and capitalism. *The Soul of the American University* (New York: Oxford University Press, 1994), chap. 21.

12. By "technologies" I mean those structures of culture that shape us and construct us by virtue of their power as determining structures of modern life and our complicit participation in them. See Albert Borgman's classic *Technology and the Character of Contemporary Life* (Chicago: University of Chicago Press, 1984).

13. By "Cartesian autonomous minds" I refer to the modern assumptions behind the idea of selves as independent autonomous thinking minds that doubt everything and believe they can make truth evaluations all on their own. We inherit this notion of the self from Descartes and modernity. But postmodernity has vigorously deconstructed this version of the self and revealed its false pretenses and hidden contradictions.

14. With these terms, I do not mean to refer only to the worship of the self-consciously charismatic or Pentecostal churches. Instead, I refer to all types of worship known for using contemporary music forms and encouraging self-expression as a signpost of good worship.

15. Marva Dawn comments substantively on the "I" nature of the choruses used sometimes in contemporary worship, in *Reaching Out without Dumbing Down: A Theology of Worship for the Turn of the Century* (Grand Rapids: Eerdmans, 1995), 170–73.

16. I am distinguishing certain elements of bodily participation that are self-expressive versus other forms of bodily participation that might be participatory and submissive to the work of God in the church. Bowing before God physically is rarely seen in typical charismatic services. It is more common among current more liturgical and so-called emergent church services. It of course is the staple of High Church liturgy where one has a kneeling bar on the back of every pew. This kind of submissive bodily ritual is contrasted to self-expressive bodily rituals like clapping, lifting hands, etc. We need both in church worship.

17. By "signpost" I mean signature, identity, marker, that which would answer the question, "How would we know we are achieving good worship?" It goes without saying that all worship is designed for the purpose of giving glory to God, and that includes traditional worship, contemporary charismatic worship, and all other kinds of worship. The

question is, "How would we know when we are doing this well?" For the contemporary Christian worshipers the signpost of good worship is the experience, often the emotional experience.

18. On this issue in Charles Finny, see Donald Dayton, *Discovering an Evangelical Heritage* (New York: Harper & Row, 1976), 16–17; George Marsden, *Fundamentalism and American Culture* (Oxford: Oxford University Press, 1980), 86–87. On Holiness revivals and experience, see Donald Dayton, *Theological Roots of Pentecostalism* (Grand Rapids: Zondervan, 1980). For Holiness and its promotion of an experience of the Holy Spirit, see Marsden, *Fundamentalism and American Culture*, chaps. 8 and 11.

19. For an exposition of these historical developments, see Charles Taylor, *Sources of the Self* (Cambridge, MA: Harvard University Press, 1988), chap. 21. See also Roger Lundin, *The Culture of Interpretation: Christian Faith and the Postmodern World* (Grand Rapids: Eerdmans, 1993), chaps. 3, 5, 9, and 10. Each traces brilliantly the subtle changes in the conception and role of the artist as well during these influences. Nancy Murphy is also helpful in tracing the intellectual history of individual "experience" as a category for religious knowledge, in *Beyond Liberalism and Fundamentalism* (Harrisburg, PA: Trinity Press International, 1996), chap. 1.

20. A helpful summary of these developments can be found in Constance Cherry, "Merging Tradition and Innovation in the Life of the Church," in *The Conviction of Things Not Seen*, ed. Todd Johnson (Grand Rapids: Brazos, 2002), 23–27.

21. Graham Ward, *Cities of God* (New York: Routledge, 2000), chap. 2.

22. I refer here to theorists such as Robert Zajonc, "On the Primacy of Affect," *American Psychologist* 39, no. 2 (1984): 117–23; Richard Lazarus "On the Primacy of Cognition," *American Psychologist* 39, no. 2 (1984): 124–29. See also Lazarus, "Progress on Cognitive-Motivational-Relational Theory of Emotion," *American Psychologist* (August 1991): 112–27, Keith Oatley and P. N. Johnson, "Towards a Cognitive Theory of the Emotions," *Cognition and Emotion* 1, no. 1 (1987): 29–50, for a convincing argument for the primacy of cognition and appraisal in the forming of human emotions.

23. See Martha Nussbaum's exposition of this in "Narrative Emotions: Beckett's Geneology of Love," in *Why Narrative?* (Grand Rapids: Eerdmans, 1989), where she says, "We learn how to feel and we learn our emotional repertoire. . . . They are taught, above all, through stories. Stories express their structure and teach us their dynamics" (217). See also *Texts of Identity*, ed. John Shotter and Kenneth Gergen (London: Sage Publications, 1991). An exposition of this theme can be found in chapter 6 of this book.

24. Alasdair MacIntyre, *After Virtue* (Notre Dame, IN: University of Notre Dame Press, 1982), 30–33; Phillip Reiff, *The Triumph of the Therapeutic* (New York: Harper & Row, 1966); Robert Bellah, *Habits of the Heart* (New York: Harper & Row, 1986), 47–48. On the same themes, see Richard Shweder, *Thinking Through Cultures* (Cambridge, MA: Harvard University Press, 1991), chaps. 4 and 6. Roger Lundin describes well the postmodern, poststructuralist move "to read the Enlightenment and romantic development of the self as a misguided attempt to internalize the divine, undertaken at a time when orthodox faith was effectively eclipsed in science, philosophy and culture." *The Culture of Interpretation*, 211. On the construction of self, see Kenneth Gergen, *The Saturated Self* (New York: Basic Books, 1991), 41–47, 145–60. For a critique of Romanticist views of emotions and experience 6–47.

25. Rodney Clapp asserts this notion is what lies behind the word *revival*. *A Peculiar People* (Downers Grove, IL: InterVarsity, 1996), 163.

26. See, for instance, Stanley Hauerwas and Charles Pinches, *Christians among the Virtues* (Notre Dame, IN: University of Notre Dame Press, 1997); Jean Porter, *The Recovery of Virtue* (Louisville: Westminster John Knox, 1990).

27. I use the term *erotics* in the sense of desire as nurtured and structured from and toward God à la Gerald Loughlin, "Erotics: God's Sex," in *Radical Orthodoxy: A New Theology* ed. John Millbank, Catherine Pickstock, and Graham Ward (London; New York: Routledge, 1999), 148–50.

28. Catherine Pickstock, *After Writing* (Oxford: Blackwell, 1998), 208.

29. There is some dispute as to whether "beauty" is a transcendental condition of being in medieval theology alongside "the one, the true and the good." Nonetheless there seems to be a consensus that beauty became a predominant part of the transcendentals either as a corollary to "the good" or as a summary of all the other conditions of "being" later in medieval theology. Therefore, it would have been difficult for a medieval scholastic to see something that is "ugly" as true. Of course they would not use "ugly" in the sensuous or degrading sense of today's overtly hedonistically obsessed culture. "Ugly" and "beauty" would refer to moral and metaphysical beauty. On beauty as a medieval transcendental, see Jan Aertsen, *Medieval Philosophy and the Transcendentals* (New York: E. J. Brill, 1996), chap. 8, especially pp. 335–37. See also Umberto Eco, *Art and Beauty in the Middle Ages* (New Haven: Yale University Press, 1986). It was part of Hans Urs von Baltasar's program to develop a theology in terms of the so-called "third transcendental" of beauty. See his *The Glory of the Lord: A Theological Aesthetic, Vol. I, Seeing the Form*, trans. E. Leiva Merikakas (Edinburgh: T & T Clark, 1982).

30. This is obviously a notion of beauty that goes beyond the truncated forms of sensuality that pass for beauty in American culture. It is also moral in nature. Something is beautiful in ascending to its created order and purposes. It is more than just visual as well. Mother Teresa was using beauty in this sense when she stated in her speech before Congress on accepting her Congressional Medal of Honor: "It is a beautiful and attractive thing to serve the poor."

31. See John Milbank and Catherine Pickstock, *Truth in Aquinas* (London: Routledge, 2001). Milbank draws extensively upon Hans Urs von Balthasar's aesthetic theology in *The Glory of the Lord*. See also Frederick Bauerschmidt, "The Theological Sublime," in *Radical Orthodoxy*, 201–19.

32. William Dyrness, *Visual Faith: Art, Theology, and Worship in Dialogue* (Grand Rapids: Baker Academic, 2001). Michael Card, *Scribbling in the Sand* (Downers Grove, IL: InterVarsity, 2002); Robert K. Johnston, "Visual Christianity," *The Conviction of Things Not Seen*, ed. Todd Johnson (Grand Rapids: Brazos, 2002), 165–82.

33. Henri Nouwen describes the function of icons in these terms in *Behold the Beauty of the Lord: Praying with Icons* (Notre Dame, IN: Ave Maria, 1987).

34. An icon "was meant to lift the soul toward the contemplation of God, to stimulate," as Bernard McGinn put it, a "contemplative movement from the perceptible 'up' to the conceptual." Dyrness, *Visual Faith*, 35. See Dyrness, *Visual Faith*, on "icons," 33–37. See also some works he refers to: Bernard McGinn, John Meyendorff, and Jean Leclerq, eds., *Christian Spirituality: Origins to the Twelfth Century* (New York: Crossroads, 1987); and Gervase Matthew, *Byzantine Aesthetics* (New York: Harper & Row, 1971).

35. For a dense discussion of the place of art amidst the end of modernity, see Gianni Vattimo's *The End of Modernity* (Baltimore: Johns Hopkins, 1985). In particular, see his treatment of Heidegger's notion of art as a "setting into work of truth." He states "the work of art has the function of founding and constituting the outlines which define an historical world. . . in the work [of art in its exhibition] each individual's sense of membership in an historical world is intensified" (61–62). These notions are pregnant with possibilities for understanding the role of art in the world devoid of foundations for truth. For Nietzsche's views on art, see Vattimo, 95–103. Whatever you think of postmodernity and its legitimacy as a philosophical position, our society is more and more captivated by art as the stage upon which to play out truth.

36. Bill Cavanaugh locates this development at the dawn of modernity in the Italian Renaissance in Marcilio Facinio's writings. The establishment of the religious impulse was part of the depoliticization of the church and the interiorizing of religious faith. William Cavanaugh, *Theopolitical Imagination* (New York: T & T Clark, 2002), 30.

37. Rene Girard, *Deceit, Desire and the Novel: Self and Other in Literary Structure* (Baltimore: Johns Hopkins University Press, 1996).

38. George Lindbeck, *The Nature of Doctrine* (Philadelphia: Westminster, 1984), 36–37.

39. I believe the apostle's point in 1 Corinthians 12–14 is just this: ecstatic experience is not a signpost indicating that one is led by the Holy Spirit in worship, rather it is the ability to confess truthfully and in integrity (and liturgically) that "Jesus is Lord" (1 Cor. 12:1–3).

40. Robert Webber, *Worship Old and New* (Grand Rapids: Eerdmans, 1994), 27ff.

41. On *lex orandi, lex credendi,* see Yves Congar, *Tradition and Traditions* (London: Burns & Oates, 1966), 429.

42. Albert Borgman makes this clear in his book *Technology and the Character of Contemporary Life,* where he says if we do not recapture orientation as a category for experience, technology shall orient us all into oblivion. I owe thanks to Steven Long for pointing me toward Borgman's excellent exposition of this concept. Albert Borgman, *Technology and the Character,* chap. 13.

43. An example of this typical bifurcation of the worship debate among evangelicals is Ortberg and Howell, in "Can You Engage Both Heart and Mind?" *Leadership Journal,* Spring 1999, 32–36. They discuss the need to combine the experiential aspect (the heart) and the propositional aspect (the mind) but do not go beyond these in their understanding of worship. I am indebted to Geoff Holsclaw, friend and co-laborer in ministry, for pointing this article out to me.

44. Lindbeck, *Nature of Doctrine* (Philadelphia: Westminster, 1984), 15–42.

45. Ibid., 32.

46. Ibid., 16–19.

47. John Milbank appropriates the work of Hans Urs von Balthasar to elaborate a similar move to overcome the modernist alternatives of fundamentalist propositionalism and Protestant liberal privatizing egoism. As opposed to Lindbeck's Wittgensteinian linguistic approach, however, Milbank builds upon a premodern Thomism and conjoins it with Baltasar's use of the medieval transcendentals, especially the transcendental of beauty. He can therefore say, "Because our cultural products confront us and are not truly 'in our control' or even 'our gift,' this allows that somewhere among them God of his own free will finds space to confront us also. The transcendental possibility of revelation is the decision of God to create the poetic being humankind, and with this the realization one can, at once, overcome a liberal, merely 'ethical' reading of religion, and also (equally modern and deviant) positivistic notion of revelation as something in history 'other' to the normal processes of historicity." *The Word Made Strange* (Oxford: Blackwell, 1997), 130. Milbank and the whole Radical Orthodoxy theological project provide enormous resources for overcoming the problems of modernity and postmodernity and a worship grounded in the epistemological categories of beauty and liturgy.

48. Lindbeck suggests the wording "absorbs" in *Nature of Doctrine* (Philadelphia: Westminster, 1984), 117. He says that "A Scriptural world is thus able to absorb the universe. It supplies the interpretive framework within which believers seek to live their lives and understand reality." The practice of worship is allowing oneself to be absorbed like this.

49. This is Graham Ward's brilliant depiction in *Cities of God* (Oxford: Routledge, 2000).

50. From Nicholas Arseniev, *Russian Piety* (London: American Orthodox, 1964), 85. I owe thanks to David Bunker for pointing me to this text and quote.

51. This notion of practice is indebted to Alasdair MacIntyre's fuller and more substantive account of "practice" in *After Virtue*, 2nd ed. (Notre Dame, IN: University of Notre Dame Press, 1982), 187–91.

52. I am using "goods" here in the way Alasdair MacIntyre has described "internal goods" and their relation to practices. He describes how a tradition's "goods can only be achieved by subordinating ourselves within the practice in our relationship to other practitioners." *After Virtue*, 191.

53. For the idea of the church as a "museum," I owe my friend David Carlson.

54. For an exploration of Thomas Cranmer and the writing of the liturgy for accessibility, see Mark Ashton, "Following in Cranmer's Footsteps," in Donald Carson, ed., *Worship by the Book* (Grand Rapids: Zondervan, 2002), 64–135. Thanks to David Whited who referred me to this reference. For an excellent description of the ongoing development of liturgy, see the preface to the *Common Book of Prayer* of the Episcopal Church 1979, 9–11.

55. See Robert Webber's description in *Worship Is a Verb* (Peabody, MA: Hendrickson, 1992), chaps. 4 and 6.

56. See the narratives of Exodus 15 and 1 Chronicles 16 as examples.

57. See Graham Ward, ed., *The Postmodern God* (Oxford: Blackwell, 1997), xvii–xxii, for a treatment of how time and space were corrupted by modernity according to a Christian perspective. See Robert Webber, *Ancient Future Time* (Grand Rapids: Baker Books, 2004), for a helpful guide on using the church calendar in church life, especially for evangelicals who might be new to the practice.

58. Again I refer to Marva Dawn, *Reaching Out without Dumbing Down* (Grand Rapids: Eerdmans, 1995), 170–73. See also Brian McClaren's insightful piece "An Open Letter to Worship Songwriters," *Worship Leader*, October 2002.

59. I am using the term as Robert Webber refers to them in his *The Younger Evangelicals* (Grand Rapids: Baker Books, 2002).

Chapter 5: The Preaching of the Word

1. "Vigilant communities" is Stephen Fowl's concept from *Engaging Scripture* (Oxford: Blackwell, 1998), chap. 3.

2. As reported in Sundar Krishnan's *Heart, Mind, Strength* (Camp Hill, PA: Christian Publications, 2003), 79. *Preaching and Pulpit Digest* analyzed two hundred sermons preached in evangelical pulpits between 1985–1989. They categorized these sermons according to four categories: (1) content and organization came from the Bible, (2) content came from the Bible but the organization came from the preacher's own preferences, (3) neither content nor organization came from the Bible but could be recognized as matters of Christian concern, and (4) neither content nor organization was recognizably Christian. Barely 25 percent fell into the first category, 22 percent fell into the second category, and over half fell into the third category. The percentage in the fourth category was negligible. An additional analysis was done that analyzed how many of these sermons were grounded in the character, nature, and will of God. Evidently fewer than 20 percent of these sermons met this test. David Wells decries how these findings show that 80 percent of sermons in evangelical pulpits are anthropocentric, not putting God at the center of the preaching. In Os Guinness and John Seel, eds., *No God But God: Breaking the Idols of Our Age* (Chicago: Moody, 1992), 184–85. The noticeable presumption in these statistics is that expository preaching (category 1) is the answer to this problem.

3. Or in the language of Schleiermachian Romanticist hermeneutics, the preacher seeks to overcome the distance between the reader and the spirit of the author.

4. Stephen Fowl refers to this notion as "determinate interpretation." He refers to Ben Witherington III as an example of a scholar who still abides by these notions of determinate interpretation. Stephen Fowl, *Engaging Scripture* (Oxford: Blackwell, 1998), 33. Another prominent scholar committed to this kind of interpretation would be James Dunn, who describes the task of biblical studies as "trying to hear the words of the texts as the writer of these words intended those words for whom he wrote to hear them. Our only real hope of achieving that goal is by setting the text as fully as possible into the historical context within which it was written." James Dunn, *Christology in the Making*, 2nd ed. (London: Student Christian Movement, 1989), xiv. This was quoted by Graham Ward, *Theology and Critical Theory*, 2nd ed. (New York: St. Martin's, 1989), 40. I suspect that many more biblical scholars from traditional evangelical seminaries hold to this same view of scriptural hermeneutics.

5. For a more extensive treatment of why determinate interpretation is unsustainable as a hermeneutical theory, see Fowl, *Engaging Scripture*, 33–40.

6. As Derrida describes it, "[C]ommunication, which, in fact, implies the transmission charged with passing, from one subject to the other, the identity of a signified object of a meaning or a concept in principle separable from the process of passage and of signifying operation." As quoted by G. Spivak in his preface to his translation of Jacques Derrida, *Of Grammatology* (Baltimore, MD: Johns Hopkins University Press, 1997), lvii. Spivak calls this idea of meaning the "notion of unified subjects of meaning as portable property."

7. I owe this example to Steve Long, given in a lecture at Garrett Evangelical Seminary.

8. Of course the same is true of topical preaching or preaching in general. But whereas topical preaching openly admits that it aims the preaching at the person's subjective needs already, expository preaching somehow claims to be more pure. It is the "preaching of the Word." It assumes that by following the text more closely, somehow the propositions will not be polluted by the pastor's or other foreign agendas.

9. Hans Frei calls this "the Cartesian error of separating out a self-contained, self-certain ego of 'understanding' from the understood world." *Theology and Narrative* (Oxford: Oxford University Press, 1993), 132.

10. Fowl, *Engaging Scripture*, 113ff.

11. Ibid., 114.

12. Unpublished paper, "The Interpretive Leader," by Jim Van Yperen, Executive Director of Metanoia Ministries, Washington, New Hampshire, 1999. Posted on website www. changeyourmind.net. This of course assumes a process of ordination and consecration into an ongoing tradition of faith.

13. Fowl, *Engaging Scripture*, 62.

14. Stanley Fish, *Is There a Text in This Class?* (Cambridge, MA: Harvard University Press, 1980), 14–15.

15. Imagine such a pastor finding sufficient Jewish and Roman backgrounds supporting the idea that lightning was associated with the Greco-Roman god Saturn. The pastor then makes the case that our resurrected bodies shall all be born of Saturn, a foreign god. This maverick interpretation is then carried out to imply we should start worshiping Saturn as part of our Sunday liturgy. The reason why a pastor could not get away with this expository preaching is not because of bad exegesis but because the interpretation violates the communal consensuses within both the immediate body of Christ, the local church, as well as orthodoxy in general as carried on by the church tradition of which it is a part.

16. Stanley Fish, *Is There a Text in This Class?* (Cambridge, MA: Harvard University Press, 1980), 193.

17. Fowl, *Engaging Scripture*, chap. 3.

18. John Howard Yoder, *To Hear the Word* (Eugene, OR: Wipf and Stock, 2001), 49.

19. James K. Smith, *The Fall of Interpretation* (Downers Grove, IL: InterVarsity, 2000).

20. Stanley Hauerwas, *Unleashing the Scripture* (Nashville: Abingdon, 1993).

21. These are Walter Brueggemann's words, from *Texts Under Negotiation: The Bible and Postmodern Imagination* (Minneapolis: Fortress, 1993). For more, see his brilliant book on preaching, *Cadences of Home: Preaching among Exiles* (Philadelphia: Westminster John Knox, 1997), 29–37, which describe what preaching must look like for the church in a postmodern post-Christian context.

22. Paul Ricouer calls what critical exergesis seeks to uncover "the world behind the text." See, for instance, his "Biblical Hermeneutics," *Semeia* 4 (1975); See also "The Hermeneutical Function of Distanciation," in Paul Ricouer, *Hermeneutics and the Human Sciences*, ed. John Thompson (New York: Cambridge University Press, 1981), 131–44.

23. Hans Frei, *The Eclipse of Biblical Narrative* (New Haven: Yale University Press, 1974), 3.

24. Paul Ricouer, *Hermeneutics and the Human Sciences* (Cambridge: Cambridge University Press, 1981), 143. To accept Ricouer on this point is not to fully embrace that "the mode of being in the world" is a phenomenological human experience created in front of the text and this is the sole referent for the text. For the problematics of this theory for both Ricouer and his follower David Tracy, see Hans Frei, "The 'Literal' Reading of Biblical Narrative," in *Theology and Narrative* (Oxford: Oxford University Press, 1993), 117–52.

25. Walter Brueggemann, *Texts Under Negotiation: The Bible and Postmodern Imagination* (Minneapolis: Fortress, 1993).

26. I take this term from Hans Frei, *Types of Christian Theology* (New Haven: Yale University Press, 1992), chap. 3.

27. Most prominently in his *The Eclipse of Biblical Narrative* (New Haven: Yale University Press, 1974).

28. There are evangelicals who jump to the conclusion that to see Scripture as primarily narrative is to strip it of its historical grounding and to make all Scripture essentially self-referential. Likewise, these same people often suggest that to remove the stability of meaning from the author's original intent is to somehow cast aside a stable relationship between what we believe as true and its grounding in Scripture. See, for example, the article (in my opinion misguided) by Bob Wenz, "Truth on Two Hills," *Christianity Today*, July 2004, 46–47. But what Wenz and like-minded others argue is simply not the case. A narrative hermeneutic need not give up any claims for an extratextual reality toward which Scripture refers or for that matter strong truth claims in general. Neither Frei nor Lindbeck made either of these two moves. See Fowl, *Engaging Scripture*, 23–24, and his reference to Bruce Marshall, "Aquinas as Post-Liberal Theologian," *The Thomist* 53, no. 3 (1989): 353–406. Likewise, to purport that a meaning unfolds in front of the text is not to necessarily infer with Ricouer's student David Tracy that the referent of the text can only be a "mode of being in the world." David Tracy, *Blessed Rage for Order* (New York: Harper & Row, 1988). For as Hans Frei makes clear, the "historicity" of humankind in general and of each self severally is the general transcendental condition which constitutes the underlying possibility of stories. "The 'Literal Reading' of Biblical Narrative," *Theology and Narrative* (New Haven: Yale University Press, 1993), 128–29. See this whole article for Frei's engagement with Ricouer on these matters. The point here is that historical reference remains part of the hermeneutical enterprise; it is, however, only possible after we have entered the language, its understood world, sufficiently to understand its meaning so as to know what it then could refer to. For another nuanced view of this issue, see Ricouer, *Hermeneutics and the Human*, 141ff.

29. For example, evangelicals have often been proponents of using psychology in sermons. Part of psychology's appeal in the church has been the authority it carries by

virtue of it being a science. Pastors can appeal to psychology because it is perceived by our congregations and culture as having an authority underwritten by modern science. In a society where Scripture is no longer a respected source of truth, the pastor can still be relevant by appealing to psychology. Psychology has successfully sold itself as a science with the same kind of veracity as other medical sciences, and since the church has adopted the authority of medicine as an adjunct to the church (albeit at times uneasily), psychology sneaks in, accepting the same authority and respect. The pastor can prove the validity of his sermons now based upon science, not just Scripture. As subtle as it might have been, the church has supplanted *sola scriptura* with the added authority of psychological science, because it seemingly felt Scripture needed some help. And although psychology can certainly help illumine some things already said in Scripture, too often the pastor's mode of interpretation has been to take the precepts of psychology and baptize them with proof texts. Psychology ends up interpreting Scripture instead of the reverse. As we have mentioned, however, the cultural intellectual milieu that has supported the authority of science and undercut the authority of Scripture has shifted. It no longer makes the same sense for pastors to pursue this line of thought.

30. On how emotions are formed in narrative, see Martha Nussbaum, "Narrative Emotions: Beckett's Geneology of Love" and Stephen Crites, "The Narrative Quality of Experience," in Stanley Hauerwas and L. Gregory Jones, *Why Narrative?* (Grand Rapids: Eerdmans, 989), 216–49. Of course Alasdair MacIntyre's work is foundational to this thesis. See chapter 7 of this book (*The Great Giveaway*) for further explication.

31. See Hermann Ridderbos' famous exposition of this in *Paul: An Outline of His Theology* (Grand Rapids: Eerdmans, 1975), 253–58.

32. For evangelicals, the individual in the pew engages Scripture as a Cartesian mind comprehending a proposition, being convicted of its truth by the Holy Spirit, and then proceeding to act upon that proposition in his or her Christian life. Much more profound is the notion that the hearer in the pew is confronted with an alternative world, indeed an alternative reality, the lordship of Christ as presented in the preaching of the Word. This alternative world of God in Christ offers the hearer the opportunity to respond to and submit to Christ's lordship, as well as to be formed into a new subjectivity. In Graham Ward's words, "the world of the text confronts the world of the reader; an experience of transcendence offers the reader possibilities for transformation." *Theology and Contemporary Critical Theory* (New York: St. Martin's, 2000), 124. I believe Ward's review of reader-response as an aesthetic experience is extremely helpful in fleshing out some of these issues (see *Theology and Contemporary Theory*, chap. 4).

33. For a convincing argument for narrative preaching, see Richard Eslinger, *Narrative Imagination: Preaching the Worlds That Shape Us* (Minneapolis: Fortress, 1995).

34. As reported in the Vineyard Association's *Cutting Edge* magazine, "An Inside Look at Solomon's Porch," *Cutting Edge* 8, no. 2 (Summer 2004): 14–19.

Chapter 6: Justice (Our Understanding Of)

1. See for instance Joel Carpenter, "Compassionate Evangelicalism," *Christianity Today*, December 2003, 40–42. George Barna (www.barna.com) has done research that shows that conservative evangelical Christians are now more likely (by a slight margin) to be involved in a justice outreach project than mainline Protestant parishioners.

2. In other words, in postmodern terms, our justice gets "spatialized" by the discourses and social forces of democracy and capitalism rendering our justice recognizable only as another form of democracy or capitalism.

3. This was the legacy of the modernist-fundamentalist controversies of the 1920s and '30s. See David Moberg, *The Great Reversal: Evangelism versus Social Concern* (Philadelphia: Fortress, 1972); George Marsden, *Fundamentalism and American Culture* (New York: Oxford

University Press, 1980), 85–93, 124–32. Evangelicalism's negative position toward social salvation was forged out of the fundamentalist's reactions to liberal Protestant positions on "social gospel" and the historical reliability of Scripture. In reaction to the "social gospel," in which liberal Protestantism marginalized the need for personal salvation, fundamentalists reasserted the need for personal salvation by rallying around a premillennial eschatology that encouraged missions and a heightened belief in the apocalyptic end of the current age. In so doing they opposed most positive views toward current society and postmillennialism, which viewed the kingdom of God being currently ushered in via the current political structures of the day. In reaction to the devaluing of scriptural historicity, the fundamentalists emphasized dispensationalist systems of understanding prophecy and the supernatural elements of Scripture. Some believe this also had a concomitant effect of a negative assessment of current culture via dispensationalism. Although by no means consistent throughout the "Great Reversal," evangelicalism had inherited these tendencies coming out of World War II. See Carl F. Henry, *The Uneasy Conscience of Modern Fundamentalism* (Grand Rapids: Eerdmans, 1947), 26–34.

4. Carl F. Henry, *Uneasy Conscience*. Henry, in the aftermath of the modernist-fundamentalist controversies of 1920s America, is writing to undercut the extreme dispensational pessimism toward the present age that characterized much of fundamentalist evangelical Christianity back then. Henry instead encouraged a more balanced view of God's "already/but not yet" kingdom and the embracing of a social agenda that is consistent with the evangelical emphasis on the historic tenets of "biblical Christianity."

5. A recent study confirms this social economic statistic by Michael Emerson of Rice University. See Michael O. Emerson and Christian Smith, *Divided by Faith: Evangelical Religion and the Problem of Race in America* (Cambridge: Oxford University Press, 2002), chap. 7.

6. Among evangelicals, it is probably Ron Sider who is best known for using and defining the term *holistic*. See Ron Sider, Philip Olson, and Heidi Unruh, *Churches That Make a Difference* (Grand Rapids: Baker Academic, 2002), 23–126. Over the last twenty years, the term has become accepted currency for most evangelicals and their U.S. seminaries.

7. Ron Sider, *Good News and Good Works* (Grand Rapids: Baker Books, 1993), 10.

8. In *Good News*, Ron Sider separates the work of evangelism from social action, claiming that evangelism is the task of converting persons into disciples and social action is the improvement of socioeconomic and psychological well-being of people here on earth. *Good News*, 161; see 158–65.

9. On the necessity of a strong visible witness of a community of faith as necessary for social action, see Ron Sider, *Good News*, 175–79; Stephen Mott, *Biblical Ethics and Social Change* (New York: Oxford University Press, 1982), chap. 7; and Jim Wallis, *The Soul of Politics* (New York: Marynoll, 1994). On the downplaying of the community as a strategy itself to engage the world, see Sider, *Good News*, 178; Mott, *Biblical Ethics and Social Change*, 138–39. Sider sees the local church's role in social justice as being the backdrop for integrity for the prophetic witness of Christians in the world. He states, for instance, "When Christian leaders go to the government to call for sweeping structural change, we have more integrity and power when we can say: 'We are part of Christian communities that are already beginning to live out what we are calling you to legislate.'" Sider *Good News*, 178. I certainly affirm this as a social strategy for the church, but in this case Sider still seems to differentiate justice in the world from salvation taking place inside the church. In the same vein, Mott states more blatantly, "The historic Anabaptist model of the church was theologically sounder . . . because it did not assert that the existence of an intentional community would lead to changes in other structures of society. . . . To suggest today that significant social change can be effected through the proliferation of Christian

communities is analogous to expecting social change from evangelism alone" (to Mott an obvious mistake). Mott *Biblical Ethics and Social Change*, 138–39.

10. The evangelical mentality behind using parachurch organizations to do the work of justice ministry was illustrated by the headline speaker at a major fundraiser of a major evangelical parachurch justice ministry. He said to the audience that "we need to let the experts do this kind of work and 'get out of their way' because they understand the needs and how to minister in these inner-city places of great social need better than we do."

11. To the extent that Mennonites have been considered evangelicals, they could be excluded from this generalization, although some would recognize that those Mennonites who have moved toward evangelicalism have also lost their sense of the centrality of the body as social witness.

12. John Milbank exposits some of the modernist roots of this distinction between individual and social in *Theology and Social Theory*, 232ff.

13. According to Marsden, this idea is as old as the holiness revivals of the late nineteenth century when, for example, the evangelical patron saint A. J. Gordon said in 1877, "[I]t is futile to preach to those with empty stomachs." Marsden, *Fundamentalism*, 83.

14. For many evangelicals, social justice ministry is justified by its ability to uncover each individual's need for salvation. This was stated in classic form by Carl F. Henry in *The Uneasy Conscience* under the section "The Evangelical 'Formula of Protest'" (76–80).

15. A typical statement is Sider's in *Good News*: "Biblical evangelism both results in and aims at social action . . . The gospel creates new persons whose transformed character and action change the world." *Good News*, 174. This is a continuation of Carl F. Henry in some respects but also reproduces the Protestant liberal justification for the church.

16. The diminishment of the church's role in society as a body and its replacement by the kingdom of God at work for the liberation of persons in democracy is the trajectory of classic Protestant liberalism from Harnack to Tillich. See Walter Rauschenbusch, *Theology of the Social Gospel* (New York: Abingdon, 1917), chap. 13.

17. Steve Long characterizes this liberal tendency as the "Protestant principle" as it is found in the work of Paul Tillich and his follower Reinhold Niebuhr. See D. Stephen Long, *Divine Economy* (London: Routledge, 2000), 136. See Paul Tillich, *Systematic Theology*, vol. 1 (Chicago: University of Chicago, 1951), 37; *Systematic Theology*, vol. 3 (Chicago: University of Chicago Press, 1963), 243–45. According to the "Protestant principle" anything that is temporal and historical is ultimately too impure to be Christian. Christ therefore is always removed from concrete politics. We cannot expect that Christ actually affects real concrete politics in an ultimate way among a people that indeed choose to follow him. H. Richard Niebuhr's social theology underwrote a similar theme in *Christ and Culture* (New York: Harper & Row, 1951) when he depicted Christ as an ideal that stands transcendent over and above culture. The temporal can be nothing more than finite or sinful existence. We should therefore not expect to see the church as a purified social ethic because it is historical. See John H. Yoder (and Glen Stassen and D. M. Yeager), *Authentic Transformation* (Nashville: Abingdon, 1996), 58–61. It is a sign of how much evangelicalism adopted this social ethic when an evangelical college like Wheaton College (Wheaton, IL) embraced Niebuhr's *Christ and Culture* during the 1970s by making it into a required class (entitled "Christ and Culture") for graduation.

18. In contrast is Roman Catholic theologian Henri de Lubac's thesis that salvation is inherently social. John Milbank characterizes de Lubac's position as follows: "It is not . . . that there is individual salvation and also a salvation of social structures." John Milbank, *Theology and Social Theory*, 226. See Milbank's important exposition on de Lubac in *Theology and Social Theory*, 225–28. See de Lubac's *Catholicism: Christ and the Common Destiny of Man* (San Francisco: Ignatius, 1988).

19. The best characterization of this approach to Scripture among evangelicals is stated by John Howard Yoder as the "fundamentalist" approach to Scripture. He states, "Fundamentalism is most fairly characterized as the denial that there is a hermeneutic task. . . . The words of the biblical text are held to be univocal, to such an extent that anyone's doubt about the rightness of my view of the text is at once an act of unbelief." John Howard Yoder, *To Hear the Word* (Eugene, OR: Wipf and Stock, 2001), 49.

20. On the necessity of a community for faithful reading of Scripture, see Fowl, *Engaging Scripture* (Oxford: Blackwell, 1998).

21. This of course hearkens to the classic liberal Protestant positions as outlined by Harvey Cox, *The Secular City* (New York: Macmillan, 1965), and Paul Van Buren, *The Secular Meaning of the Gospel* (New York: Macmillan, 1963), where Christians were challenged to change their mission mind-set from extending mission into the world to instead joining up and participating with what God is already doing in the world and make it more human.

22. This is similar to the bifurcation made by Reinhold Niebuhr between individual and social life. The first can be motivated by religious conscience and love, while the second must be organized according to inherent self-interest and liberal justice. Therefore, the best the church can do is individually love in an already compromised democracy. Reinhold Niebuhr, *Moral Man and Immoral Society* (New York: Charles Scribner's Sons, 1960). H. Richard Niebuhr's *Christ and Culture* advocates this same bifurcation. Christ is an ideal that stands outside culture that can never be realized in culture. Therefore, the best we as Christians can do is end up being individual Christians working for the transformation of culture. See this interpretation of Niebuhr by John H. Yoder in his *Authentic Transformation*, 58–60.

23. For an example, see Stanley Fish, *There's No Such Thing as Free Speech and It's a Good Thing Too* (New York: Oxford University Press, 1994); see also Richard Rorty, *Objectivity, Relativism and Truth* (New York: Cambridge University Press, 1991), 175–202.

24. This point was illustrated most vividly when Iraq was opened up to American evangelical relief agencies after the American incursion into Iraq. Certain Islamic groups refused to allow Christian groups into Iraq because they viewed these attempts to give relief as the preamble to proselytize the minds of Islamic people with Christianity. In fact, many of the Christian relief agencies openly acknowledged their relief work was an attempt to open Iraqi minds to the presentation of the evangelical message of the gospel. The point here is that for one side, the evangelical relief work was a manifestation of God's justice, while for the Islamic side, the work of relief was an incursion of Western imperialism aimed at indoctrinating susceptible populations into Western Christianity. One person's justice was another person's injustice. This also highlights how evangelicals continue to bifurcate social justice from personal salvation relegating acts of social justice to becoming pragmatic means to convert people.

25. The best discussion of the way "human rights" have lost currency as determinants of justice in American democracy is by Alasdair MacIntyre, *After Virtue*, 66–73.

26. Alasdair MacIntyre, *Whose Justice? Which Rationality?* (Notre Dame, IN: University of Notre Dame Press, 1988), 335, bracketed comment mine.

27. MacIntyre, *Whose Justice?* 345. On this subject, the whole of chapter 17 in *Whose Justice?* is essential reading.

28. Ibid., 346.

29. Stanley Hauerwas, *A Community of Character* (Notre Dame, IN: University of Notre Dame Press, 1981), 79.

30. Stanley Hauerwas, *After Christendom: How the Church Is to Behave If Freedom, Justice, and a Christian Nation Are Bad Ideas* (Nashville: Abingdon, 1991), 68.

31. Ibid., 48–49.

32. Hauerwas is known for this phrase in lectures. Elsewhere he says, "Christian social ethics should not begin with attempts to develop strategies to make the world more 'just,' but with the formation of a society shaped and informed by the truthful character of God we find revealed in the stories of Israel and Jesus." *Community of Character* (Notre Dame, IN: University of Notre Dame Press, 1981), 92.

33. On "ontological violence," see Milbank, *Theology and Social Theory*, chap. 10, especially p. 314.

34. See William Cavanaugh, "The City," in *Radical Orthodoxy*, 182–98. See D. Stephen Long, *Divine Economy* (London; New York: Routledge, 2002), 258–60.

35. Here Milbank follows Henri de Lubac's contention that the fall dispersed the created unity and brought the distinction between what is mine and what is yours, the distinction of individual versus individual. See Henri de Lubac, *Catholicism: Christ and the Common Destiny of Man* (San Francisco: Ignatius, 1988). See John Milbank, *Theology and Social Theory* (Oxford: Blackwell, 1993), 226ff.

36. A good summary of Milbank's position is by William Cavanaugh, "The City" in *Radical Orthodoxy*, 186, where he states, "As John Milbank has argued, modern politics is founded on the voluntarist replacement of a theology of participation with a theology of the will, such that the assumption of humanity into the Trinity by the divine logos is supplanted by an undifferentiated God who commands the lesser discrete wills of individual humans by sheer power." Milbank's classic delineation of this development is in *Theology and Social Theory*, 12–15.

37. On Milbank's view that capitalism is heresy, see Long, *Divine Economy*, 258–60.

38. Ron Sider, *Just Generosity* (Grand Rapids: Baker Books, 1999), 28.

39. Ibid.

40. Ibid., 45.

41. Ron Sider, *Rich Christians in an Age of Hunger* (Downers Grove, IL: InterVarsity, 1977), 40.

42. Stephen Long, *Divine Economy*, 236.

43. Ibid.

44. Catherine Pickstock gives a compelling account of how medieval Christian charity was given through actual kinship and neighborly relation. In the Middle Ages, through liturgical cycles of feasts and festivals, the economic was subordinated to the "liturgical order" and capital excess was freely given over to the liturgical processes. Later, however, the accumulation of capital became an immanent teleology all its own, displacing the liturgical order of giving and receiving all provisions as from God. Thereafter, charity became privatized into a duty or customary tax to help those less fortunate. It was removed from the rhythms of an integrated social body. *After Writing* (Oxford: Blackwell, 1998), 143–44. It seems the challenge in relation to capitalism for evangelicals lies precisely in the task of recapturing this communal notion of charity as a work of God and not personal benevolence.

45. I cite just a few of the governmental issues Sider addresses in *Just Generosity*.

46. James D. G. Dunn and Alan Suggate, *The Justice of God* (Grand Rapids: Eerdmans, 1993), 33.

47. Ibid., 38–39.

48. Ibid., 37.

49. Ibid., 42.

50. To bifurcate justification from the outworking of that justification as righteousness in the believer as well as the people of God is the mistake made by those who would commodify salvation into an individual act-decision, which produces a crass legal exchange that justifies the new believer in God's court of law. In effect justification is the entrance into a new covenantal relationship with God and his people upon which each individual

receives justification. So to separate the acceptance of this justification from the entrance into the new covenant is a gross distortion. As Dunn states, "The Christian doctrine of justification by faith begins as Paul's protest not as an individual sinner against a Jewish legalism, but as Paul's protest on behalf of gentiles against Jewish exclusivism." Dunn, *Justice*, 25. In other words, for Paul, justification isn't for the relieving of the guilty Jewish conscience, which is always striving to maintain the standard of God's law. It is for the establishment of a new righteousness in a people through Christ, not the fulfillment of the law. It is a righteousness of a new covenant, not the old covenant of the law. The ground-breaking critique of Luther's reading into Romans the idea of an individual sinner with guilty conscience before the God of Jewish legalism came from Krister Stendahl, "The Apostle Paul and the Introspective Conscience of the West," found in *Paul among Jews and Gentiles* (Philadelphia: Fortress, 1976), 78–96. It was put to the forefront by John H. Yoder in his classic *The Politics of Jesus*, 2nd ed. (Grand Rapids: Eerdmans, 1994), chap. 11. And this thesis is further carried out in Dunn's *Word Biblical Commentary, Romans 1–8* (Waco: Word, 1988) and *Word Biblical Commentary, Romans 9–16* (Waco: Word, 1988).

51. The notion of "unlimited liability" was first articulated using these words by Ron Sider, *Rich Christians in an Age of Hunger* (Downers Grove, IL: InterVarsity, 1979), 101.

52. Again I refer to Charles Taylor's powerful descriptions of pseudo community in modernity. *Sources of the Self* (Cambridge, MA: Harvard University Press, 1989), 508. Sadly this has often been an accurate description of North American evangelical churches.

53. Sider again calls this "unlimited liability." He details how private property was not abolished or looked down upon in the primitive church. Rather it was economic *koinōnia* that demanded that all people were equally liable financially one to another. *Rich Christians*, 95–110; 113–30. See Stephen Long's comments on communal property in *The Goodness of God* (Grand Rapids: Brazos, 2002), 239–48.

54. I refer here to Kelly S. Johnson's writings on this topic. See for instance her "Koinonia and Almsgiving: Remarks in Response to David Janzen," on the ekklesiaproject .org website.

55. Sider, *Rich Christians*, 106.

56. The classic argument here is from John Howard Yoder, *The Politics of Jesus*, 2nd ed. (Grand Rapids: Eerdmans, 1994), chap. 3. On page 70 Yoder disavows that Jesus prescribed "Christian communism" as a way of Christian corporate life.

57. For instance the struggles of the Jesus People U.S.A. community in Chicago in this regard have been reported by the *Chicago Tribune*, April 1, 2001. The credibility of the *Chicago Tribune's* reporting is very disputed. Nonetheless, the controversy illustrates that even intentional communities are not automatically immune from at least the potential of capitalism's corrupting influence.

58. See William T. Cavanaugh, *Theopolitical Imagination* (New York: T & T Clark, 2002), 15–20, where he describes how John Locke argued for private property as the outgrowth of one's own human labor applied to that property, which allows its abundance to be made manifest. Private property therefore enables one to protect one's property, the fruit of one's own labor, from the encroachment of other individuals. This is a distinct departure from Roman Catholic, medieval, and Thomist understandings of property rights as founded in the stewardship of the property for the common good of all humanity.

59. Oliver O'Donovan, *Desire of the Nations* (Oxford: Cambridge University Press, 1996), 265.

60. William Cavanaugh, *Theopolitical Imagination*, 119. For Cavanaugh this practice is the Eucharist. Although I wish to make the case here that the same organizing powers can be unleashed in the benevolent fund for issues of justice, I do not mean to diminish the centrality of the Eucharist for justice as Cavanaugh has done. In fact, benevolence practices must be the product of the Eucharist to have any legitimacy at all.

61. See Ronald Vallet, *Congregations at the Crossroads: Remembering to Be Households of God* (Grand Rapids: Eerdmans, 1998), 67–72, for the history of "benevolent fund" practices in Protestantism.

62. There is of course caution needed. As MacIntyre implies, "Benevolence in the eighteenth century is assigned very much the scope which the Christian scheme of the virtues assigned to charity. But, unlike charity, benevolence as a virtue became a license for almost any kind of manipulative intervention in the affairs of others." *After Virtue*, 232.

63. This echoes John Howard Yoder's statement that "legislative implementation is only meaningful when it extrapolates or extends the commitment on a part of the Christian community which has already demonstrated the fruitfulness of that commitment." *For the Nations* (Grand Rapids: Eerdmans, 1997), 88. See also Sider, *Good News*, 178.

64. Such a community-centered formation of Christ's justice should in no way be construed as a retreat from concern or engagement in the world. First of all, such a strategy should in no manner devalue social activism and mercy outreach outside the church. Second, such a communal-based strategy most certainly would have vigorous impact upon a society at large all on its own. Consider if in wartime, a draft was resisted communally by fifty evangelical churches all refusing their children to go fight war based upon theological objections and the filing for conscientious objection status. Consider that these fifty communities welcomed in all soldiers to be cared for and nurtured back to health from any wounds whether physical or emotional. Given the current place of evangelicals in America politically, not only would this witness have profound effect upon the culture at large, it would also bring the evangelical church as a whole into discernment over the issue, and it would lend power to any furthering of additional activism and protest movements.

65. I paraphrase the following description by William Cavanaugh of how the church witnesses against the torture of Pinochet's Chile: "If the church is to resist disappearance [torture tactics of Chile], then it must be publicly visible as a body of Christ in the present time, not secreted away in the souls of believers or relegated to the distant historical past or future." *Torture and the Eucharist* (Oxford: Blackwell, 1998), 234.

66. An example of such a ministry is the Christian Community Health Fellowship, an organization focused upon living out the gospel by providing health care to the uninsured and underinsured through the local church. It began in one church, the Allegheny Center Alliance Church in Pittsburgh, Pennsylvania, with the church's pastor Bruce Jackson, as an attempt to extend health care to the poor out of the church's relationships to the surrounding poor and medical doctors within its community.

67. William Cavanaugh, *Torture and Eucharist* (Oxford: Blackwell, 1998).

68. In some ways, I am asking whether the reinvigoration of the practice of benevolence in our churches can take Cavanaugh's thesis in *Torture and Eucharist* concerning "the Eucharist as an organizing of space" one step further. I do not, however, mean to diminish the singular foundational nature of the Eucharist as that which lies at the basis of the whole church's existence and indeed as the basis for the practice of benevolence.

Chapter 7: Spiritual Formation

1. For example, James Hillman and Michael Ventura, *We've Had a Hundred Years of Psychotherapy—and the World's Getting Worse* (San Francisco: HarperCollins, 1992).

2. For example Phillip Rieff, *The Triumph of the Therapeutic* (New York: Harper & Row, 1966). See also Hillman and Venture, *We've Had a Hundred Years*.

3. Most notably by Robert Bellah, *Habits of the Heart* (New York: Harper & Row, 1985), 47, who follows Alasdair MacIntyre's critique in *After Virtue* (Notre Dame, IN: University of Notre Dame Press, 1982).

4. Most brilliantly by MacIntyre, *After Virtue*, 73ff. But also Jürgen Habermas, *Knowledge and Human Interests* (London: Heinemann, 1972), 247ff.; Paul Ricouer, *Freud and Philosophy:*

An Essay on Interpretation, trans. Denis Savage (New Haven: Yale University Press, 1970); Edward E. Sampson, "The Deconstruction of the Self," in *Texts of Identity*, ed. John Shotter and Kenneth Gergen (London: Sage Publications, 1991), 1–19, to name just a few.

5. Most famously by Michel Foucault, *Madness and Civilization: A History of Insanity in the Age of Reason* (New York: Pantheon, 1965).

6. Thus the growth of Christian graduate programs in psychology such as Mars Hill Graduate School of Psychology, Wheaton Graduate School of Psychology (of Wheaton College, Wheaton, IL), Rosemead School of Psychology (of Biola University, La Mirada, CA).

7. Jürgen Habermas, classified more often within modernity, nonetheless speaks of the "self-misunderstanding of psychoanalysis as a natural science" and has suggested that the relationship between the therapist and his or her client is an unequal power relationship, enforcing a certain interpretation upon the analysis. See Habermas, *Knowledge and Human Interests* (London: Heinemann, 1972), 247ff.

8. The main impetus behind this view is Thomas Kuhn's famous *The Structure of Scientific Revolutions* (Chicago: University of Chicago Press, 1962). On the social sciences, see Paul Ricoeur, "Science and Ideology," in *Hermeneutics and the Human Sciences* (Cambridge: Cambridge University Press, 1981); Alasdair MacIntyre, *After Virtue*, 2nd ed. (Notre Dame, IN: University of Notre Dame Press, 1984), chap. 8.

9. Religions have of course their own set of "facts," events occurring in history out of which arrive these religious narratives and accounts of human living. For the Christian, the most important of these events ("facts" ignores that all events have an observer and therefore a subjective interest and interpreter) are the cross of Christ and the resurrection.

10. Paul Ricouer, *Freud and Philosophy: An Essay on Interpretation*, trans. Denis Savage (New Haven: Yale University Press, 1970). According to Graham Ward, the center of psychoanalytic work is the subject to whom the analyst gives a language. For structural analysis, however (in the work of Jacques Lacan and others), the center of analysis becomes "the differential system," the structure to which the self belongs and gives it an identity. Graham Ward, *Theology and Contemporary Theory* (New York: St. Martin's, 2000), 19. See Ward's entire discussion on Freud and Lacan on pages 19–21.

11. Jürgen Habermas, "The Hermeneutic Claim to Universality" in *The Hermeneutic Tradition*, ed. Gayle Ormiston and Alan Schrift (Albany, NY: State University of New York Press, 1990), 254–65.

12. Michel Foucault, *The History of Sexuality: An Introduction, Volume 1* (New York: Vintage Books, 1990), 67.

13. Robert Bellah, *Habits of the Heart* (New York: Harper & Row, 1985), 47–48.

14. Phillip Rieff, *The Triumph of The Therapeutic*, 13, as recited in Roger Lundin, *The Culture of Interpretation* (Grand Rapids: Eerdmans, 1993), 5.

15. The problem with most therapy is the manner it which it trains the patient to see that "everything is about me." The therapist's questions and the patient's response is a form of liturgy that trains the patient to always examine every emotional issue in terms of the questions: "What does that say about you?" "Where is that coming from?" "What does that trigger inside of you?" The reference point for the formation of the self is not external to the self; it is always the formation of emotions in terms of personal choices and undoing past history in a productive and positive manner for the living of one's life in democracy and capitalism. There is therefore a narrative in play, and it is the narrative of the Western democratic self. The goal is to resolve oneself to live a more productive life in terms of capitalist democracy. There can be no formation away from self-absorption in the capitalist self-interested sense, without something bigger than oneself to submit to, participate in, and be formed into. For Christians, this is the life of God and his work in Jesus Christ.

16. Jung was too prolific and varied in his thought for anyone to be able to attach any particular brand of Jungian thought onto him. My characterization of Jungian therapy in this chapter is just one of the many outworkings of Jung in therapeutic form. I use the Jungian school represented by Robert Moore, Douglas Gillette, and the men's Warrior movement, a men's organization that conducts psychologically intensive, therapeutic weekends for men to become integrated emotionally, as an example of Jungian therapy in order to illustrate the point of chapter. My main purpose is not to critique Jung or Moore but to show how all psychology in one form or another is a specific interpretation of life from a narrative that by its very nature is distinct, different, and in some senses in competition with the Christian narrative.

17. For examples of Christian adoption of Jungian therapeutic methods, see "Willow Creek Disavows ex-Pastor," *The Daily Herald* (Chicago), September 30, 1996, which offers an account of the famous church's issues with former pastor Jim Dethmer's Jungian counseling methods. See also Vern Becker, *A Real Man* (Grand Rapids: Zondervan, 1992), a Christian reflection on his own journey through the Jungian Warrior's movement. See the now endless examples of Christian Jungian men's books: Sam Keen, *Fire in the Belly* (New York: Bantam, 1991); Gordon Dalby, *Fight Like a Man* (Wheaton: Tyndale, 1995); *Healing the Masculine Soul* (Dallas: Word, 1988). Robert Moore and Douglas Gillette, *King, Warrior, Magician, Lover* (New York: Harper, 1990), have been major figures in the movement and represent the easy compatibility between modern liberal theological method and Jungian psychology.

18. I recognize this is only one of many interpretations of sin and its application to the Christian life available out of Scripture and the church. My purpose here is not to define specific ways Christians should interpret their lives over against Jungian therapy, only to illustrate how different the outcomes can be.

19. See Martha Nussbaum's exposition of this in "Narrative Emotions: Beckett's Genealogy of Love," in *Why Narrative?* (Grand Rapids: Eerdmans, 1989), where she says, "We learn how to feel and we learn our emotional repertoire. . . . They are taught, above all, through stories. Stories express their structure and teach us their dynamics" (217). See also Kenneth Gergen, *The Saturated Self* (New York: Basic Books, 1991), 8–27.

20. On this, see the debate between Richard Lazarus and Robert Zajonc. R. Zajonc, "On the Primacy of Affect," *American Psychologist* 39, no. 2 (1984): 117–23; R. Lazarus "On the Primacy of Cognition," *American Psychologist* 39, no. 2 (1984): 124–29. See also R. Lazarus, "Progress on Cognitive-Motivational-Relational Theory of Emotion," *American Psychologist* (August 1991): 112–27; Keith Oatley and P. N. Johnson, "Towards a Cognitive Theory of the Emotions," *Cognition and Emotion* 1, no. 1 (1987): 29–50, for a convincing argument for the primacy of cognition and appraisal in the forming of human emotions.

21. Moore, *King, Warrior, Magician, Lover*.

22. Joseph Campbell, *The Hero with a Thousand Faces* (Princeton, NJ: Princeton University Press, 1949).

23. Anthony Stevens, *Archetypes: A Natural History of the Self* (New York: Morrow, 1982).

24. At first glance many of Moore's archetypes (King, Warrior) appear to have strong affinities with Christian ideals. The King archetype is the energy that the man channels that allows him to "encourage the wife when she decides she wants to go back to school . . . take time off from work to attend his son's piano recital . . . confront the rebellious subordinates at the office without firing them" (62). This canalization allows the man to take control in productive ways. There is the Warrior's "transpersonal commitment or loyalty" (84), which could translate into the kingdom of God for Christians. But what view of the world, what beliefs, reasons, or commitments drive the character behind this behavior? It appears to be the desire for order with the King or the drive for conquering for a greater

cause with the Warrior. These motivations may be good, but nothing about them makes them Christian. In fact, I suggest that Christians give up control and the ordering of the world to a sovereign God and instead pursue the following of Christ. And Christians have a transpersonal commitment, but it is a specific one: the kingdom of God. This specific transpersonal commitment will profoundly change one's experience of the world versus other transpersonal commitments. So it is misleading to "follow" these archetypes and then label them as Christian. To this author, Moore's archetypes most resemble the highest ideals of the tradition of Western, democratic, "enlightened" Kantian liberalism.

25. Michel Foucault, *The History of Sexuality* 1 (New York: Vintage, 1991), 63–67. For a quick introduction to Foucault's work on the "technologies of the self," see *The Foucault Reader*, ed. Paul Rabinow (New York: Pantheon Books, 1984), 7–12.

26. On the evolvement of the classical Christian self of medieval times to the modern subject of liberal society via the ways scientific discourse and psychiatric institutions, see the fascinating interview with Foucault in *The Foucault Reader*, 359–72.

27. The understanding that "binding and loosing" is not only about forgiveness and reconciliation but also about discernment and making commitments is detailed in John Howard Yoder's essay "Binding and Loosing," in *The Royal Priesthood*, ed. Michael Cartwright and Richard Mouw (Scottdale, PA: Herald, 1994), 323–58.

28. You can find the rules for the class meeting in "Rules of the Band Societies," *The Works of John Wesley*, vol. 9 (Nashville, Abingdon, 1989).

29. The succumbing of the Wesleyan class meeting to modernity is chronicled in David Holsclaw's Ph.D. dissertation, "The Demise of Disciplined Christian Fellowship: The Methodist Class Meeting in Nineteenth Century America," University of California-Davis, 1979. Also see John H. Yoder's positive historical appraisal of the class meeting as well as other small group processes of confession and discipline in "Binding and Loosing," *The Royal Priesthood* (Scottdale, PA: Herald, 1998), 338–41. He states, "The fundamental local experience that the 'methodist' believer had week by week, and the real reason for the movement's practical success, was the regular encounter with the 'class.' This was a circle of persons meeting regularly, committed to one another and bearing one another's burdens in every way, with special attention to reproof and restoration. This has been true of movements of revival and renewal in every age" (340).

Chapter 8: Moral Education

1. For data on this issue I recommend George Barna, *Third Millennium Teens* (Ventura, CA: Revel Books, 2002).

2. Dewey was not a modern individualist in the ways addressed in this book (for instance, see his very communal descriptions in *The Public and Its Problems*, reprinted in John Dewey, *The Later Works, 1925–1953*, ed. Jo Ann Boydston (Carbondale, IL: Southern Illinois University Press, 1988), 2:235–374). Nonetheless, it was his emphasis on critical preparation for democracy that led the way for the progressivist school of education led by his student W. H. Kilpatrick of Teacher's College (New York), which emphasized the child-centered education, the development of critical thinking, and the natural romanticist development of the child's inborn personality and curiosity as the basis for education. This later development symbolizes more than anything else the modern consensus in the American education establishment.

3. The modern notion of education is adequately summarized by Oliver O'Donovan when he states, "It [modern education] conceived ignorance, like every other inequality, as a problem of social organization, to be met by social technique. From this perspective it seemed possible to ignore the implications of the rarity of wisdom and of prophecy. Education concerned itself with the task of disseminating information. It was then for individuals to make what use of it their natural or supernatural endowment would

allow." O'Donovan then summarizes the postmodernist critique as follows: "There is no information that exists outside of any discourse. The idea of a purely formal education is a phantasm. To extract the dissemination of information from the goal of wisdom is to promote thoughtless knowledgeableness." Oliver O'Donovan, *The Desire of the Nations* (New York: Cambridge University Press, 1996), 282.

4. This assumes that children cannot help but be in the world, which is no longer Christian. In other words, our children cannot avoid living in the media deluge and overwhelming cultural forces of public schools and capitalism. Unlike the medieval world, therefore, the current post-Christian cultural conditions make for a better argument for adult baptism and a defining of a "separation" in every young person's life.

5. See, for instance, evangelical Wheaton College's CACE's bulletin *Discernment* 9, no. 1, (Spring 2004), entitled "Character Education in the Public Schools." See particularly Jillian Lederhouse, "Which Values Ought We to Teach in Public Schools, and Can They Be Identical to the Ones We Teach at Home?" 8–9. Evangelical spokesman Chuck Colson wrote an article for his Breakpoint radio program entitled "Reviving the Virtues," where he supported Bill Bennett and character education (www.christlife.org). Bennett's book was the number three recommended book for Christian homes in an article published by an evangelical magazine: Bonne Steffen and Randy Bishop, "Ten Christian Books No Child Should Miss: A Panel of Judges Lists the Books to Be Read and Reread by Children and Adults," *Today's Christian*, September/October 1999. Bennett's *Book of Virtues* also made several best seller lists during 1994 that segregated books as sold through Christian bookstores associated with the predominantly evangelical Christian Booksellers even though *Book of Virtues* was considered a crossover book. This information can be located through the archives of *Publishers Weekly* among others. This is just some of the anecdotal evidence available of the general supportive attitude of evangelicals toward the idea propagated by Bennett to promote teaching virtues in the broad culture including the public schools.

6. William J. Bennett, *The Book of Virtues* (New York: Simon & Schuster, 1993).

7. See Edward Wynne and Kevin Ryan, *Reclaiming Our Schools: A Handbook on Teaching Character, Academics and Discipline* (Englewood Cliffs, NJ: Macmillan, 1993); Thomas Lickona, *Educating for Character* (New York: Bantam Books, 1991); William Kilpatrick, *Why Johnny Can't Tell Right from Wrong* (New York: Simon & Schuster, 1992).

8. According to the special interest group Character Education Partnership, forty-seven states now receive federal money for teaching character in public schools. See *Discernment* 9, no. 1 (Spring 2004): 1.

9. See note 5.

10. See the debates on character education in *Educational Leadership* 51, no. 3 (November 1993) and 43, no. 4 (December 1985/January 1986).

11. Bennett, *Book of Virtues*, 13.

12. Bennett, *Our Children and Our Country* (New York: Simon & Schuster, 1988), 79.

13. William Bennett, *Our Children*, 165, 179, 180–82.

14. Bennett, *Our Children*, 179, 194. See further William J. Bennett, *The Devaluing of America* (New York: Simon & Schuster, 1992), 59.

15. Alasdair MacIntyre, *After Virtue* (Notre Dame, IN: University of Notre Dame Press, 1984), 188.

16. MacIntyre, *After Virtue*, chap. 14; Stanley Hauerwas, *A Community of Character* (Notre Dame, IN: University of Notre Dame Press, 1981), 112–13, 124–28.

17. Stanley Hauerwas, *Character and the Christian Life* (San Antonio: Trinity University Press, 1985), 203.

18. As seen advertised on the Blaine Junior High School sign of the Chicago public school system in 1999.

19. Alasdair MacIntyre, *After Virtue*, 186.

20. This example is taken from Jean Porter, "Virtue and Sin: The Connection of the Virtues and the Case of the Flawed Saint," *Journal of Religion*, Fall 1995, 525.

21. Hauerwas, *Community*, chaps. 6 and 7.

22. Jerome Bruner, *Acts of Meaning* (Cambridge, MA: Harvard University Press, 1990); *Actual Minds, Possible Worlds* (Cambridge, MA: Harvard University Press, 1986).

23. This point is substantiated significantly in various fields of psychology: by Jerome Bruner in the field of developmental psychology, Richard Shweder in the field of cultural psychology, and Donald Spence among others in narrative psychology. See Jerome Bruner, *The Culture of Education* (Cambridge, MA: Harvard University Press, 1996); Jerome Bruner, *Acts of Meaning* (Cambridge, MA: Harvard University Press, 1990); Richard Shweder, *Thinking Through Cultures* (Cambridge, MA: Harvard University Press, 1991); Donald Spence, *Narrative Truth and Historical Truth: Meaning and Interpretation in Psychoanalysis* (New York: Norton Press, 1982).

24. To put it another way, Bennett's so-called "common Western heritage" cannot be enough to teach children virtue because if we are to teach our children a character of substance, we require a tradition of substance. And if the Western heritage becomes a tradition of substance, it is automatically excluded from the pluralist setting of the public school. Strategically then, the public schools are inevitably left with "lowest common denominator" virtues that have a short shelf life. These virtues, however, are not benign because the commitment to tradition-neutrality (that supports these virtues) takes on a value agenda all its own.

25. Ultimately, this is the outworking of a modernist epistemology inherited from Immanuel Kant and the Enlightenment. It was Kant who separated knowledge of the physical world from knowledge of God and made any knowledge of God as the postulate necessary to believe in morality. As a result, the knowledge of the public world (science, social sciences, historiography, math) was separated from religious knowledge, which at best could be private and personal. Evangelicals reveal again their staunch alliance with modernity in their accommodation with post–World War II public schools, which embraced public instruction on math, science, and social sciences but carefully scrutinized the enforcement of private moral beliefs.

26. The Sunday school movement developed from an attempt to teach basic literacy and mathematical skills to the children of the poor, who had been left without any schooling after industrialization came to America, to a school aimed at attracting unchurched children into schools for the purposes of evangelism in the purest of revivalist senses. As the public schools began to emerge, the two schools began to conflict. The accommodation that was accomplished was that the leaders of the denominations would teach in the Sunday schools the religious knowledge that public schools could no longer teach. They would also provide more deliberate moral instruction that denominational leaders felt the new public schools could not do. The result was a split. The new public schools would teach so-called value-neutral subjects, that is, reading, writing, arithmetic, geography, etc. The Sunday schools would pick up the slack and provide moral and religious foundational knowledge. As Robert Lynn and Elliott Wright assert, "To solve a mathematical equation or to study Shakespeare, according to one leader, was a 'mere mental gymnastic.' But the Sunday School was unique because its fruits included 'practical truth.' What could be more practical than choosing the right destiny?" Robert Lynn and Elliott Wright, *Big Little School* (Birmingham, AL: Religious Education Press, 1980), 78. As for the revivalists (Dwight L. Moody, et al.), the Sunday schools became the means to evangelize young children's souls (Anne M. Boylan, *Sunday School: The Formation of an American Institution* [New Haven: Yale University Press, 1988], 94). Catechesis was rejected for more expedient evangelistic goals (William Bean Kennedy, *The Shaping of Protestant Education*, [New York: YMCA, 1966], 42). On the developments of this history, see William Bean Kennedy, *The Shaping*

of Protestant Education, chap. 1, "The Sunday School and the Public School"; Anne M. Boylan, *Sunday School*, chaps. 1–2.

27. The current evangelical battles over evolution and creationist science (e.g., intelligent design) might appear to be an exception to this because of evolution being an issue of science. Some might argue that creation was argued as an issue of good science, not a moral issue. Yet this also could be construed as a modernist approach because again the evangelicals attacked a single informational issue in an argument about getting the facts straight. Looking back, evangelicals probably could have had more success arguing it as an issue of moral concern.

28. Craig Gay, *The Way of the (Modern) World* (Grand Rapids: Eerdmans, 1998).

29. For an admittedly controversial account of modernity's influence upon the formation of educational theory in North America, see E. D. Hirsch Jr., *The Schools We Need* (New York: Doubleday, 1996), especially chaps. 3–4.

30. Evangelicals have often succumbed to the romanticist modernist notions of education, which center education around the individual. This is noticeable even in the way we carry on curriculums in our Sunday schools and children's ministries programs. We adopt, for example, methods similar to the Montesorri approaches, which turn the classroom into a more "child-centered" classroom and the children interact with a "box of gizmos" that illustrate a lesson. (See, for example, Thom Schultz and Joanie Schultz, *Why Nobody Learns Much of Anything in Church and How to Fix It* [Loveland, CO: Group Publishing, 1999].) Many of these approaches are philosophically indebted to the post–Deweyian Progressive schools of education in the United States from the 1930s to the present. Schools that are modernist in this manner emphasize the development of individual creative and critical thinking skills and resist processes of induction into a cultural foundation of knowledge. See Richard Pratte, *Contemporary Theories of Education* (Toronto, ON: Intext, 1971), 123–25; and Steven Tozer, Paul Violas, and Guy Senese, *School and Society: Education Practice as Social Expression* (New York: McGraw Hill, 1993), 140–44. Although Dewey believed in the role of community and social formation, his work provided the seeds for the full-blown individualist educational movement of Progressivism that followed him. See John Dewey, *Democracy and Education* (Carbondale, IL: Southern Illinois University Press, 1985), 49–50, 100. See Dewey's follower William H. Kilpatrick, "The Project Method," *Teachers College Record* 19 (1918); and William H. Kilpatrick, *Foundations of Method* (New York: Longmans, 1925). William H. Kilpatrick, a post-Deweyian popularizer of Progressivism, emphasized education as the development of critical skills over against the acquiring of a set subject matter (see note 2 above). Evangelical Christian educators, when they use educational methods that are child-centered and promote self-flourishing, reveal their indebtedness to modern notions of the self and education.

31. See chapter 1 of this book, under the section entitled "Do Decisions Count Where There Is No Sanctification?"

32. On the idea that authoritative communities are essential for healthy moral development in children, see a study entitled "Hardwired to Connect: The New Scientific Case for Authoritative Communities," conducted by the Commission on Children at Risk (New York: Institute of American Values, 2003). Such a community "ideally brings together people of all ages: the young, the middle aged and the old. A sizeable body of scholarship confirms what most people sense intuitively: Children benefit enormously from being around caring people in all stages of the life cycle. . . . In addition, a community that is multi-generational is significantly more likely to reflect, as a core part of its identity, the quality of shared memory, a key dimension of human connectedness. . . . Shared memory can help to deepen identity and define character, largely by giving the child clear access to lessons and admirable persons from the past" (37). It seems then that if character and

identity in Christ is lacking in our children as they leave home, the lack of a viable living community might be the reason.

33. As Yoder suggests, "'Transformation' is meaningful and accountable only when those who call for it have a stance." John H. Yoder, "How H. Richard Niebuhr Reasoned: A Critique of Christ and Culture," in Glen Stassen, D. M. Yeager and John H. Yoder, *Authentic Transformation: A New Vision of Christ and Culture* (Nashville: Abingdon, 1996), 74.

34. Since there is no universal basis for virtue, no neutral objective interpretation of virtue, and since virtue is so deeply formed by the specifics of our stories and the things we believe, we are all dependent upon communities of interpretation to sort out life in a society that has become fragmented. See John H. Yoder, "How H. Richard Niebuhr Reasoned," 74. See also Joseph Dunne, "Beyond Sovereignty and Deconstruction: The Stored Self," *Philosophy and Social Criticism* 21, nos. 5/6 (1995): 137–57; Stanley Hauerwas, *Sanctify Them in the Truth* (Nashville: Abingdon, 1998), chap. 5; Alasdair MacIntyre, *After Virtue*, chap. 15.

35. I recommend Robert Webber's *Journey to Jesus* (Abingdon, Nashville, 2001) as a source for such initiatory processes.

36. Our church uses the "Our Life in Christ" curriculum of the Lutheran Church–Missouri Synod from Concordia Publishing, St. Louis, Missouri.

37. In "How H. Richard Niebuhr Reasoned," John Yoder teaches us that just because there is no longer one common, monolithic culture from which Christians can engage moral concerns, does not mean that Christians withdraw from engaging such a culture(s). It does imply, however, that the fulcrum of transformation transfers from Niebuhr's category of "culture" to the space of the church. Out of this space, where Jesus is recognized as Lord, Christians can engage the powers of culture one by one, rejecting it, including it, or capturing it for transformation, expanding the sphere of his lordship in the process. Yoder teaches us that Christian engagement with culture requires such a standpoint: a cultural place of evaluation from which we critically engage the forces of the principalities and powers of the world. In other words, we need not reject the entire enterprise of anyone from anywhere teaching our children virtue. Instead, each occasion becomes an opportunity to concretely engage and discern whether "the rebelliousness of a given element of culture can be overcome, (and) where its tools can be used Christianly" (71). Each educational situation is an opportunity for critical engagement by the Christian, out of our stance in the church. Given the content of Christian virtue worked out in the church, we can determine whether there are elements to embrace in the public school's virtue or whether it is to be rejected and on what grounds. There is, in this process, the opportunity for our children to learn their virtue better as well as the opportunity for witness to what our life means before the world.

38. A proposal for the schools to invite children of all traditions to defend and critique their traditions is offered by Robin Lovin, "The School and the Articulation of Values," *American Journal of Education*, February 1988: 143–61.

Conclusion: Let Us Return to the Practices

1. Gerhard Lohfink, *Does God Need the Church?* (Collegeville, MN: The Liturgical Press, 1999), 27. Thanks to Dave Carlson, who reminded me of this quote at his father's funeral.

David E. Fitch (Ph.D., Northwestern University) is pastor of Life on the Vine Christian Community of the Christian and Missionary Alliance, Long Grove, Illinois, and an adjunct professor of ministry, theology, and ethics at Northern Seminary in Lombard, Illinois. He is also co-founder of Up\Rooted (up-rooted.com), a collaborative gathering for Chicago area church leadership engaging the postmodern context.